THE GROWTH AND DEVELOPMENT OF THE CATHOLIC SCHOOL SYSTEM IN THE UNITED STATES

THE
GROWTH AND DEVELOPMENT
OF THE
CATHOLIC SCHOOL SYSTEM
IN THE UNITED STATES

BY

REV. J. A. BURNS, C.S.C., Ph.D.

President Holy Cross College, Washington, D.C.,
Author of " The Catholic School System in the United States; its Principles,
Origin, and Establishment"

New York,   Cincinnati,   Chicago
BENZIGER BROTHERS
PRINTERS TO THE | PUBLISHERS OF
HOLY APOSTOLIC SEE | BENZIGER'S MAGAZINE

1912

Permissu Superiorum.

Nibil Obstat.

REV. REMY LAFORT, D.D.,
Censor Librorum.

Imprimatur.

✠ JOHN CARDINAL FARLEY,
Archbishop of New York.

NEW YORK, June 3, 1912.

PREFACE

In a previous volume, entitled "The Catholic School System in the United States: Its Principles, Origin, and Establishment," the history of the Catholic school movement in this country was outlined from its origin in early Colonial times down to the great immigration, about the year 1840. The present volume is a continuation of the same study. The characteristic feature of the school movement during the long period covered by the first volume was the slow but steady growth of the schools. During the period that is now studied, this feature continued to be predominant as long as the first great influx of Irish and German immigration lasted; but about the time of the Second Plenary Council of Baltimore, which was held in 1866, a new era in American Catholic school history may be said to have begun, an era that was characterized by the efforts made to develop and perfect as well as to expand the existing system. The author has, accordingly, aimed at bringing out into clear relief these two essential features of growth and development that marked the course of the school movement from the beginning of the Immigration Period to the present time. The first four chapters, as well as the sixth, deal with the continued expansion of the school system; the succeeding chapters take up, one after another, in broadly historical sequence, those various elements of the Catholic school which became the objects of the efforts put forth for its improvement; while towards the end of the work a study is made of the growth of the schools of the foreign nationalities.

It is the author's hope that the present volume, like the preceding one, may interest non-Catholic as well as Catholic students of education. His conviction, in undertaking and carrying on these studies, has been that so vast and important a thing as the Catholic parish school system, which has been built up at a cost of such great and continual sacrifice, which was begun in good faith at a time when denominational schools were the order of the day, and which long antedates the federal and the state constitutions, must command the respect if not the admiration of non-Catholics when they come to know it such as it is and such as it has been; and that it can not fail to enlist the good will and sympathy of all those who can be brought to appreciate the real purpose for which it stands. It is only through a better mutual understanding in this way that Catholics and non-Catholics can ever arrive at a settlement of the " school question " that will be satisfactory to both.

Chapters I, V, and VIII appeared in the *Catholic Educational Review* during 1911-12; and Chapter XI formed part of an article contributed to the *American Ecclesiastical Review* for May, 1911.

JAMES A. BURNS, C. S. C.

HOLY CROSS COLLEGE,
  WASHINGTON, D. C.,
    MARCH 7, 1912.

CONTENTS

CHAPTER IV

TEACHING BROTHERS DURING THE IMMIGRATION PERIOD

CHAPTER V

SCHOOL LIFE AND WORK DURING THE IMMIGRATION PERIOD

CHAPTER VI

IN THE FAR WESTERN STATES

CHAPTER VII

SCHOOL LEGISLATION

CHAPTER VIII

GROWTH OF SCHOOL ORGANIZATION

CHAPTER IX

CATHOLIC SCHOOLS AND THE STATE—DISCUSSION OF PRINCIPLES

CHAPTER X

STATE-SUPPORTED CATHOLIC SCHOOLS

CHAPTER XI

THE ECONOMIC SIDE OF THE SCHOOL QUESTION

CHAPTER XII

SCHOOLS OF FOREIGN NATIONALITIES

CHAPTER XIII

SCHOOLS OF FOREIGN NATIONALITIES (CONTINUED)

CHAPTER I

CATHOLIC SCHOOLS IN THE IMMIGRATION PERIOD

ECONOMIC AND SOCIAL FACTORS

THE YEAR 1840 introduced a period of unprecedented economic prosperity in the United States, which lasted until the Civil War. The opening up of new and quicker routes of travel and traffic by canals and railroads, together with the steady development of manufactures, gave abundance of work, and the demand for labor brought a constantly increasing stream of immigrants from the Old World. The attraction which America had for the laboring classes, owing to the favorable conditions here, was intensified by the conditions existing in those countries from which they came. The Irish famine, particularly, which began in 1846, drove the inhabitants in immense numbers to this country, over a million and a quarter arriving during the ten years, 1845-1855.[1] Most of these, naturally, were Catholics. As the Catholic population in the United States in the former year was only 1,071,800,[2] these figures mean that, within a single decade, the Catholic immigrants arriving from Ireland alone were sufficient in number to double the Catholic population of the

[1] Commons, Races and Immigrants in America, p. 66.
[2] Cath. Almanac, 1845.

11

United States. German Catholics, too, came in
large numbers. The stream of German emigration grew gradually and steadily from the year
1820, until, in 1851, it surpassed even that from
Ireland. The proportion of non-Catholics was
greater among the German immigrants than
among the Irish, but a very large proportion of
the Germans came from the Rhine provinces, and
were staunchly devoted to the faith and religious
traditions of their fathers. Ireland and Germany
furnished nearly all the Catholic immigrants to
the United States up to the Civil War.

THE CHURCH

It is necessary to bear these economic and
social factors in mind, if we would penetrate to
the causes of the extraordinary activity of the
Church in the United States during the period
between 1840 and the Civil War, and particularly
on the educational side. Never before, perhaps, in her long and eventful history, did the
Church exhibit a growth at once so great, so
orderly, and so solid. The phenomenon is doubtless to be ascribed, in the last analysis, to the vitality inherent in the Church herself; but much must
be attributed to the favorable economic, social,
and political conditions under which Catholic
immigrants found themselves in America, and
much must also be attributed to the character of
the immigrants themselves. They were far too
numerous to be simply absorbed. The organic
frame-work of the Church had to extend itself,
to reproduce and multiply itself over and over in

order to make room for them. During the twenty years from 1840 to 1860, almost twice as many dioceses were organized as had existed at the beginning of this period. Nearly all of these new dioceses were west of the Alleghanies.

The bishops or vicars appointed to the new sees were, without exception, men devoted to the cause of Catholic education. Trained themselves, generally speaking, under Catholic auspices, they were not less profoundly imbued with the idea of the necessity of the Catholic school than had been the great prelates of the preceding generation. And they gave abundant evidence of the educational faith that was in them. The maxim of Bishop Hughes, "The school before the church," was given many a practical exemplification in the pioneer towns and settlements that dotted the great prairies and wildernesses of the West. Most often, however, the accepted educational policy ran, "The school alongside the church." As a matter of fact, both church and school were frequently begun about the same time, and, if there was but one building, it was usually made to serve the double purpose of church and school.

There was no question raised as to the advisability of erecting distinctively Catholic schools. Here and there, where circumstances were specially favorable, support was gotten for the local Catholic school out of the common school funds; but this was exceptional. Catholics were called upon by their bishops and priests to pay a tax for their own schools, besides paying for the public schools. There was a hope that some day the American people would be led to see the injustice of this; but the feeling was strong among Catholics that they must have their own schools, even if they had to pay double for them. The pioneer bishops and priests of the West during this period, like those of the East before them, were practical men—men who were used to wrestling with rough conditions and had learned by hard practice how to produce practical results. It was their own experience that led them to the conviction of the absolute necessity of the Catholic school. The stupendous task they were undertaking in attempting to provide for a complete school system for the entire Catholic population, from the voluntary contributions of Catholics themselves, did not frighten them, although its immensity and difficulty were keenly apprehended; no more than did the equally stupendous task of building up the mighty material organization of the Church. In both cases, they were prompted by faith; in both, they brought to the task the absolute confidence that springs from faith.

THE IMMIGRANTS

Besides the favorable conditions existing here, and the Church, with her wonderful organism and inherent vitality, another primal factor in the Catholic educational development during the Immigration Period remains to be mentioned— the immigrants themselves. Something has already been said of their number and nationality. The pioneer bishops and priests in the new dioceses were, as a rule, of this class. Catholic immigrants were, almost without exception, poor. Driven from Ireland and Germany by famine or oppression, they were glad, on their arrival here, to get any kind of work, and the work they took up was usually of the hardest and least lucrative kind—out on the railroad tracks or in the grimy railroad shops, in the streets of the city or in the fields. They were the poorest of the poor of their day and generation. As we look back at it from the distance of half a century, the marvel is how men who received but the slender dollar-a-day of the average immigrant, with growing family to support, and newly purchased home to pay for, could, nevertheless, contribute not only to the building of churches and the support of pastors, but to the building of schoolhouses and the support of Catholic teachers as well. In thriving towns throughout the Middle West, traditions still linger which bear witness to the heroic quality of the self-sacrifice of the Catholic pioneers in behalf of religion and education. An instance which may be cited—for it appears to have been not infrequent—was that of men who had no money to give coming night after night, after their hard day's work of twelve hours, and laboring as long as there was light, at the work of laying the foundations or raising the walls of the new church and school building. It was out of such self-sacrifice, in fact, that the solid structure of Catholic education was everywhere reared. The story of the first Catholic schools in Milwaukee and Chicago recalls the early school history of New York, Baltimore and Boston, just as the first foundations of the great teaching orders in the West

West recall the heroic story of the Georgetown Convent and of the Sisters of Emmittsburg.

Catholic immigrants did not need to be convinced of the necessity of Catholic schools. They were of one mind with their pastors and bishops on the subject. Centuries of struggle to preserve their faith and their national traditions had taught the Irish and the Germans the value of the religious school, and the immigrants to America simply brought with them the educational ideas which had become a part of their inheritance and their faith. This is why there was no question with the laity any more than with the clergy as to the wisdom of attempting to establish a separate system of Catholic schools. Like their pastors, the laity accepted this alternative as a matter of course, although the additional financial burden it brought to every home was keenly felt. There were many instances where a group of Catholic families, who were either not numerous enough or able to secure a priest, hired a Catholic teacher themselves and started a Catholic school, although public schools were within easy reach. The Catholic school was thus simply the concrete, practical expression of an educational ideal that was common to all Catholics, and that was enrooted in the minds of the laity no less than the clergy. Leaders of course there had to be, and it was natural that bishops and priests should have taken the lead in the work of Catholic education. But it was never argument that was needed, so much as practical direction, and often, as has been said, the leadership of the clergy was not waited for in the matter of establishing schools. Circumstances sometimes precluded the founding of Catholic schools. People were, in places, too poor; or, not numerous enough; or, a teacher could not be had. In such cases it often happened that years passed before a Catholic parish had a school of its own. The ideal, however, and the fixed purpose was everywhere the same; and this was, a Catholic school and a Catholic training, from start to finish, for every Catholic child.

If we consider the widely diversified elements that went to form the Catholic population in the new dioceses, this unanimity of thought and purpose must be matter for wonder. It was shared by Frenchman and Catholic native American, by German and by Irishman. It is still more wonderful, perhaps, that this unanimity was preserved, notwithstanding the widely differing circumstances into which the component elements of the Catholic population were thrown. Everywhere, and everywhere almost at the same time, Catholic schools were springing up, in the great cities of the East, as well as in pioneer settlements in the West; in Protestant strongholds like Massachusetts and Connecticut, as well as in ancient Catholic centers like Detroit; in Catholic settlements scattered through the Alleghany Mountain region, and in the rising towns that dotted the great plains of the Mississippi Valley.

There was no noise or agitation, such as accompanied the great educational movement making for the betterment of the public school system during the same period. The Catholic educational movement was not intellectual, but religious.

It sprang from the heart rather than the head, and was the result of a common impulse flowing from a common religious ideal. The fanatical anti-Catholic agitation and outbreaks that marked the growth of the Native American and Know-Nothing parties had little permanent influence upon the Catholic school movement. Here and there a school was burned or temporarily closed, and in Massachusetts Bishop Fitzpatrick deemed it prudent for the time being to stop the building of schools. But, generally speaking, Catholics kept bravely on with the work. If anything, the fanatical spirit of the times rather helped on the Catholic school movement, by making Catholics more sensible of the danger to the faith of their children which lurked in the atmosphere of the public school.

EDUCATIONAL CONDITIONS

"The Great Awakening," as the educational movement started by Horace Mann about 1839 was called, had little influence upon Catholics, although it spread from one end of the country to the other. The problems of Catholic education at the time were different. The existing religious communities, under the stimulus of European influence, had already accomplished for their teachers and schools much of what "The Great Awakening" came to do for the public schools and their teachers;[3] and the newly arrived or newly forming communities were still struggling for existence. Even the existing communities were

[3] Cf. The Cath. School System in the U. S., Chapter viii.

straining every nerve to meet the demand made
upon them by the sudden and extraordinary
growth of the school system. The two movements, therefore, although contemporaneous, had
little, if anything, in common. The purpose of
the one was to raise the standard of the public
schools, especially by improving the quality of the
teaching; the purpose of the other was to provide
schools and teachers for a population that was
growing so fast as almost to double itself within
a few years. Both movements were chiefly concerned, it is true, with the teacher; but, in the
one case, it was the better training of the teacher
that was sought for, while, in the other, it was
simply the getting of a sufficient number of teachers with the necessary religious and other qualifications.

There were at least two hundred Catholic parish schools in the country in the year 1840. More
than half of these were west of the Alleghanies.
It was due to the educational zeal or genius of
Bishops Flaget and Dubourg that, at the above
date, the dioceses of Kentucky and St. Louis were
better off for schools and teachers than the more
populous dioceses of the East.[4] Bishop Kenrick,
of Philadelphia, in 1843, complained of the im-
possibility of finding teachers enough for the
schools. Bishop Hughes, of New York, after the
school controversy, made several trips to Europe
partly for the purpose of securing teachers for
his schools. Both of these dioceses had the Sisters
of Charity of Emmittsburg, but, rapid as was the
growth of that community and its branches, the

[4] Cf. op. cit., c. viii.

supply of teachers was entirely inadequate to the demand. It was to Europe that Hughes and Kenrick and their contemporaries turned, as Flaget and Dubourg had done, in order to get teachers enough for their schools.

Teaching communities were plentiful in France and Germany, and many of these were induced to send colonies to the United States during the period, 1840-61. So numerous were these colonies, in fact, and so rapid was their growth, once they were fairly settled, that their members soon outnumbered the members of the religious orders existing here before them, just as the immigrants did the native Catholic population.

The religious orders were really the nuclei of Catholic educational growth during this period. Their growth was both coincident with and causative of the advance of the school movement. They represented also, generally speaking, whatever there was of organization of Catholic educational forces. Of diocesan school organization there was little more than the name. There had to be schools, before schools could be united and governed as a system, and the attention of both bishops, priests, and religious superiors was absorbed by problems connected with the indispensable prerequisites for the school as an individual thing.

It is best, therefore, in dealing with this period, to take the religious teaching community, rather than the diocese, as the unit of organization, since it was practically, although not formally, such. This arrangement is the more convenient, since the purpose of this study is to show the causative influences that have been at work in the development of the Catholic school system. In the post-Revolutionary period it was the diocese that gave definite and final shape to the school system and determined the character of the teacher. That period was the turning-point in the history of Catholic education in the United States, and the diocesan influence was then supreme. But the diocese, while remaining supreme in authority, ceased to be such as a causative or determinative educational influence during the Immigration Period. The supreme factor, so far as growth is concerned, was the religious teaching community. Taking it, then, as the organization-center, the effort will be made to show, in the three following chapters, the influence which the various teaching communities of the time had upon Catholic school development. The diocesan organization, however, will not be lost sight of. Particular dioceses will be frequently referred to in the study of the teaching communities. The rise of the diocesan school systems in the Far West remains still to be outlined. Furthermore, the study of the development and perfecting of the diocesan system will be taken up in the chapters on School Legislation and Organization.

CHAPTER II

TEACHERS AND TEACHING COMMUNITIES IN
THE IMMIGRATION PERIOD

A GENERAL VIEW

AT THE beginning of the period of the Great Immigration there were thirteen religious communities in the United States engaged in parish school work. All of these were communities of women. In the Archdiocese of Baltimore there were the Visitation Nuns, the Sisters of Charity, and the Oblate Sisters of Baltimore; in the Diocese of Philadelphia, the Sisters of Charity of the Blessed Virgin; in South Carolina, the Sisters of Mercy and the Ursulines; in New Orleans, the Ursulines; in the Diocese of St. Louis, the Ladies of the Sacred Heart and the Sisters of St. Joseph; in Kentucky, the Sisters of Loretto, the Sisters of Charity of Nazareth, and the Dominican Sisters; and in Detroit, the Poor Clares.[1]

During the period we are now to consider, twenty-five new communities entered the field. Several of these were founded in this country, but the greater number came from Europe. Be-

[1] Cf. The Catholic School System in the U. S.

sides these, a number of independent orders grew up from branch establishments previously existing here, or from branch establishments which were formed during this period. All but six of the new communities were sisterhoods. Efforts were made by several bishops to procure more Brothers for boys' schools, but it was very difficult to induce the existing brotherhoods in Europe to found branch establishments at a distance, so great was the demand for the Brothers at home. Moreover, it was found hard to get vocations for the brotherhoods here, much harder, in fact, than it was abroad. There was a financial advantage, also, in favor of the Sisters, in that they could live more cheaply, and consequently were content with a lower salary. These last two factors have continued to operate in favor of the employment of Sisters rather than Brothers as teachers in parish schools, and their influence will be considered more fully later on.[2]

Although most of the new teaching orders came from abroad, and their first members—usually either French or German—were unable to speak English upon their arrival, their Americanization was both rapid and complete. The first members were obliged to learn English at once, in order to take up the work of teaching; the recruits that were gathered to the little immigrant colonies were, of course, Americans, although often of foreign birth; and it thus came about that the general personnel of the community became, in a generation or so, thoroughly American. In quite a number of instances, too, the American branch,

[2] See especially chapter on Economic Side.

owing to one cause or another, broke away from the parent stem and became an independent religious organization, obtaining the formal approval of the Holy See.

In respect of organization religious communities may be divided into two classes: those whose several houses are dependent in government upon a common central establishment, besides being bound by a common rule; and those whose several houses are independent in government, while all living under a common rule. Both types were represented among the religious orders which came to the country during the Immigration Period, as they were also among those which existed here before. Again, in the case of communities that have a common central government, while the form of government is, in general, much like that of the Sisters of Charity,[3] there is considerable diversity in respect to the relationship of the branch houses to the central establishment. With some, this relationship is very close; in others, it is much less so. It is necessary to bear this in mind, in order to understand the phenomena met with in studying the growth of the teaching orders during this period. This fact, taken in connection with external influences, helps to explain the splitting up of some communities, as well as the development of others on a national scope, with an organization comprising hundreds and even thousands of subjects, united under a common government, and with schools in every section of the country and in almost every State.

[3] Cf. The Cath. School System in the U. S., "Sisters of Charity of Emmittsburg."

The chief factor, however, in the making of the community was, generally speaking, its leadership. The community which grew great and powerful was made so by some extraordinarily gifted man or woman who had the shaping of its early destiny. Leadership counted for more than external circumstances. Where feeble organizations grew feebler or disintegrated altogether in the face of difficulties, other communities better officered grew strong, and were able to harness even adverse circumstances to their service. This is especially true of the development of the community on the purely educational side. The spirit of a single great teacher often passed to the entire community as an inheritance for all time. Special attention will, therefore, be given to the great educational leaders in the religious communities.

As the aim of the author is an historical study of the Catholic *school system,* it would be obviously impossible, within the limits of this work, to give a complete historical sketch, or anything approaching to it, of each religious order. The aim will consequently be, simply to show the influence of the various orders which engaged in school work during this period upon the growth and development of the Catholic system of schools; and the history of each will be dealt with only to the extent deemed requisite for the accomplishment of this purpose. The space devoted to each community will necessarily vary accordingly. The facts and features of each order's growth will likewise be selected with this end in view. The order of historical sequence will be followed so far as convenient, first in the case of the teaching communities of women, and afterwards with respect to the teaching brotherhoods.

SISTERS OF CHARITY OF THE BLESSED VIRGIN— MOTHER FRANCES CLARKE (1833)

This community, which owed its origin as a religious body to the zeal of Rev. T. J. Donaghoe, pastor of St. Michael's, Philadelphia,[4] sent a party of five Sisters to Dubuque in 1843, in response to the urgent appeal of Bishop Loras, who was eager to secure religious teachers for his growing schools. The greatness of the opportunity offered in the West, and the obstacles to their work in Philadelphia, owing to the Know-Nothing movement, combined to induce the founder and the Sisters who had remained behind to move the entire community to Dubuque the same year. The place then contained about seven hundred inhabitants. A tract of land ten miles southwest of the city, named St. Joseph's Prairie, was chosen as the site for the mother-house; but the buildings were destroyed by fire soon after the Sisters had settled there. Father Donaghoe, who had come with the community to Dubuque, set himself courageously to repair the damage, and soon new buildings arose. The number of novices, as well as the number of pupils in the academy which had been founded, increased until, fifteen years later, a large new building was erected on a bluff overlooking the Mississippi and just within the city limits. To this site, known as Mt. Carmel, the mother-house was transferred.[5]

[4] Cf. Cath. Sch. Sys. in U. S., p. 263.
[5] The Cath. Ch. in the U. S. of A., I, p. 311.

Bishop Loras builded even better than he knew in bringing the community to his diocese. They not only aided him in the extension of education in the diocese, but furnished teachers to neighboring dioceses as well. Throughout the West, to which its work has been confined, the community has had a potent influence upon Catholic educational work, especially in the development of parish schools. This was the primary purpose of the congregation, and it was firmly held to this purpose during the long administration of the first superior, Mother Frances Clarke, who lived till the year 1887. Academies and high schools were taken charge of in time, but the main work has always been considered to be the parish schools.

Mother Frances, although a woman of great ability, was personally strongly inclined towards elementary school work. She was remarkable for a humility that caused her to seek to lead a hidden life, even when directing the affairs of the entire community. Gentle and at the same time firm, she labored in the retirement of the mother-convent to mold the community according to her ideal, seeking to make religious who would be, above all, humble and self-sacrificing, and teachers who would strive to excel all others in the doing of their work, even though that work was in the elementary school. Like many of the great founders or superiors of the sisterhoods during this period, Mother Frances succeeded in impressing her spirit and her ideals permanently upon the community. The rules of the new society, so far as concerns methods of teaching, were framed from ideas acquired in the actual practice of the class-room. Sister Margaret Mann, one of the original members, was the right hand of Mother Frances in the administration, and was distinguished by her activity in promoting the educational interests of the community. In the work at Dubuque Sisters Mary Joseph O'Reilly, Catherine Byrne, and Rosalia Ryan were also distinguished among the pioneers.[6]

Upon their arrival at Dubuque the Sisters had taken charge of St. Mary's School (now St. Raphael's), and later on another academy was opened within the city limits. For a period of twenty-four years no permanent foundation was made outside of Iowa. But during that time, an academy and two schools were opened at Davenport as well as parish schools in other important towns of the State.[7]

Under Sisters Agatha Hurley and Agnes Burke the work of the community was extended to Illinois. The Sisters took charge of St. Aloysius (now Holy Family) School, Chicago, in 1867, and, the next year, of the Sacred Heart School. From now on, for a period of eighteen years, the rapid development of the parish school system in Illinois and Iowa absorbed the energies of the community. Many schools were opened by the Sisters in the growing Catholic centers of these two States. The concentration of the work of the community upon elementary education made very greatly for the efficiency of the Sisters as teachers. In Chicago the demand for their ser-

[6] Records of the mother-house.
[7] Ib.

vices has been particularly urgent, and the number of their establishments there has steadily increased, until at present they have charge of one high school and eighteen parish schools, some of the latter being among the largest and most important in the city.[8]

In assuming charge of the Holy Rosary School in Milwaukee, in 1885, the community entered upon an era of wider expansion. The western limit of this movement was marked by the opening of a school in San Francisco the next year, and since then many schools and several academies have been opened in the far western States. New schools have also been taken by the community during this period in Milwaukee, as well as in various places in Illinois and Iowa.[9]

In 1908 the community contained over 1,000 members, having under its direction 25,000 pupils.[10]

SISTERS OF ST. JOSEPH—MOTHER ST. JOHN FOURNIER (1836)

The coming of the first Sisters of St. Joseph to America and their establishment at Carondelet, near St. Louis, in 1836, has already been described.[11] After taking charge of school-work in St. Louis, in 1844, the community increased rapidly, and was soon strong enough to send bands of Sisters to distant places. In 1847, a perma-

[8] Records of the mother-house.
[9] Ib.
[10] The Cath. Ch. in the U. S., I, p. 312.
[11] Cf. Cath. Sch. Sys. in U. S., p. 310.

nent foundation was made in Philadelphia. While
continually extending their work in St. Louis and
vicinity, the Sisters also opened schools among
the Sioux and Winnebago Indians in 1850, and
the year following founded the first house of the
order in St. Paul. At Wheeling, Buffalo, Rochester, Brooklyn, and several places in Canada foundations were made within the next few years. A
house was established at Troy, N. Y., in 1861,
and at Tucson, Ariz., in 1869. Thus, within
twenty years after being solidly established at St.
Louis, the community had a dozen widely spread
branch-houses, reaching from the Atlantic almost
to the Pacific, each surrounded by a growing
Catholic population. The result was shown in
the rapid growth of these branch-houses, and
their important educational influence. Each was
independent of the original mother-house, and
from several of these primitive branches, in turn,
new independent communities were soon formed.[12]

A plan to unite all the branches of this great
community under a central government, with a
superior-general at its head, inasmuch as all wore
the same garb and followed substantially the same
rule, originated with Archbishop Kenrick, of St.
Louis. In the year 1860 representatives from the
various houses met at Carondelet, and formulated
a plan of government which was approved by the
majority of those present, and later received the
formal approbation of the Holy See. Many of
the branch-houses were thus re-united to the original mother-house, the Congregation so formed
being known as "The Sisters of St. Joseph of

[12] Rivaux, Life of Mother St. John Fontbonne, p. 208 seq.

Carondelet." The houses in the East, as a rule, acting under the advice of their respective bishops, remained outside of the union. The congregation includes four provinces: St. Louis, comprising the schools in charge of the Sisters in Missouri and the neighboring States; St. Paul, including principally the establishments in Minnesota; [13] Troy, including those in Central New York; and Los Angeles, those in California and Arizona. The members of the congregation, in the year 1910, numbered 1751; there were 126 schools, with upwards of 41,000 pupils. [14]

The oldest of the branch-houses, at Philadelphia, grew rapidly under the fostering care of Bishop Kenrick and his successors. Beginning parish school work at Pottsville, the Sisters took charge of St. John's Orphan Asylum in Philadelphia in 1847, and some years later of the schools at old St. Joseph's Church and St. Philip's. From now on, the community was able to furnish teachers for many of the parish schools which Bishop Neumann's burning zeal was raising up on every side, and its membership was increased correspondingly. As the Orphan Asylum was unsuitable for a novitiate, this was transferred to McSherrystown, in 1854, but four years later a beautiful estate at Chestnut Hill was acquired, and the novitiate and mother-house permanently established there. An academy was opened at the same time. This institution, from the tiniest beginnings, has developed into a large modern academic

[13] An independent branch of the St. Paul Community was established at Cleveland, in 1872. The Sisters conduct diocesan schools, and also an academy.

[14] Cath. Dir., 1910; The Cath. Ch. in the U. S. of A., p. 382

and collegiate plant, and is known as Mt. St. Joseph's Collegiate Institute. The community has won an enviable place among Catholic teaching bodies, and for this credit is due in part to Bishops Kenrick, Neumann, and their successors, but chiefly to the foundress, Mother St. John Fournier, and those who came after her in the administration. Mother St. John belonged to one of the pioneer bands of the Sisters, reaching St. Louis in 1837. She was a woman of courage, and her activity was not only incessant, but prudent and far-seeing. It was she who began the school work in St. Louis. She founded the community in Philadelphia, and governed it for nearly thirty years, except for an interval of three years during which she was recalled to the West, to found the first schools in St. Paul. Mother John Kieran, who succeeded her in 1875, enlarged the work of the foundress to meet the changing conditions— re-organizing the novitiate, amplifying its educational facilities, and modernizing its pedagogical training. The policy of her predecessors was continued, in spirit and purpose, by Mother Clement Lannen, who became the superior-general in 1887. The number of Sisters, in 1910, was 716, with 40 schools, and 24,642 pupils.[15]

Besides continually enlarging their work in eastern Pennsylvania, the Sisters took charge of schools in New Jersey and Maryland, which have remained subject to the mother-house in Philadelphia. Several independent offshoots were also

[15] Records of the Phila. mother-house; Rivaux, Life of Mother St. John F., p. 223 seq.; Cath. Ch. in U. S. of A., p. 383; Hist. Sketches of the Cath. Churches in Phila., p. 192; Cath. Dir.

formed. One of these was at McSherrystown,
Pa., where the academy was continued and where,
upon the creation of the Diocese of Harrisburg,
in 1868, an independent mother-house was established.[16] Another was at Toronto, in 1851, from
which other independent colonies in Canada were
formed.[17]

The most important branch of the Philadelphia community, however, was the establishment
at Brooklyn, founded in 1856. Two Sisters, with
Mother Mary Austin, began the work by opening
St. Mary's Academy and a parochial school, a
novitiate being also established. The community's
development was rapid, owing, in great part, to
the personal exertions of Bishop Loughlin in their
behalf. Soon the novitiate and academy were
removed to a more suitable site at Flushing. Subsequently, they were removed to Brentwood, L. I.,
where an extensive establishment has been built
up. The community has been quick to respond to
appeals for teachers, sending out a number of
colonies, which became new centers of the work
of the order, independent of their mother-house.
One of these was established at Erie, Pa., in 1862,
from which a colony was sent to Kansas in 1887.
Another was first established at Ebensburg, Pa.,
in 1864, the mother-house being afterwards
moved to Baden, in Beaver County, where Mt.
Gallitzin Academy was opened. Another was
sent to Boston, in 1873, where the growth of the
community has been large, while other diocesan
communities were founded at Rutland, Vt., in

[16] Life of Mother St. John F., p. 237.
[17] Ib., pp. 228, 256.

1876, and at Springfield, Mass, in 1880. The number of Sisters in the Brooklyn community, in 1910, was 584, with 11,000 pupils under their care.[18]

The Philadelphia branch has thus been almost as prolific as the original colony at St. Louis. But besides the houses in Philadelphia and St. Paul, several other important branches were formed from Carondelet. A colony was sent to Wheeling in 1853, at the request of Bishop Whelan, where they founded an academy and novitiate, which became the center of a series of schools.[19]

Another colony from Carondelet founded a novitiate and academy at Canandaigua, in 1854, at the instance of Bishop Timon, the mother-house and novitiate being transferred to Buffalo several years later, where the community opened an academy and assumed charge of the diocesan schools. From Buffalo, several Sisters were sent to Rochester, in 1864, and, after the erection of this place into an episcopal see, the Sisters were organized as a separate community by Bishop Mc-Quaid. The Rochester community, with its academy and schools, has kept pace with the striking development of the diocese educationally, and from it, in 1883, a colony was sent to Concordia, Kansas, where a flourishing community was formed—the Concordia community, again, establishing an independent branch at La Grange, a suburb of Chicago. From Buffalo a second diocesan community was founded at Watertown, N. Y., in 1880. An independent branch of the Water-

[18] Op. cit.
[19] Life of Mother St. John F., p. 228.

town community was settled at Tipton, Ind., in 1888.[20]

In communities historically connected with Carondelet, there were, in the year 1908, about 4600 Sisters, with approximately 110,000 pupils.[21]

MOTHER THEODORE GUÉRIN AND THE SISTERS OF PROVIDENCE (1840)

The comprehensive educational plans of Bishop Bruté involved the procuring of Sisters for the parish schools throughout Indiana, and it was partly in fulfilment of this purpose that his Vicar-General, Father C. de la Hailandière, was sent to France shortly before the former's death.[22] The vicar-general, being chosen as the new bishop, applied to the Sisters of Providence, a recently founded teaching community at Ruillé, with the result that, on Oct. 5, 1840, a band of six Sisters, with Mother Theodore Guérin as superior, arrived at New York, and commenced the long stage-journey to Vincennes.[23] The Sisters had, on leaving France, less than six hundred dollars. Upon arriving at their destination, near Terre Haute, they found, in the midst of a dense forest, a small frame farm-house, partly occupied by a Catholic family, with a log chapel not far away. The Sisters were crowded into a single

[20] Life of Mother St. John F., p. 228; The Cath. Ch. in U. S. of A., pp. 384, 385; The Diocese of Ft. Wayne, p. 468; Cath. Dir.
[21] Cath. Dir., 1908.
[22] Cf. The Cath. School System in the U. S., Diocese of Vincennes.
[23] Life and Life-Work of Mother Theodore Guérin, pp. 99, 126; Alerding, Hist. of the Dioc. of Vincennes, p. 573.

room, an attic which had been used as a corn-loft serving as the dormitory. Such was the first humble home of the Sisters of Providence in America. St. Mary's of the Woods was the name appropriately given to the place. The land was purchased through the generosity of friends in Europe.

The Sisters labored diligently to acquire English, and to fit themselves for the work of teaching. An academy and school was opened in July of the following year.[24] Only four pupils presented themselves for the opening; but the number gradually increased, as the Sisters became better equipped for their work, and especially when, in the succeeding years, more members came from France. There were postulants, too. Four of these, in fact, were at St. Mary's to meet the Sisters on their arrival, and others came before long from various parts of the State. Before the end of the second year, schools were opened in Father Kundeck's parish at Jasper and at St. Francisville, Ill.[25] From the latter place, the Sisters were transferred two years later to St. Peter's, replacing the Brothers of St. Joseph. Soon afterwards they took charge of the school at Vincennes.

The rapid progress of the community during these first years was due in part to the energy and devotion of the Sisters themselves, and in part also to the active and generous interest of the mother-house at Ruillé. Mother Theodore was a woman of exceptional ability as well as of singular holiness of life, and deserves a distinguished

---

[24] Mother Theodore Guérin, p. 200.
[25] Ib., p. 219 seq.; Alerding, op. cit., p. 580.

place among the great Catholic educational pioneers of this period. During the sixteen years of her administration she succeeded, not only in guiding the young community safely through difficulties, but in permanently impressing upon its character the stamp of her own personality. A descendant of an illustrious family, she was a Religious of mature experience when she assumed the responsibilities of the new establishment in America. Quick to realize the educational possibilities of the time and place, she made it her aim from the very first to offer in the academy at St. Mary's, notwithstanding the poverty and the meager attendance at the beginning, a curriculum comparable with that of the best schools for girls in her native land.[26] She entertained the loftiest ideals, too, in regard to the preparation of teachers destined for the parish schools, and she was inflexible in insisting upon the full carrying out of all that the community rules required on this point.

Never in the history of religious orders in America, however, was a superior more sorely tried. The authorities in France thought the establishment too remote to be governed from there, and the Sisters at St. Mary's, although desirous of remaining united to France, were thus brought under diocesan jurisdiction. The difficulties and troubles caused by the acts and policy of the bishop with respect to the community do not, fortunately, fall within the scope of this work, since they had only a secondary bearing upon education, and they were, moreover, not lasting, the

[26] Life of Mother Theodore, p. 215.

bishop resigning in 1847.[27] Suffice it to say, that Mother Theodore bore herself throughout these painful trials with the simplicity and devotedness of a faithful Religious as well as with the fortitude befitting an heroic character.

Under Bishops Bazin and St. Palais, she resumed the direction of affairs, and from this time on the development of the community and the extension of its work was steady and rapid. Mother Theodore had able coadjutors, chief among whom were Sisters Francis Xavier and Cecilia, the latter succeeding her as superior-general.[28] At the time of Mother Theodore's death, in 1856, fourteen establishments had been formed, the principal ones being schools at Madison, Fort Wayne, Terre Haute, Evansville, and Columbus, besides the central institution at St. Mary's, which had been greatly enlarged.[29] Under Mother Cecilia the community continued to grow and to spread. Schools were opened at Washington and Indianapolis. The work of the Sisters was also gradually extended to other States, establishments being founded in Michigan and Illinois, as well as in States as far away as Maryland, Massachusetts, and Nebraska. In 1910 the community had 957 Sisters, with 68 parish schools, 15 academies, and 18,160 pupils.[30]

[27] Cf. op. cit., passim.
[28] Cath. Ed. Rev., I, p. 143.
[29] Alerding, op. cit., p. 585.
[30] Records of the mother-house; Cath. Dir., 1908.

SISTER LOUISE—THE SISTERS OF NOTRE
DAME (NAMUR) (1840)

Cincinnati had become a center of Catholic
educational work and influence even during the
episcopate of Bishop Fenwick, and the policy of
establishing schools alongside the churches became a cardinal principle of the Rt. Rev. John B.
Purcell, who succeeded him in the year 1833.[31]
Bishop Purcell recognized the necessity of providing a body of professional teachers for his growing schools. In 1839 he journeyed to Europe for
this purpose, and soon had the satisfaction of
engaging for the diocese a band of Sisters from
one of the most promising religious institutes of
the Old World—the Sisters of Notre Dame, a
teaching community founded after the French
Revolution by the venerable Mother Julia Billiart,
with its mother-house at Namur, Belgium.

The party, which arrived at New York on
Oct. 19, 1840, was composed of eight Sisters, all
of whom had offered themselves as volunteers,
Sister Louis de Gonzague being the superior. In
the group was a native of Holland, named in the
world Josephine Vonder Schriek and in religion
Sister Louise, who was destined a few years later
to assume the leadership of the community in
America and to be the directing spirit of its development during a period of over forty years.

The Sisters began their work in a humble way.
A small house on Sycamore Street, opposite the
present Jesuit church of St. Francis Xavier, was

[31] Cf. The Cath. School System in the U. S., p. 331.

rented; but as the building was too small and miserable for school work of any sort they bought a large and finely appointed house about a dozen yards from the former, on Sixth Street, for $24,000, and here school was opened January 18, 1841.[32] The Sisters looked with simple faith to Providence to enable them to pay for the new place. Only one of them, Sister Louise, could speak English, yet pupils came in increasing numbers. An academy as well as a parochial school was opened, and in a few months the pupils, boarders and day-scholars, numbered sixty. Two years later, three more Sisters came from Namur, and the institution was enlarged by the purchase of an adjoining house, which was soon filled with pupils. In 1845 six more Sisters arrived from the mother-house. A school was now opened in Toledo, and Sister Louis de Gonzague appointed as superior, while Sister Louise was named as her successor in Cincinnati.

It was evident that the people of Cincinnati held the Sisters in high esteem, for Protestants as well as Catholics patronized the institution. Their ability as teachers made itself felt from the very beginning, in spite of their lack of English, and as this difficulty gradually grew less, and the number of Sisters increased, new schools were opened in Cincinnati, especially in the newly forming German parishes, as well as in other places.[33] In 1849 Sister Louise was made superior of all the houses branching from the original founda-

[32] Memoirs of Sister Louise, p. 47 seq.; Hist. Cath. Ch. in U. S. of A., I, Sisters of Notre Dame.
[33] Memoirs of Sister Louise, p. 80 seq.

tion.   Previous to this, in 1843, eight Sisters had
been sent from Namur to Father De Smet's missions in Oregon, in response to his urgent appeal.
After laboring there under great privations and
hardships, these devoted pioneers were, in 1851,
transferred to San José, Cal., where, with the aid
of four Sisters from Cincinnati, a school was
opened which became in time the mother-house
of an extensive series of establishments along the
Pacific Coast.

Under Sister Louise academies and schools
began to multiply.   Vocations were numerous,
thirteen postulants being received in six months
during the year 1850-51.   An establishment at
Dayton was founded in 1849, and the same year
witnessed the beginning of the Sisters' work in
the East, on their taking charge of the girls'
school in St. Mary's Parish, Boston.   Later on,
they took up their residence on Berkeley Street,
in the Back Bay district, where they opened an
academy, while still continuing to teach at St.
Mary's.   In 1853 a school was opened at Lowell,
Mass., and the year following an academy was
founded at Roxbury.   Additional schools and
academies were opened in Massachusetts in the
succeeding years, the Archdiocese of Boston becoming eventually one of the most important
centers of their work.   Invitations to establish
schools and academies, in fact, poured in from
all sides.   In 1856 they opened an academy in
Philadelphia, where, several years later, Mother
Julia laid the foundations of the well-known institution on Rittenhouse Square.   Other schools
were opened from time to time in Philadelphia,

which became another important center of their
work in the East. Ohio and the Middle West
also continued to witness the growth of the community through the foundation of new institutions.
The mother-house in Cincinnati was enlarged in
1859 by the removal of the boarding-school to
"Mount Notre Dame," then at some distance
from the city. Another design of Sister Louise,
the removal of the novitiate to a site outside the
city, was accomplished about a year after her
death, when Mother Julia purchased the magnificent property at East Walnut Hills.[34]

The rapid, solid growth of the community,
evidenced in these outlines, has few parallels in
the history of religious orders in the country.
It was largely due to the esteem in which the Sisters were held, but this again was attributable to
the spirit of the order and the training of the
Sisters both as religious and as teachers. Circumstances, of course, were favorable. The chief
credit, however, was due to the wise and firm
administration of Sister Louise, who continued as
superior of the community until her death in 1886.
She had all the qualities of an ideal religious
superior, and the exercise of her talents and virtues was unceasingly directed to the development
of the work of the institute of which she was the
head. Her fine religious zeal seemed to be communicated to all her spiritual children, and the
generation which came after her needed only to
continue along the lines she had laid down. She
trained Mother Julia, who succeeded her, and one

[34] Memoirs, pp. 69-162; Records of the mother-house, Cincinnati.

of her last acts was to appoint this very able woman as assistant-superior.[35]

It is remarkable that, although Sister Louise was more anxious to establish parochial schools than academies, the community was led more and more into the field of secondary and collegiate work. This was due, doubtless, to the high regard entertained for the ability of the Sisters as teachers, joined to the academic needs of the times. This tendency culminated, in the year 1900, in the foundation of Trinity College, at Washington, D. C., by Mother Julia, an institution which is almost alone among Catholic institutions of higher education in the United States in not receiving students below the Freshman year, and which also occupies a unique position among colleges for women by reason of the administrative relations it bears to the Catholic public.

In 1910 the Sisters numbered 1248, with 12 academies, 64 parish schools, and 30,974 pupils.[36]

SISTERS OF THE HOLY CROSS—MOTHER ANGELA (1843)

In two important respects the history of the Sisters of the Holy Cross is like that of the other great sisterhoods in the United States: there was a fiery furnace of trial in the beginning, and there was the creative influence of a great personality in the Order's development. Founded in 1841 by the Abbé Moreau, who had established the Con-

[35] Memoirs, pp. 69-162; Records of the mother-house, Cincinnati.
[36] Cath. Dir., 1910. These figures do not include the statistics of the California Province, which was founded directly by the mother-house of Namur.

gregation of the Holy Cross a few years before, the first Sisters in the United States arrived at Notre Dame two years later, in response to the appeal of Father Sorin. As Bishop de la Hailandière refused to authorize the opening of a novitiate, this institution was, in 1844, established at Bertrand, just outside the Indiana diocese, where an academy and school were also opened.[37] A few children from the neighborhood formed the attendance the first year. There were several English-speaking novices, and with the aid of these and professors from Notre Dame the French Sisters were soon able to begin to teach in English. Money was an unknown commodity, we are told, provisions being brought from Notre Dame. The next year, however, a grant of five thousand francs by the Society for the Propagation of the Faith, and the donation of seventy-seven acres of land by the inhabitants of Bertrand, brightened the prospects considerably. Their first home was a small frame building, rented from Mr. Bertrand; now, a new building was erected —a two-story frame structure, and by the end of the year 1845 the total number in the community had increased to fourteen.[38]

The following year more Sisters came from France. The years from 1848 to 1855 were the

[37] A Story of Fifty Years, p. 22. It is interesting to record that the Sisters re-opened the Indian school which had been established by Father Badin near Bertrand some fourteen years before, and taught by Miss Campeau. The school was taught by the Sisters from 1845 until 1852. Its closing was necessitated by the dispersion of the remaining Indians, owing to the coming of the whites and the development of the country. Ib., p. 56.

[38] Ib., p. 32; Hist. Cath. Ch. in U. S. of A., I, p. 370 seq.

period of organization, when the life and spirit
of the community was being shaped under the
direction of Father Sorin, and its academic ideals
fostered and developed by the training of the
Sisters, professors being secured from Notre
Dame and other places for the purpose. By 1850
the academy showed an attendance-roll of fifty
boarders. In 1855 the entire institution was
moved from Bertrand to a beautiful tract of land
about a mile west of Notre Dame, on the picturesque St. Joseph River, near the point where
La Salle and so many other voyagers after him,
leaving the river, struck across the ancient Indian
portage for the headwaters of the Kankakee. "St.
Mary's of the Immaculate Conception," as the
new home of the Sisters was named, grew rapidly
from this time on. Building was added to building,
and the academy soon took a high rank among
educational institutions of its class, the work in art
and music especially giving it reputation. In 1869
the community received recognition at Rome as
an Order independent of the parent body in
France.

Father Sorin was the dominant personality in
the development of the community up to the time
of the Civil War, and, as its ecclesiastical superior,
he continued to have a great influence in shaping
its growth and policy down to the time of the
approval of the rules and constitutions by Rome
in 1889. There was another remarkable personality, however, to which the community owes no
less than to Father Sorin. This was Mother
Angela, who was appointed as head of the academy at Bertrand in 1854, and who "for more

than thirty years governed the growing community, formed its members, and directed its manifold energies." [39]   Mother Angela's great endowments of mind and heart excercised a quickening and permanent influence upon the community in several ways. From a modest boarding school, the academy was raised to a plane of high educational efficiency and given definite intellectual ideals. She devoted herself particularly to the training of the Sisters who were to teach. In this as in other respects, the standards she set were beyond the power of the community to realize during her time, and were handed down to the generation that came after her as the most precious heritage of the past.

Mother Angela, like Father Sorin, was an ardent patriot, and when the Civil War broke out the services of the community were offered to the Government. It is to the glory of the Sisters of Holy Cross, as well as of the American teaching profession, that the energies of this devoted body of women were, for the time being, diverted very largely from the schools and turned to the service

[39] A Story of Fifty Years. pp. 40-188.   Mother Angela (Eliza Maria Gillespie) was born in Pennsylvania in 1824, and died in 1887.   As a child, she was the companion of her cousin, the future statesman, James Gillespie Blaine.   She was educated at the Dominican Convent at Somerset, Ohio, and at the Visitation Convent, Georgetown.   Stopping at Notre Dame in 1853, while on her way to join a religious community in Chicago, she was attracted by the life and work of the Sisters at Notre Dame and Bertrand.   Father Sorin sent her to France at once, in order to study to better advantage while making her novitiate, and on her return the following year she was placed at the head of the academy.   "Mother Angela's personality had a fascination about it; she was courteous, tactful, sympathetic, a rare conversationalist; in fine, a woman of highest culture and truest spirituality."—Ibid., p. 133 seq.

of their country in tending to sick and wounded soldiers in the camps and military hospitals. Many of the best teachers of the order were sent South, Mother Angela herself being one of the first to go. The war records bear the names of nearly four-score Sisters of Holy Cross. Great were the sacrifices, in an educational way, which this work of charity and patriotism entailed. "No other order," it has been said, "made for the purpose sacrifices as did the Holy Cross." [40]

Previous to the Civil War schools or academies had been founded at South Bend (Lowell), Laporte, Michigan City, Chicago, Philadelphia, Washington, and Baltimore.[41] The schools at Philadelphia, although flourishing, were given up, while in the two latter places the work of the Sisters continued to develop after the War, especially in Washington, where the educational interests of the community came to include several boarding academies, as well as a number of parish schools. In the West the Chicago foundation, although most promising, was also relinquished; but many schools were opened in Indiana and Illinois as well as in States farther West. In 1875 an academy was founded at Salt Lake City, a place which became a center for the work of the Sisters in the Far West, other schools being opened in Utah, as also in Idaho and California.[42]

The community in the year 1909 numbered almost one thousand members. The work of the

[40] Archbishop Ireland, Sermon on the Occasion of the Golden Jubilee of Father Sorin, 1888, in op. cit., p. III.

[41] Ib., p. 57.

[42] Ib., p. 148 seq.; Records of the Mother-house.

Sisters is about equally divided between parish schools and academies.

MOTHER WARDE——THE SISTERS OF MERCY

(1843)

The religious teaching orders, as has been pointed out, may be divided into two main classes: those which have a closely knit organization, with a series of establishments dependent upon a common center or mother-house, whether within the limits of a single diocese, or without diocesan limitation; and those whose establishments are independent, although under a common name and rule, and with a common historic origin. In the case of the latter, there is often a relation of more or less dependence between a series of houses and the establishment to which they owe their origin. The Sisters of Mercy belong rather to the former class, and are diocesan in organization.

The foundation of the Order in America dates from the time of the arrival in Pittsburgh of Mother Mary Frances Xavier Warde with six other Sisters, from the convent of Carlow, Ireland, Dec. 21, 1843.[43] Mother Warde was cast in the same heroic mold as the saintly foundress of the order, Mother Catherine McAuley, and she has left the impress of her life and work upon our land for all time. She was born at Mountrath, Queens County, Ireland, about the year 1810. Of a lively, fun-loving disposition, the youthful Frances was at the same time strongly

[43] Rev. Mother M. Xavier Warde, p. 97; Life of Catherine McAuley, p. 506.

drawn to religion from her earliest years.
Naturally bright, she was educated after the best
standards of the time. Her character, according
to those who knew her most intimately, was "a
combination of candor and common sense, of
sweetness and firmness." [44] Her heart overflowed
with love and sympathy for others, and when she
came into contact with the educational and chari-
table work of Catherine McAuley in Dublin, it
needed only the touch of the personal influence
of the foundress to cause the accomplished girl
of eighteen to turn away from the dazzling prospects the world was offering to her, and join the
little band of devoted women who were laying the
foundations of the Sisters of Mercy in Ireland.
Father O'Connor—afterwards bishop—brought
the Sisters to Pittsburgh, where, some months
after their arrival, they opened a school in the
basement of their first convent on Penn Street.
Mother Warde, who had been superior at Carlow, was now a woman of ripened judgment, and
her experience, added to a rare insight and courage, fitted her peculiarly for the rough trials
incident to the pioneer educational and religious
work she was called upon to do.

Many subjects soon entered the novitiate,
among whom was Miss Eliza Tiernan, known as
Sister Mary Xavier, the daughter of a wealthy
banker.[45] The school attendance also rapidly increased. A generous Catholic, Mr. Kuhn, having
donated one hundred and ten acres of land for the
purpose, the Sisters were induced to erect a board-

[44] Mother M. Xavier Warde, p. 16.
[45] Ib., p. 98 seq.

ing-school, which became known as St. Xavier's Convent and Academy. In 1846 Mother Warde, fulfilling the prophetic hopes of Bishop Bruté,[46] took with her six religious, with Sister M. Agatha O'Brien as superior, and proceeded to Chicago, then "a small wooden city, with about fifteen thousand inhabitants." They took up their residence at first in a wretched little house at the corner of Michigan Avenue and Madison Street. A dilapidated frame building adjoining was turned into a schoolhouse; and soon, we are told, it was metamorphosed into "the prettiest and best equipped school building on the shores of Lake Michigan." [47] Such were the humble beginnings in Chicago, where, under the guidance of prudent superiors, the work was destined to grow to such extensive proportions.

It was a rough, roundabout trip from Pittsburgh to Chicago in those days. The Sisters had gone by way of the Great Lakes. Mother Warde came back alone, in the depth of winter, traveling in a kind of stage-wagon, drawn part of the way by oxen. For two days and nights she had neither food nor drink, and for days and nights at a time she never dared for a moment to close her eyes. She arrived at Pittsburgh in a state of utter collapse, her garments saturated with water and mud. But her iron will was never known to bend under personal suffering or adversity—truly, a woman worthy to build upon the foundations laid by a Badin and a Bruté.

Under such leadership the order grew and

[46] Cf. Cath. Sch. Sys. in U. S., p. 357.
[47] Mother M. Xavier Warde, p. 135 seq.

spread very rapidly. The house in Chicago developed and became in time the mother-house of many schools and academies in the city, as well as of some at a distance. One of its branch-foundations was at Ottawa, Ill. In fulfilment of a wish of Father Gallitzin, "the Apostle of the Alleghanies," Mother Warde, in 1848, sent a colony to Loretto, Pa., which became an important center of the work of the order. The mother-house of this branch was afterwards changed to Cresson.[48] In later years the Pittsburgh house sent new colonies to found independent centers at Titusville and Wilkesbarre, Pa. In 1851, the indefatigable foundress, taking with her four of the nuns at Pittsburgh, opened a school in Providence, R. I., and thus laid the foundation of the work of the Sisters of Mercy in New England.

Mother Warde also founded institutions for the sick and the poor, but she realized that the supremely appealing work of mercy for the age was the establishment of Catholic schools. "What work so Godlike," she would repeat, "as the care of the development of these young intellects and the cultivation of their pure hearts!" [49] The work prospered in Providence, and from there its influence soon spread far and wide. Free schools were opened in the city, and a fine large academy built. Missions were founded in Hartford and New Haven in 1852, the former becoming one of the largest and most important centers of the order. The development of the work in Connecticut was

[48] Life, p. 153 seq.; The Cath. Ch. in the U. S. of A., Vol. I, The Religious Communities, p. 398.
[49] Life, p. 158.

due chiefly to Mothers Pauline Maher and Angela Fitzgerald.[50] From Providence Mother Warde, in 1857, took a band of Sisters to Rochester, which became in turn an independent center. Foundations were also made at Newport, Pawtucket, Cranston, and other places in New England, as well as at St. Augustine, Fla., and Nashville, Tenn. During the Know-Nothing excitement of 1855 Mother Warde stood firm at her post in Providence, refusing to leave the city at the request of the timid mayor, and raising by her example the courage of the little band of Catholics.

Her last great foundation was the convent at Manchester, N. H. With a few Sisters from the house in Providence she began to work under the most discouraging prospects, but bigotry melted away at her touch, and the children of the "Granite State," Protestants as well as Catholics, flocked to the free schools and academies she established. The academy at the mother-house, known as Mt. St. Mary's, has had an important influence upon Catholic education in New England. From there also colonies were sent out to form new centers at Philadelphia, Omaha, Yreka, Cal., Jersey City, St. Johnsbury, Vt., and Portland, Me. Mother Warde died at Manchester, Sept. 17, 1884.

Besides the original colony of the Sisters of Mercy which accompanied Mother Warde, several other bands of the Sisters came from Ireland to the United States. One of these established St. Catherine's Convent and Academy, New York City, in 1846, from which, as the mother-house,

[50] Life, p. 186 seq.

new centers were formed at Brooklyn, St. Louis,
Albany, and Rennselaer, N. Y. In 1868 Bishop
McCloskey brought seven of the community in
St. Louis to Louisville, Ky., where, with the
growth of the new convent, the Sisters opened
two academies and took charge of many of the
parish schools.[51] Another colony from Ireland,
consisting of thirteen Sisters, with Mother Agnes,
a woman of rare tact and energy, at their head,
founded St. Elizabeth's Convent and Academy, at
Middletown, Conn., in 1872, and St. Bridget's
at Meriden, in the same State. From St. Elizabeth's branch-houses were established at Bridgeport, Greenwich, Portland, Newtown, and Nauga-
tuck; while from St. Bridget's, which became an
independent mother-house, schools were opened
at Norwalk, Derby, Rockville, New London, and
Torrington, with academies at Ansonia and Mil-
ford.[52] Other colonies from Ireland settled at
Little Rock, Ark. (1850), San Francisco (1854),
Cincinnati (1858), and Philadelphia (1860).[53]

In the year 1910, the Sisters of Mercy in the
United States numbered 4395, about one-half of
whom were engaged in teaching in secondary and
elementary schools. The latter contained about
70,000 pupils.

[51] Records of the Louisville Convent.
[52] The Cath. Ch. in the U. S. of A., Vol. I, p. 395 seq.
[53] Life of Catherine McAuley, p. 506 seq.

URSULINES

From the venerable Ursuline establishment in
New Orleans, two bands of Sisters were sent out
during the Immigration Period which have had an
important educational influence in the Southwest.
One of these opened an academy and free school
in Galveston, Jan. 16, 1847; and the other, an
academy and free school in San Antonio, Sept. 7,
1851. From each of the two establishments new
foundations were made in these cities, and academies and schools were also opened at Bryan,
Laredo, and Dallas. Until recently, the convents
of the Ursuline Order have been, like those of
the Dominican Sisters, independent.[54]

Another historic center of the Ursuline Order
was founded when, in 1845, eleven nuns were
brought by Father Machebeuf from Ursuline convents in France and established at St. Martin's,
Brown County, Ohio, where they opened an academy and school. A convent of the order was
established at Cleveland in 1850, and from Cleveland new convents were founded at Toledo, Tiffin,
and Youngstown, each the center of a number of
schools.[55] The mother-house for the Cleveland
branch, with its numerous schools in that city, has
been established at Villa Angela, in Cuyahoga
County, where a flourishing academy has also
grown up. From St. Martin's also Bishop Lynch
brought a band of six Sisters to Columbus, S. C.,

[54] Records of the Ursuline Convent, N. O.; Cath. Dir.
[55] Howlett, Life of Rt. Rev. J. P. Machebeuf, p. 133; Houck,
A Hist. of Catholicity in Northern Ohio, pp. 82, 721 seq.

where they began an academy and school.
A branch of the Columbus school has recently
been started at Greenville, in the upper part of
the State.[56] Another band of Sisters from St.
Martin's founded an academy at Santa Rosa, Cal.,
in 1880, a branch of which was later established
at St. Helena.

The Toledo group, in 1884, sent a band of
Sisters to Montana, where a number of academies
and schools for Indians, and also for whites, were
developed, the most important being the Academy
of Mt. St. Angela. An interesting offshoot of the
Montana foundation was the sending of three
Ursulines to open a school at Akularak, Alaska,
in 1905.[57]

An even more important Ursuline foundation
—viewed from the standpoint of historic development—was made at St. Louis, Mo., in 1848, by
nuns from Austria. From their mother-house in
that city, schools were taken up by these Sisters
in many parishes through Missouri, and several
branch-houses were established which have
achieved considerable educational importance.
The first and most important of these branch-
establishments was founded in 1855, when ten
nuns from St. Louis opened an academy at East
Morrisania, New York City. The academy and
mother-house was removed to a handsome site at
Bedford Park in 1892. Besides this institution,
the "Bedford Park" group of Ursulines founded
an academy at Wilmington, Del., and have two
academies and several schools in New York City.

[56] The Cath. Ch. in the U. S. of A., p. 451.
[57] Ibid.

In 1873 the convent at East Morrisania put forth another branch, when Sisters were sent to take charge of the schools of St. Theresa's Parish. The work grew rapidly, a novitiate was established there, and an academy and school at Middletown. Another academy was founded at New Rochelle, where, under the energetic direction of Mother Irene, the Sisters opened St. Angela's College in 1904, an institution which, with its new buildings, able teaching staff, and modern curriculum, promises much for the higher education of Catholic women.[58]

The St. Louis convent sent another colony of nuns to Alton, Ill., in 1859, who founded an academy there, and opened a number of schools through the diocese. A school was also established at Lake City, Minn., and the Villa Maria Academy opened at Frontenac, in the same State.[59]

Several other colonies of Ursulines from Europe established themselves in the United States. One of these, consisting of three nuns from Bavaria, founded an academy at Louisville, in 1859. With the growth of the convent, the Sisters were able to establish another academy, known as Mt. St. Joseph's, in western Kentucky. The academy in Louisville has developed steadily, new buildings being erected in 1899. A large number of the parish schools in Louisville, as well as some outside of the city, are in charge of the Ursulines, and they have several other schools beyond the diocese.[60]

[58] The Cath. Ch. in the U. S. A., I, pp. 443, 444.
[59] Ib., p. 446; Cath. Dir.
[60] Ib., p. 449.

A band of Ursulines driven from its German home by the Kulturkampf, after establishing several schools in the diocese of Peoria, opened a school at York, Neb., which became the center of a group of schools in the dioceses of Lincoln and Omaha.[61] Independent Ursuline convents have also been established at Pittsburgh, Grand Forks, N. Dak., Waterville, Maine, Muskegon, Mich., and Malone, N. Y.[62]

A most important event in the history of the Ursuline Order occurred in 1900, when delegates from many houses throughout the world met, at the invitation of the Holy See, for the purpose of forming an administratively organic body out of the scattered convents, with a constitution, a superior-general, and provincial superiors for the various countries. The action of the Holy See was based upon the conviction that the houses of the Order, as anciently constituted, "being autonomous, could neither lend one another help and assistance, nor yet spur themselves on to higher and better things, by reciprocal rivalry."[63] A large number of convents joined the union, although many have thus far remained outside of it. In the United States the united convents are divided into two provinces, the Southern, with its center at San Antonio, and the Northern, with its provincial-house at Middletown, N. Y.

The Ursuline Order is exclusively devoted to teaching. The total number of members in the United States in 1910 was 1932, of whom about

[61] The Cath. Ch. in the U. S. of A., I, pp. 443, 444.
[62] Cath. Dir., 1908.
[63] Cath. Ch. in U. S. of A., p. 441.

two-thirds belonged to independent convents. The total number of pupils was about 17,000.[64]

SISTERS OF THE MOST PRECIOUS BLOOD

(Sanguinist Sisters) (1844)

The Fathers of the Precious Blood, like the Redemptorists, did a great work for the Church in ministering to the German immigrants who were pouring into the Middle West during this period. German Catholics demanded Catholic and German schools, and it was to meet this demand, which was being heard from German settlements through Ohio and Indiana, that the Rev. Francis S. Brunner, Provincial of the San-guinist Fathers, brought a colony of six Sisters from Switzerland to New Riegel, Seneca County, Ohio, in the year 1844. Their first convent was a loghouse, most primitively furnished; but the Sisters had come prepared for hardship, and they bravely set to work, some to clear and till the land, so as to provide the necessaries of life, others to teach in the neighboring parish school or in the school which they began at their log-convent along with a novitiate.[65]

The self-sacrificing labors of the Sisters appealed to the sturdy German immigrants and their children. The novitiate grew, new schools were opened, and new convents formed. The earliest of these was at Thompson, in the same county, in 1845, the first convent building being built of logs. This convent, as also that estab-

[64] Cath. Dir.
[65] Houck, Hist. of Catholicity in Northern Ohio, p. 759.

lished at Glandorf, Putnam County, four years later, became one of the centers of the school work of the Order.[66] The mother-house and novitiate of the community was established permanently at Maria Stein, in Mercer County. Outside of Ohio, the Sisters took charge of a number of schools in the Diocese of Fort Wayne, and of several in dioceses still farther west.[67]

An independent branch of the same Order developed from the coming of a band of the Sisters from Gurtweil, Bavaria, in 1869, and the establishment of a convent and novitiate at Piopolis, Ill., in the Diocese of Alton. As with the Ohio branch, the principal theater of their school work has been the State in which their first foundation was made. Some schools, however, have been taken up in States across the Mississippi, the greater number of these being in the Diocese of Wichita. In 1876 the mother-house was transferred from Piopolis to Ruma, Ill.[68]

A third independent branch of the Order was established when a large band of the Sisters, driven from Gurtweil by the Kulturkampf, arrived at St. Louis. The mother-house and novitiate were fixed at O'Fallon, Mo., which has become the center of a series of parish schools conducted by the Sisters, mostly in the Archdiocese of St. Louis.[69]

The educational work of the order is done chiefly in parish schools. In 1910 there were 1043 Sisters, divided as follows: Maria Stein

[66] Houck, Hist. of Catholicity in Northern Ohio, pp. 760, 757.
[67] Cath. Dir.; The Diocese of Ft. Wayne, p. 468.
[68] Cath. Dir.; The Cath. Ch. in the U. S. of A., p. 411.
[69] Ib.

Community, 662; Ruma Community, 180; O'Fallon Community, 201. The total number of pupils in charge of the three branches was 11,928.[70]

SISTERS-SERVANTS OF THE IMMACULATE HEART OF MARY (1845)

Monroe, Mich., where Father Richard had sown the seed of Catholic education by teaching school himself, was the birthplace of this community.[71] The successors of Father Richard had tried to keep up the school, and by the year 1830 an academy for young ladies had been started.[72] The Redemptorists, who took charge of the parish some ten years later, labored to improve the school, while endeavoring to secure Sisters. In 1845 two Sisters of Providence came from Baltimore, and, being joined by several of the young ladies who had been teaching, a religious community was formed under the direction of the pastor, Father Gillet, with the approval of Bishop Lefevre. Their first home was the old log schoolhouse. The next year, however, a large frame building was erected for an academy, the attendance having grown to twenty boarders and 140 day scholars. Father Joos, who became pastor in 1857, wrote the constitution and revised the rules of the community.[73]

[70] Cath. Dir., 1910.
[71] Cath. School System in the U. S., p. 187; Le Père Juste, by Very Rev. Dean O'Brien, Kalamazoo, p. 33.
[72] Cath. School System. p. 341.
[73] Le Père Juste, p. 34 seq.; The Cath. Ch. in the U. S. of A., Sisters-Servants of the I. H.

In 1858 Bishop Neumann, of Philadelphia, called the Sisters to his diocese. Their first foundation was an academy at St. Joseph's, Susquehanna County, near Scranton. A year later an academy was opened at Reading. Each of these foundations has had an important development. The Sisters in the Diocese of Philadelphia, soon after their arrival, were formed into an independent community, while in 1871 those in the newly created Diocese of Scranton were also organized by Bishop O'Hara independently.

The Scranton community opened a second academy and school at Susquehanna in 1861. This institution served as the central establishment until a new mother-house, together with an academy and school, was erected in Scranton in 1872. Several years later, the novitiate and training-school was removed to Carbondale. In 1902 a magnificent new mother-house and academy was completed at Scranton, at a cost of $200,000. As the community grew schools were opened in the city and diocese and even, in more recent years, in such distant States as Oregon, Idaho, and Washington.

The community in the Philadelphia Diocese developed no less vigorously. A military academy at West Chester was purchased, and here the mother-house was established, under the title, "Villa Maria." Hither also the academy at Reading was removed, and with the new buildings erected and the extensive additions and improvements, a large and finely appointed institution for the education of girls as well as for the training of Sisters has been built up. The work of the

community has been confined to the Archdiocese
of Philadelphia and the Diocese of Harrisburg.
They have had a prominent part in the development of the school system of the Archdiocese, and
at the present writing they have charge of 34 of
its 142 parish schools.[74]

The parent-community at Monroe, although
badly crippled by the loss of the Sisters who
joined the eastern branches when the separation
occurred—only eleven Sisters remained in the
West—gradually recovered its strength, under the
wise government of Mother Mary Joseph and
the zealous aid and direction of Father Joos. A
new building was erected, as the attendance at the
academy increased and new vocations came.
Under Bishop Borgess a normal school for the
better training of the Sisters was established at
Monroe, and through his influence each parish
school was brought into touch with the academy.
A fine new academy building has lately been
erected.[75] The work of the community has been
confined chiefly to the Diocese of Detroit, where
they have had charge of a steadily increasing
number of parish schools.

The number of Sisters in the parent community
in 1910 was 368; in the Philadelphia community,
481; and in that of the Scranton Diocese, 365.
Together, the three communities have charge of
upwards of 35,000 pupils.[76]

[74] Cath. Directory; Hist. of the Cath. Ch. in the U. S. of A.,
I, p. 430-433; Hist. Sketches of the Cath. Churches and Insts.
of Phila., p. 204; Rep. of Supt. of Par. Schools of Phila, 1910.
[75] Le Père Jeste, p. 40 seq.
[76] Cath. Dir.; Hist. Sketches, etc., loc. cit.

CHAPTER III

TEACHERS AND TEACHING COMMUNITIES IN THE IMMIGRATION PERIOD (CONTINUED)

SISTERS OF CHARITY OF MT. ST. VINCENT, N. Y.

(1846)

THE RELIGIOUS community founded by Mother Seton would undoubtedly have grown to be the largest and most influential of the teaching sisterhoods in the United States, had it not been for the splitting up of the parent organization into a number of independent communities.[1] Bishop Hughes was strongly convinced that it would be for the best if the Sisters of the order in New York were organized as a separate body, with the rules of the original community; and in the year 1846 the bishop's wishes were acceded to through an amicable agreement with the superiors in Maryland. Begun in 1817, the work of the Sisters in New York had gradually developed until, at the above date, the diocese counted forty-five Sisters, with two academies—one in Oliver Street and another on East Broadway—and a number of parish schools and orphan asylums. Thirty-five Sisters chose to remain to form the new com-

[1] For the causes which led to this result in the case of the Emmittsburg sisterhood, as well as of other communities, cf. "The Cath. School System in the U. S.," pp. 219, 220.

munity, and Sister Elizabeth Boyle was chosen as the first superior.[2]   One of the early companions of Mother Seton, Sister Elizabeth had been for three terms assistant-mother and for many years mistress of novices at Emmitsburg.[3]   Her first act was to open a novitiate in the establishment on East Broadway, but in the following year the novitiate and mother-house were removed to an estate which was purchased at McGown's Pass, at One Hundred and Ninth Street and Fifth Avenue, within the present limits of Central Park, where, at the same time, the Academy of Mount St. Vincent was also opened.[4]   In 1857 the academy and mother-house were removed to a picturesque site known as Fonthill, on the east bank of the Hudson, fourteen miles above the city.

Meanwhile changes had occurred in the administration, Sister Elizabeth being succeeded by Mother Jerome Ely.   Mother Angela Hughes, a sister of the great archbishop, was also for a time the head of the administration.   Each of these three women contributed much, by sagacious and far-seeing direction as well as by energetic personal service, to the development of the community during its formative period; but Mother Jerome was the predominant influence in shaping its early history, by reason both of superior quali-

[2] When the Emmitsburg community was affiliated to the Sisters of Charity in France, the rules, dress, and customs of the original society established by St. Vincent de Paul were adopted by the American branch. The New York community, on the other hand, retained the rules, dress, and customs inaugurated by Mother Seton.—Sadlier, Elizabeth Seton, p. 282.
[3] Brunowe, A Famous Convent School, p. 30.
[4] Ib., p. 32; Cath. Encyclopedia, III, p. 608; Shea, Hist. Cath. Ch. in U. S., IV, p. 110.

ties of leadership and length of service. Entering the order in the year 1827, at the age of sixteen, she was for over fifty years prominent in Catholic educational work in New York. A woman of quiet self-possession, she was, nevertheless, active and energetic and of unfailing resourcefulness in emergencies.[5] Under her prudent initiative new buildings were erected, the membership of the community was multiplied, and schools, orphanages, asylums, and hospitals were opened in various parts of the city and State as well as in neighboring States.

The immense and rapid growth of the metropolis, following soon after the organization of the community, offered an ample field for the educational activity of the order, and schools were opened in quick succession under the vigorous educational policy of Bishop Hughes. For many years the Sisters of Charity were almost exclusively in charge of Catholic female education in New York, and even with the multiplication of teaching orders in the city within recent decades, they have always remained the chief educational agency of the diocese in elementary school work. While endeavoring to meet the ever growing demand for teachers in the metropolis, the community was also able to extend its energies in other directions. Schools were opened in Brooklyn and New Jersey, as well as in the Diocese of Harrisburg. The schools in New Jersey, as we shall see, led to the formation of a separate branch of the community, while the establishment founded by a little band of the Sisters at Halifax, Nova

[5] Brunowe, op. cit., p. 94.

Scotia, in 1849, likewise developed into an independent order. In 1910 the Mt. St. Vincent community counted 1400 Sisters, in charge of 20 academies, 6 high schools, an industrial school, 5 orphan asylums, and 77 parish schools, with over 50,000 pupils in all.[6]

SISTERS OF CHARITY, OF CINCINNATI, OHIO—
MOTHER MARGARET GEORGE

When the Sisters of Charity of Emmitsburg affiliated with the Daughters of Charity in France, Sister Margaret George was the superior of the Sisters in Cincinnati, where they had charge of two schools and two orphanages, the first Sisters having been brought there by Bishop Fenwick in 1829.[7] Sister Margaret had entered Emmitsburg in 1812, and was one of the original incorporators of the community. She stood very close to Mother Seton, occupying the position of secretary and treasurer, and teaching in the academy. The proposed change of rules and constitutions, traditions and costume, was distasteful to Sister Margaret as well as to her companions, and, with the concurrence of Bishop Purcell, it was arranged that the Sisters of Charity in Cincinnati should continue as before, but independent of Emmitsburg, and under the authority of the bishop of the diocese. The Sisters have thus retained all the essential characteristics of the religious organization of which Mother Seton was the saintly foundress.[8]

[6] Cath. Enc., loc. cit.; Cath. Dir.
[7] Cf. Cath. Sch. Sys. in the U. S., p. 330.
[8] Mother Seton, pp. 46, 54, 64 seq.

The Sisters in Cincinnati at this time numbered seven. A novitiate was soon opened, however, and twenty candidates presented themselves during the first year. As the community grew in numbers its work was pushed on vigorously and extended. The mother-house was transferred to a beautiful property outside the city, where the Cedar Grove Academy was opened. In 1869 the mother-house was finally located at Mt. St. Joseph, on the Ohio, where the chief academic institution conducted by the community was developed. During the period of these changes, which had in view the strengthening and perfecting of the central establishment, the work of the community was gradually expanding. Beginning with 1853 schools were opened in one parish after another in Cincinnati and the diocese, the average being one new school a year.[9]

The Civil War brought this academic development to a sudden stop. The Sisters were among the first to answer the call for nurses; and from May, 1861, to the close of the war, many of them left behind their school-rooms, to care for the stricken defenders of the nation, in the military hospitals and camps. Like the Sisters of the Holy Cross, the Sisters of Charity glory in having sacrificed for the time being their most precious temporal interests at the call of patriotism.[10]

After the war, however, the extension and consolidation of the work of the community proceeded very rapidly. The most notable among

[9] Records of the mother-house; Cath. Telegraph, July 15, 1909. Mother Margaret George, a Brief Biographical Sketch. (1911).
[10] Cath. Tel., loc. cit.

the many branch-houses established during this period was that at Santa Fé, N. M., where the Sisters went in 1865 to lay the foundations of the great educational work undertaken by Bishop Lamy and Father Machebeuf.[11] In 1870 another group of Sisters began the work of the community in Colorado. Several schools were opened in Tennessee, while in Michigan a series of flourishing schools has also been developed. The Sisters were among the pioneers in the Catholic high school movement, having opened a parish high school at Bay City, Mich., as early as 1873.[12]

The Sisters exercised an important influence in the formation of the new community of the Sisters of Charity in New Jersey, under Bishop Bailey.[13] In 1870 they helped to found another important branch of the order at Pittsburgh by training a number of candidates Bishop Domenec sent them for the purpose, and also by sending two able Sisters to remain permanently with the new community—Mother Aloysia Lowe, who was made superior, and Sister Ann Regina Ennis, mistress of novices. The mother-house and principal academy of this branch is now at Greensburg, Pa., and the community numbers over 300 Sisters.[14]

Mother Margaret was a woman of scholarly tastes, and a writer as well as a linguist. During the two terms of office allowed her by the constitution she labored to imbue the teachers with her own pedagogic and academic ideals while, at

[11] See " New Mexico," in chapter on " Far Western States."
[12] Cath. Tel., loc. cit.
[13] See following pages, Sisters of Charity, Convent Station, N. J.
[14] Cath. Dir.

the same time, as a wise and devoted superior, she
sought earnestly to perfect them in the religious
life. At the time of her death, in 1869, she was
the last of the original Emmittsburg band. She
was succeeded as superior by Mother Josephine
Harvey, who in turn was replaced by Mother
Regina Mattingly, both of these Sisters having
been among the founders of the Cincinnati community.

Mother Margaret left a lasting monument of
her life and labors in the tradition of intellectual
thoroughness which she established in the community. It is this spirit which has characterized
the work of the Sisters in the parish schools, and
achieved for them a general recognition as skilful
as well as devoted religious teachers.[15]

In 1910 there were about 700 Sisters, with
22,000 pupils in their schools.

SISTERS OF CHARITY, OF CONVENT STATION, N. J. —MOTHER MARY XAVIER MEHEGAN (1859)

When Bishop Bayley took possession of the
newly erected See of Newark in 1853, he found
parochial schools in charge of lay teachers in most
of the larger parishes, but only two schools—one
at Newark and the other at Jersey City—under
the direction of religious. These were Sisters of
Charity from Mt. St. Vincent's, New York. After
some negotiations the bishop obtained the consent
of the superiors of the community to organize an
independent branch of the order for his diocese.
Mother Mary Xavier Mehegan, who was at the

[15] Records of the mother-house; Mother Seton; Cath. Tel.

time in charge of the Newark establishment, was selected as the superior. Five young ladies who had applied for admission were sent to Cincinnati to be trained in the novitiate of the Sisters of Charity there, and upon their return the Sisters from Mt. St. Vincent's were withdrawn, with the exception of Mother Mary Xavier and Sister Mary Catherine Nevin. The new community was thus formally constituted Sept. 29, 1859, with the establishment of St. Mary's, Newark, as the mother-house.[16]

The progress of the new institute was rapid and steady. In the following year the mother-house was removed to Madison, and an academy opened. In 1880 both were removed to their present location at Convent Station, near Morristown. The academy—known as St. Elizabeth's—has always occupied a front rank among Catholic girls' schools. Its rapid development was largely due to the energy and intellectual ability of Sister Mary Agnes O'Neill, who presided over it for a period of nearly twenty years, acting, at the same time, as assistant to the mother-general. Another lifelong assistant, to whom the community was greatly indebted, was Sister Mary Catherine. But it is to the prudence, piety, and business ability of Mother Mary Xavier, that the rapid progress and almost uninterrupted prosperity of the community is, under God, to be ascribed. A woman of remarkable simplicity of character, combining

---

[16] The habit and constitutions of the Sisters of Charity of Mt. St. Vincent's were retained by the new sisterhood. In 1874, however, the black cap originally adopted by Mother Seton was replaced by a white one with a black veil.

gentleness with firmness, and an heroic faith with a native shrewdness in practical affairs, Mother Mary Xavier merits a high place among the distinguished Daughters of St. Vincent de Paul in America. Her policy has made for the training of the teacher along the most modern and efficient pedagogical lines, while holding fast to the religious spirit and traditions which are essential to the really Catholic school. The development of the community has consequently been marked by a corresponding growth in efficiency of the parish schools throughout New Jersey.[17] Schools were also gradually taken up by the Sisters in other States, notably in the dioceses of Hartford and Harrisburg, and in the Archdioceses of New York and Boston. In the year 1910, there were 1150 Sisters in the community, in charge of 1 college, 6 academies, and 80 parish schools, with upwards of 40,000 pupils.[18]

MOTHER CAROLINE FRIESS—SCHOOL SISTERS
OF NOTRE DAME (1847)

It was in response to the need of teachers for the parish schools which were being organized for Catholic German immigrants that the first School Sisters of Notre Dame came to the United States. The Redemptorist Fathers were specially devoted to work among the Germans, and it was through their influence that the authorities of the Order at its mother-house in Munich, Bavaria, sent out

[17] The venerable foundress, in 1909, attained the eighty-fourth year of her age.
[18] Cath. Directory, 1908; Cath. Enc., III, p. 608; Flynn, The Cath. Church in New Jersey, p. 587 seq.

the first colony, consisting of six Sisters, the party arriving at New York, July 31, 1847. Only a few years had elapsed since the re-establishment of the Order in Europe, and it was still in a weak and struggling condition. The little colony sent to America had no better prospect, humanly speaking, than any of the other religious colonies which arrived here during this period. Its material resources were of the scantiest—amounting practically to no more than money enough to meet the expenses of the journey. Its members spoke only their native tongue, and were almost wholly unacquainted with the character and institutions of the land whose youth they came to teach. To add to their difficulties, the school they had engaged to take charge of, according to the agreement of the superiors with Bishop O'Connor, of Pittsburgh, was at a newly formed Catholic German settlement called St. Mary's, in the wilds of western Pennsylvania. The journey was by stage from Baltimore, and such were the hardships to which they were exposed that one of the Sisters died on the way.[19]

In the little colony, however, was a young Sister whose name in the world had been Caroline Friess. Of German and French parentage, and combining in her character, as an eloquent eulogist has said, "the vivacity, the ardor, the quickness and daring of the French with the steadfastness, the honesty, the perseverance and simplicity of the German," [20] Sister Caroline Friess, although only twenty-three at the time, was a

[19] Abbelen, Mother Caroline Friess, p. 80 seq.
[20] Rt. Rev. John Lancaster Spalding, in ib., Introduction.

woman who seemed to be providentially fitted to grapple with the difficulties that beset the infant community on every side. Quick to see the opportunities of the moment, and as quick to act, gifted with indomitable courage and resolution, she was one of those rare souls who unite in their natures the highest intuitions of the spiritual order with a genius for the practical. The school Sisters would doubtless have prospered in America, even without Sister Caroline. They were needed, and the elements of growth were richly provided for by place and time. But the numerical pre-eminence to which the community attained in Catholic school work, in spite of its untoward beginnings, was due neither to circumstances nor to extraneous aid: its history for the succeeding forty years is practically only the story of her life and work.

Although only twenty-three at the time of her arrival, Sister Caroline was, three years later, made superioress. Schools were opened, soon after their arrival, in the Redemptorist parishes in Baltimore. More Sisters came from Munich, and the work was quickly extended to Pittsburgh, Philadelphia, and Buffalo—a striking instance of the unifying influence the religious orders have had upon the Catholic school system, as against the tendency towards particularism set up by territorial barriers. Sister Caroline foresaw that the community rule of enclosure would lead to difficulties in the carrying on of school work, and succeeded, by a journey to Europe in the year 1850, in securing a modification of this feature. Another step of importance was taken when, on her return, she proceeded to Milwaukee, and definitely established the mother-house of the community there. Bishop Henni, upon whose invitation this change was made, was eager for the establishment of Catholic schools, and, together with his clergy, co-operated with Mother Caroline in the work of building up a strong central establishment in his episcopal city.

From this time on the growth of the community was as rapid as it was solid and widespread in its influence. Mother Caroline became a true American, and her policy and sympathies were as broad as the nation. Although feeling that the Sisters had been called to this country to labor among the Germans, she welcomed candidates for the sisterhood from all nationalities, and, in the course of time, she took schools among the Poles and Bohemians as well as among English-speaking Catholics.[21] She aimed at the establishment of parish schools, rather than boarding-schools or academies, and, in this respect likewise, the tradition she established has been adhered to. One of the chief factors in the success of the community has been the thoroughness of the training in the normal school and novitiate, no effort being spared to give the candidates the benefit of the most experienced teaching and of the most efficient courses of instruction in the science and art of pedagogy.

In 1876 the community had become so large as to make advisable a division of the administration, and the eastern houses were erected into a separate province, with the Baltimore convent as the mother-house. A third province, consisting

[21] See chapter on Schools of the Foreign Nationalities.

of the southern houses, was formed in 1897, with
the mother-house near St. Louis. At the time of
Mother Caroline's death, in 1891, there were
over 2000 Sisters, with nearly 70,000 pupils and
1500 orphans. By the year 1910, the Sisters had
increased to 3786, the pupils to 102,622, and the
branch-houses to 274.[22]

SISTERS OF ST. DOMINIC (SINSINAWA, WIS.)

(1847)

The beginnings of this teaching community,
which has had such an important educational influence in the Middle West, date back to the pioneer
labors of the Dominican missionary, Father Mazzuchelli, who conceived the idea of founding a
community of Dominican Sisters for the education
of girls in elementary schools and academies.[23]
In 1844 he purchased an estate of 800 acres at
Sinsinawa Mound for $6500, the money being
procured mainly from Italy.[24] A college for boys
was established; and on December 26, 1847, two
young ladies, Miss Mary Fitzpatrick and Miss
Margaret Conway, were admitted as novices for
the projected sisterhood, receiving the names of
Sister Ignatia and Sister Clara. Before the end
of the year two more novices were admitted, Miss
Judith Cahill (Sister Josephine) and Miss Ellen
Conway (Sister Rachel). The little community
was now given an organization, and Sister Clara
appointed prioress. On August 15, 1849, the four

[22] Op. cit., p. 159; Cath. Directory, 1910.
[23] Cf. The Cath. School System in the U. S., pp. 246, 339.
[24] Golden Bells in Convent Towers, p. 56.

novices were admitted to the religious profession.
Such was the humble commencement of the work.
In 1852 Father Mazzuchelli, having resigned the
charge of the college, returned to his parish at
Benton, Wis., where he provided a home for the
Sisters, and where, the following year, they
opened St. Clara's Academy. Four Sisters came
from the Dominican Convent at Somerset, Ohio,
to instruct the infant community in the rules and
spirit of the Dominican Order; but only one of
the four, Sister Joanna, remained. Soon after
she was elected prioress, an office which she continued to hold until her death in 1864.

The years 1852-1864 were the formative
period for the community. From Father Mazzuchelli it took its ideals, and also its religious
life and spirit. The great missioner, who had for
twenty years and more been building pioneer
churches and schools throughout Wisconsin, Iowa,
and Minnesota, saw that he could give perma-
nency to his educational work only by means of a
stable organization of teachers. At Benton,
accordingly, he gave himself up to the work of
forming this teaching body. A brilliant scholar,
he taught the Sisters mathematics and the natural
sciences, besides Latin, French, and Italian. It
is not surprising, therefore, to read that the
standard of teaching in the little academy at Benton was high, and that, by 1860, there was not
room in the small frame convent for all the pupils
who applied for admission.

Under Father Mazzuchelli's direction work
was progressing on a new and larger building of
stone, when the year 1864 ushered in a period of

misfortunes and trials which only the strong religious spirit implanted by the founder enabled the
community to survive. The venerable priest died
in February. One after another the Sisters who
were the leaders in the community were stricken
down. Four of the pupils were carried off by
typhoid fever, and, by the close of the year everything "seemed to be tottering helplessly towards
inevitable ruin."

The community was saved, however, by the
spirit of the Sisters. Mother Regina Mulqueeny
took up the work of Father Mazzuchelli and
Mother Joanna, and upon her death, two years
later, Sister Emily Power, at the time sub-prioress,
was elected superior. One of the new superior's
first acts was to purchase the property of the
Dominican Fathers at Sinsinawa, negotiations for
which had been begun by Mother Regina. St.
Clara's was now moved to Sinsinawa, where, the
first year, the attendance numbered one hundred
and fifteen. The community, too, now began a
period of rapid and healthy growth. Up to the
time of the founder's death there had been only
thirty-two members, while during the first decade
at Sinsinawa eighty-five new members were
received, and sixteen new schools opened in Wisconsin and Illinois.

Branch establishments of the Dominican Sisters may be independent of the mother-house,
but there was a strong desire on the part of
the new foundations to continue in a dependent
relation to Sinsinawa. In 1877 Mother Emily
journeyed to Rome, where she succeeded in having the mother-house at Sinsinawa and its branch

houses, in various dioceses of America, consti-
tuted as a united body, under the title of "The
Dominican Congregation of the Most Holy
Rosary." [25]

The second decade at Sinsinawa witnessed the
accession of one hundred and sixty-four new members to the community and the establishment of
many parish schools.   In 1888 the constitutions
were approved by the Holy See.   In considering
the growth of the community since then, the
features that stand out more prominently are: the
constant enlargement and advancement of the
academy at the mother-house, which culminated
in its being chartered as a college in 1901; the
opening of new schools and academies, especially
throughout the Middle West; and the constant
effort to raise the standard of scholarship and of
practical efficiency, especially by the systematic
organization of summer-institute work, in which
the community was one of the pioneers.   Mother
Emily continued as superior until her death, in
1909, and to her wisdom and prudence in government, and, above all, to her insistence upon the
highest pedagogical standards in the training of
teachers, is due the splendid progress of the community and the high rank it has attained among
Catholic teaching orders in the United States.

In 1910 there were 800 Sisters, 1 college, 9
academies, 45 parish schools, with a total attendance of 17,000 pupils.[26]

[25] Golden Bells in Convent Towers, p. 64 seq.; 96; Records
of the mother-house.
[26] Cath. Dir., 1910.

OTHER SISTERHOODS OF ST. DOMINIC

The convents of the Dominican Sisters, like those of the Benedictines, are usually independent. Several new convents were formed from the primal American Dominican community established in Kentucky in 1822, or from its Ohio offshoot of a little later date;[27] many others have been derived from colonies of Dominican Sisters from the convent at Ratisbon, who came to this country during the Immigration Period for the purpose of teaching the children of the German immigrants.

One of these colonies settled in Brooklyn in 1853, and became diocesan in organization. It sent a group of Sisters to California in 1876, where an important series of establishments grew up, dependent on the house at Mission San José. Another group from Brooklyn established a convent at Great Bend, Kansas, in 1902.[28] The Brooklyn community numbered 560 Sisters in the year 1910.

The second of the Ratisbon colonies established itself in New York in 1859. From this foundation, as it developed, schools were opened in a number of widely separated dioceses, the new establishments preserving a relation of dependence to the New York house. Several of the new convents, too, became independent communities, with mother-houses respectively at Grand Rapids, Mich., Blauvelt, N. Y., and Jersey City. The

[27] Cf. The Cath. School System in the U. S., p. 243.
[28] Cath. Directory, 1908.

mother-house of the New York community is at
present at Newburg, and the number of Sisters
is 357.[29]

The third Ratisbon colony settled at Racine,
Wis., from which a number of dependent schools
have been developed, most of these being in Wisconsin.[30]

It was through the personal influence of Abbot
Wimmer, founder of St. Vincent's, Pa., that the
first Sisters from Ratisbon were induced to cross
the ocean. The foundress and first superior of
the Brooklyn establishment was Mother Josepha
Witzelhofer, but it was to Mother Seraphina
Staimer, who succeeded the former in 1864, that
the rapid growth and enduring influence of the
Brooklyn sisterhood is chiefly due. Mother
Seraphina established a novitiate at Amityville,
with a course of studies and training for the future
teachers of the order. Her influence upon Catholic education is shown by the fact that, during the
quarter of a century of her superiorship, the number of Sisters increased from nine to three hundred.[31] Mother Benedicta Bauer, foundress of
the Racine community, deserves remembrance also
for her educational influence. It was indeed due
largely to her, as prioress of the convent at Ratisbon, that the first Sisters came to this country.
She continued to send teachers for the growing
schools until finally, coming in person to America,
she consecrated her remaining years to the work

[29] Records of the N. Y. mother-house.
[30] Cath. Dir.
[31] The Cath. Ch. in the U. S. of Amer., I, p. 329; Dominican
Year-Book, 1912, p. 61.

of teaching and organizing schools among the neglected Catholic German immigrants.

A group of Dominican Sisters from Dublin, Ireland, established a convent in New Orleans, in 1860, where they have charge at present of several schools and academies. They have also founded a convent at Reno, Nev.[32]

SISTERS OF ST. FRANCIS (1851)

A significant feature of the welcome which the Catholics of Philadelphia gave to Bishop Neumann, when he came to take possession of his See, was the announcement that they had, in honor of the event, erected a new parish school. The act recalled the fervor of the early Catholics of the city in the cause of Christian education, and it was a fitting symbol of the spirit and policy of the new bishop, who had once turned schoolmaster himself rather than leave the little ones of his flock without Christian education.[33] Bishop Neumann labored hard to multiply, and to increase the efficiency of, the Catholic schools. The difficulty of getting teachers was met, partly, by bringing in other religious orders, and partly by the organization of a new religious order in Philadelphia. Acting under the advice of the Pope, the bishop, on April 9, 1855, instituted the first community of Franciscan Sisters in the United States, with Mother Mary Frances Bachmann as the superior.[34]

[32] Cath. Dir.
[33] Cf. The Cath. Sch. Sys. in the U. S., p. 279.
[34] Life of Ven. John N. Neumann, p. 365.

While teaching was one of the objects of the new society, it was to be devoted principally to the work of caring for the sick and the poor. Nevertheless, as time went on, the work of teaching assumed a larger and larger place proportionately in the activities of the community. The first school was opened in St. Alphonsus' parish in 1858, and here also the novitiate was established. For a number of years the growth of the community was slow, as only Germans were admitted. Under Archbishop Ryan, however, this limitation was removed. Parish schools were gradually taken in charge, in Philadelphia and vicinity, and branch establishments at a distance formed.

In 1871 the novitiate was removed to a fine property at Glen Riddle near Philadelphia. Since then the growth of the community has been rapid and its territorial expansion correspondingly great. There are now three provinces under the jurisdiction of the mother-house at Glen Riddle. The Eastern Province comprises many establishments in Pennsylvania and New Jersey, as well as several in New England; the Southern includes schools in Baltimore, Wilmington, and other places in the South; while in the Western Province there are establishments in Oregon, Washington, and Wyoming, several of these being devoted especially to the education of the Indians. The number of Sisters in 1910 was 863, with a total of 65 schools.[35]

The first mission of the order established from

[35] Souvenir of the Golden Jubilee of the Third Order of St. Francis; The Messenger of Our Lady of Angels, Apr., 1900; Cath. Dir., 1910; Hist. Sketches of Cath. Chs. and Insts. of Phila., p. 200.

Philadelphia was at Buffalo, in 1861. The development of the Buffalo community, which became independent two years later, ran in lines parallel with those of the parent organization. While clinging to the primitive ideal of charity-work, the Sisters were drawn to take an ever greater share in the work of education. The novitiate, which remained at the mother-house in Buffalo for many years, was lately transferred to Gardenville. Although the immediate educational interests of the community have been confined to the conduct of parish schools in the city and Diocese of Buffalo, an important branch-foundation was made at Millvale, near Pittsburgh, in 1868, which became independent, and the center of a series of schools in the dioceses of Pittsburgh and Altoona. As an offshot of the Pittsburgh branch, a new independent community was formed in recent years, with its mother-house on Staten Island. The Buffalo community numbers at present almost 300 Sisters.[36]

From the original mother-house in Philadelphia, another important branch-foundation was made at Syracuse, N. Y., in 1862. Besides conducting schools in Syracuse, the Sisters, with increase of numbers, took charge of several schools in the neighboring Diocese of Albany, and also of several in dioceses more remote.[37]

Of the Franciscan communities unconnected with the above, the oldest is the Sisterhood of St. Francis, which was founded at Oldenburg, Ind., in 1851. The pastor, Father Rudolf, had sought

[36] Cath. Dir.; The Cath. Ch. in the U. S. of A., p. 332.
[37] Cath. Dir.

in vain for Sisters for his school, until at length
two were allowed to come from the Franciscan
Convent in Vienna. One of the two, disheart-
ened, turned back. The other, Sister Theresia,
the foundress of the community, continued on
courageously, arriving at Oldenburg toward the
end of the year 1850. She at once opened a
school. Several postulants were admitted the next
year, and in 1852 the convent was canonically
established, and an academy opened. More postulants came from Europe, and several from the
vicinity, and other parish schools were accepted.
The complete destruction of their newly built
home by fire could not daunt souls of the mettle
of Mother Theresia or Father Rudolf. Another
and larger building was immediately put up. New
and larger buildings have, in fact, marked each
successive stage of the community's growth at
Oldenburg. When Mother Theresia was succeeded, in 1860, by Mother Antonia—a brave-
hearted woman of the same mold—there were
39 Sisters, while at the latter's death in 1872
there were 140 Sisters, with 28 parish schools.
The educational work of the community is chiefly
in the Archdioceses of St. Louis and Cincinnati
and the Diocese of Indianapolis. In 1910 there
were 574 Sisters, with 6 parish schools and over
13,000 pupils.[38]

The community known as the Franciscan Sisters of Perpetual Adoration was formally organized at Milwaukee by Archbishop Heiss, in

[38] Records of the mother-house, Oldenburg; Cath. Dir.;
Alerding, The Diocese of Vincennes, pp. 378, 587 seq.; Hist.
of Cath. Ch. in U. S., p. 331.

1853. Although obliged for years to struggle to
maintain its existence, the community, under the
guidance of Mother Antonia, overcame little by
little the difficulties of their situation. The first
schools were taken at Jefferson, Wis., in 1864.
Six years later the mother-house was moved to
La Crosse. Efforts were steadily made to improve
the teaching, and the number of parish schools
in charge of the community has constantly grown.
In 1910 there were 60 schools, with 8450 pupils
and 484 Sisters.[39]

Another independent community whose mother-
house is at Joliet, Ill., was founded by a Franciscan superior, Father Pamifolo da Magliano, in
1865. The growth of this community, however,
falls outside of the period we are now considering.
Its field of work is the parish schools, and in 1910,
there were 327 Sisters, with 9325 pupils, and 31
schools.[40]

Several other communities of Franciscan Sisters were founded in the United States as a consequence of the German Kulturkampf.

BENEDICTINE SISTERS (1852)

In introducing the Benedictine Fathers into the
United States and establishing the Monastery of
St. Vincent's, Westmoreland County, Pa., the
Rev. Boniface Wimmer, O. S. B., was creating
influences that were to give a mighty impetus to
the Catholic school movement. The work of the
early Benedictines was chiefly among the Ger-

[39] Cath. Dir.; The Cath. Ch. in the U. S., p. 350 seq.
[40] Ib.

mans. The Order spread and multiplied throughout the country, each new monastery becoming the
nucleus of a circle of schools. One of the first
things Father Wimmer did, after being firmly
established at St. Vincent's, was to bring Benedictine Sisters from Eichstadt, Bavaria, for the
work of the schools. Three Sisters, with Mother
Benedicta Riepp at their head, arrived at St.
Mary's, Elk County, July 22, 1852, and took up
their residence in the house which had been occupied for two years by Mother Caroline Friess
and her Sisters.[41] They taught in the public or
district schools, and the salary received was for a
time their chief means of support. But vocations
were plentiful, and other Sisters continued to
arrive from Bavaria. Boarders began to come,
too, and a part of the convent was set apart for
an academy. By 1855 the community numbered
forty members.[42]

The house having become too small for the
number of inmates, in the following year Mother
Scholastica Burkhard and six Sisters established
St. Benedict's Convent, Erie, Pa. The Sisters
had been called to Erie to teach in the German
school, but an academy was also started, and
parish schools were taken in other cities round
about. Among Benedictine convents, the Erie
establishment, in point of educational influence, is
second only to St. Mary's, its own venerable
mother-house and the cradle of the Benedictine
Nuns in America. In 1859, the convent having

[41] See Mother Caroline Friess—the School Sisters of Notre
Dame.
[42] The Cath. Ch. in the U. S. of A., p. 294.

become independent, Mother Alexia Lechner was
sent from Erie to Covington, Ky., with five Sisters, to take charge of St. Joseph's Parish School,
and during the following year three other Sisters
from Erie founded a convent of the Order in
Chicago.[43]

Both of these branch establishments of the
Erie house have special historical importance.
The Covington school, under the wise and patient
administration of Mother Alexia, grew from the
humblest beginnings to a large and successful institution, known as St. Walburg's Convent and
Academy. Another academy, known as "Villa
Madonna," has lately been opened on a beautiful
spot a few miles out from Covington. Parochial
schools were also taken up, and several foundations were made which developed into new and
important centers of the Order's work. One of
these was at New Orleans, and was founded in
1870. Later on, parish schools in Alabama were
opened. But the most important of the foundations from Covington was made at Ferdinand,
Ind., a few miles from St. Meinrad's Abbey and
College. Here three Sisters from the Covington
convent came in 1867. Teaching in the adjacent
parish schools, tilling with their own hands the
rough soil, training the candidates that came to
them, in a word, teaching, laboring, praying, and
hoping even against hope—such was the life of
this little Indiana community during its early
years. Slowly but steadily it grew. An academy
was opened, and German schools were taken up
in various places in Southern Indiana. Larger and

[43] The Cath. Ch. in the U. S. of A., p. 294.

more modern buildings for both convent and
academy were erected at Ferdinand, while independent branches were also formed, chief among
which was an establishment at Shoal Creek, Ark.,
in 1878, which has become an important convent
and academy, supplying teachers for many parish
schools throughout that State.[44] The Chicago
foundation also became an independent establishment, comprising a convent, academy, and
parish schools. From the Chicago convent St.
Mary's Convent and Academy, Nauvoo, Ill., was
founded in 1870, to which is also attached a series
of parochial schools. Other offshoots are the
Bohemian Benedictine Convent and Academy, in
Chicago, with its series of Bohemian schools, and
the Benedictine community in Colorado, with its
academy at Cañon City, and several parish
schools.[45]

We have followed the extension of this Order
which sprang from the Erie foundation, the first
offshoot. The wide-ranging movement just described is typical of a series of similar growths
that had their origin at St. Mary's, the original
mother-house.

One of these, which began a year after the
foundation of the house at Erie, had for its object
the foundation of a school at Indiana, Pa. Circumstances not being favorable, however, the
Sisters went to Newark, N. J., the same year,
opening a convent and school there, and, later on,
at Elizabeth, which became an independent

[44] The Cath. Ch. in the U. S. of A., p. 297; Cath. Dir.;
Alerding, Hist. of Dioc. of Vincennes, p. 597.
[45] The Cath. Ch. in the U. S. of A., p. 297; cf. Chapter on
Schools of the Foreign Nationalities.

center of a series of parish schools and also the
parent convent of the Benedictine establishment at
Manchester, N. H.   The mother-house of the
Newark branch was subsequently transferred to
Ridgley, Md.   From Ridgley, a colony was sent
to Iowa, but it settled eventually in Oklahoma,
where the Sisters have charge of an academy at
Guthrie and of a number of parish schools.[46]

A few months after this movement eastward,
yielding to the appeal of Bishop Cretin, of St.
Paul, another colony left the mother-house which
was destined to do much for the educational up-
building of the West.   With Mother Benedicta,
the superior of St. Mary's, at their head, this
colony of six Sisters settled first at St. Cloud,
Minn., opening an academy there and a school at
St. Joseph, Stearns County, which was made the
mother-house.   The community had years of trial
and hardship to endure, but it increased with the
rapid growth of the Northwest, extending its
work by taking up new schools and founding new
convents as centers.   It has become the largest
of the numerous Benedictine communities, counting over four hundred Sisters, with schools
in the Archdiocese of St. Paul and the dioceses
of St. Cloud, Duluth, Fargo, La Crosse,
and Seattle.   Six years after their arrival in Minnesota, the Sisters sent a colony to Atchison,
Kan., where an independent convent was established, in which teachers were formed for a series
of parish schools in Kansas, Nebraska, and Iowa,
and from which a new convent has been founded
at Nebraska City.   Another independent branch

[46] Cath. Ch. in U. S. of A., p. 294.

of the community was formed in 1892, with its center at Duluth, the Sisters having charge of an academy in that city, besides quite a number of parish schools.[47]

In 1868 another colony from the original mother-house went southward to Richmond, Va., where an academy and school were opened, the mother-house being subsequently removed to Bristow, in the same State.[48]

The last colony sent out from the venerable convent at St. Mary's founded houses at Carrolltown and Johnstown, Pa., in 1870. The latter establishment was transferred to Alleghany, which became the mother-house of the new community. Besides establishing an academy at Alleghany, and taking charge of a number of parish schools, the Sisters founded an academy and a new center of the work of the Order at San Antonio, Fla., in 1889.[49]

In addition to the Benedictine communities historically connected with St. Mary's, a number of others exist; but as these were founded after the Immigration Period, they do not lie within the scope of the present chapter. It may be noted, however, that most of these later European colonies have gone to the Far West, and that their development has been rapid. Mention may be made of the independent communities at Clyde, Mo., Yankton, S. Dak., Cottonwood, Idaho, and Mt. Angel, Ore., which were founded by Sisters from Switzerland.[50]

---

[47] Cath. Ch. in U. S. of A., p. 294.
[48] Ib.
[49] Ib.
[50] Ib.

According to the ancient constitution of the Benedictine Order, each regularly established convent was to be independent. This was the ruling principle in the developments that have just been described, the usual condition being that of a self-centered convent having attached to it a number of minor establishments or schools. But there has also been a tendency towards the formation of congregations, after the example of the Benedictine congregations of men.[51] Several of the Benedictine communities of women now have a strongly centralized government, like the more modern sisterhoods.

In 1908, there were 1884 Benedictine Sisters in establishments connected historically with the first mother-house at St. Mary's, having in charge about 30,000 pupils.[52]

SISTERS OF THE INCARNATE WORD (1853)

From the Monastery of the Incarnate Word at Lyons, France, several colonies of Sisters were sent to Texas during the Immigration Period. The first of these came in 1853, and established a convent and academy at Brownsville. Other convents and academies were subsequently founded at Rio Grande City, Corpus Christi, and other places in the same State. The houses are independent, under diocesan jurisdiction. Over one hundred Sisters were, in 1910, engaged in teaching in these diocesan branches of the Order,

[51] For an historical sketch of the development of the congregational system in the Benedictine Order, see Cath. Encyclopedia, II, art. Benedictines.
[52] Cath. Dir., 1909.

under the name of Sisters of the Incarnate Word and Blessed Sacrament.[53]

The most important foundation in Texas from the monastery at Lyons was made in the year 1866, when Bishop Dubuis, in search of religious for the work of education and charity in the vast State under his care, applied at length to the superior of this monastery, Mother Angelique. She agreed to set apart several candidates who should form the nucleus of a new congregation. The mission of the new teaching order, which was given the name of Sisters of Charity of the Incarnate Word, was thus expressly dedicated to America, and particularly to the State of Texas. After a brief stay at Lyons, the three Sisters chosen arrived at Galveston towards the end of the same year. Within a few years several other bands were sent out by Mother Angelique, and the Sisters at Galveston were enabled to found new establishments. The most important of these was at San Antonio.

The community at San Antonio, in fact, which was founded by three Sisters who were sent there in 1869 by Bishop Dubuis, has grown to be the most numerous teaching body in the Far Southwest. It was established under great difficulties, but under the wise guidance of Mother St. Madeleine Chollet, the first superior, and of her successor, Mother St. Pierre Cinquin, who has been called the "organizer and soul" of its principal undertakings, the community not only increased greatly in membership, but also in educational resources and efficiency. In 1870, it was made

[53] Cath. Dir.

an independent center, according to the statutes
then in force in the Order. From the mother-
house at San Antonio, numerous missions were
founded, both in the Diocese of San Antonio and
in neighboring dioceses, as well as in Mexico.
These branch-establishments have remained
united with the mother-house, through the adoption of an organization like that of the modern
teaching congregations. The community is known
as the Sisters of Charity of the Incarnate Word.

The mother-house and novitiate were removed,
in 1897, to a spacious site near Alamo Heights,
outside the city of San Antonio, and here also,
several years later, the Academy of the Incarnate
Word was opened. The Sisters have another
academy within the city. Besides many parish
schools, they have academies in a number of the
more important cities and towns of Texas, and
over a dozen in Mexico.

In 1910, there were 538 Sisters in the community.[54]

SISTERS OF THE PRESENTATION (1854)

There are many academies and schools in the
United States conducted by the Sisters of this
Order. The convents are, as a rule, independent
of each other. The oldest establishment is that
at San Francisco, founded in 1854, from which
several branch-houses in California were formed.
The work of the Sisters is devoted to academies,
rather than to parish schools. The other inde-

[54] The Cath. Ch. in the U. S. of A., I, p. 313; Cath. Dir.,
1910.

pendent centers were formed by colonies from Europe after the Immigration Period.[55]

SISTERS OF THE HOLY NAMES OF JESUS AND MARY (1859)

This institute, founded in the Province of Quebec in 1844, sent Sisters to Portland, Ore., in 1859, at the request of Bishop Blanchet. They made the journey by way of Panama and, arriving at their destination, then a little town of 2000 inhabitants, opened St. Mary's Academy. The work of the Sisters grew with the growth of the city and the State. Besides opening another academy in Portland, and taking charge of many of the parish schools of the diocese, they founded academies at Seattle and Spokane which have developed into important institutions. A novitiate was established at the mother-house in Portland, in 1871.[56]

Another colony of the Sisters was brought from Canada to Albany, N. Y., in 1865, by Bishop Conroy. About the same time, Bishop Verot secured some of the Sisters for the Diocese of St. Augustine, where academies or schools were opened at Key West, Tampa, and several other places. These two groups of establishments were united to form a new province of the Order, with the mother-house at Schenectady, where an academy was founded, as also at Albany. The Sisters conduct several parish schools in the diocese of Albany.

[55] Cath. Dir.
[56] See chapter on The Far Western States—Oregon and Washington.

A group of Sisters was sent from Canada to Oakland, Cal., in 1868, where the College of the Holy Names was founded, and a novitiate opened for candidates for the community. They took charge of several parish schools in the vicinity of the mother-house at Oakland, and extended their work southward, opening academies at Pasadena, Pomona, Santa Monica, and Shorb.

In addition to the establishments in the above provinces, there are a number of other schools of these Sisters in the United States which were founded directly from Quebec, and which are dependent on the mother-house there.

In 1910, there were 783 Sisters of the Holy Names in the United States, with over 18,000 pupils.[57]

SISTERS OF THE HOLY CHILD JESUS (1863)

As this community came to the United States near the end of the period now being studied, the account of it here will be brief. Founded by a native of Philadelphia, Mrs. Cornelia Connelly, a convert to the Church, the society sent a colony of Sisters to America from the mother-house at Derby, England, who opened an academy and school in Philadelphia in 1863. At the head of the little band was Mother Xavier Noble. Previous to their establishment in Philadelphia, where they came at the invitation of Father Car-

[57] The Cath. Ch. in the U. S., I, p. 379; Cath. Dir., 1910; Gleanings of Fifty Years—The Sisters of the Holy Names in the Northwest, *passim*.

ter, Vicar-General of Archbishop Wood, they had endeavored to found an academy at Towanda, Pa. Father Carter soon purchased for the Order a beautiful property at Sharon Hill, where a novitiate was opened and an academy. Another academy was established in West Philadelphia a few years later. With the growth of the novitiate, more parish schools were taken in charge in the city, and the work of the community was slowly extended. An academy and school were opened at Cheyenne, Wyo., in 1884. Another academy and school were opened in New York City. The Sisters' principal field of work, however, has continued to be the Archidocese of Philadelphia.

In 1910, there were 190 Sisters, and 4720 pupils.[58]

SISTERS OF DIVINE PROVIDENCE (1866)

Through the efforts of Bishop Dubuis, two Sisters of this community came to Texas from Lorraine, in 1866, and established a school at Castroville. The mother-house was subsequently removed to San Antonio. The community has had an important influence upon the Catholic school movement in Texas,[59] but the history of its growth falls outside the scope of the present chapter.[60]

[58] The Cath. Ch. in the U. S. of A., I, p. 368; Hist. Sketches of the Cath. Chs. and Insts. of Phila., p. 207; Cath. Dir.
[59] See Chapter on The Far Western States—Texas.
[60] Cf. The Cath. Ch. in the U. S. of A., I, p. 324; Cath. Dir.

CHAPTER IV

TEACHING BROTHERS IN THE IMMIGRATION PERIOD

GENERAL CONDITIONS

THE POLICY of the Catholic Church in the United States has, from the very beginning, favored the separation of the sexes in the school at an early age. In the schools of the early missionaries, the tendency was to hire male teachers for the boys, wherever this could be done. When the first sisterhoods came, a boys' school, with a hired teacher, was often to be found side by side with the Sisters' school for the girls. There was a persistent effort, on the part of the great pioneer schoolmen, whether bishops or priests, to bring teaching brotherhoods from Europe, or, failing in this, to institute new ones at home. Thus, Father Nerinckx, early in the last century, organized a brotherhood in Kentucky, and, upon its extinction, the project was renewed by Bishop Flaget. Bishop Dubourg brought some teaching Brothers with him to St. Louis from France, and an attempt was made to start a teaching order of men in New York City, under Bishop Dubois.[1] Bishop O'Connor planted a colony of the Irish

[1] Cf. Cath. Sch. Sys. in U. S., pp. 231, 313, 274.

Brothers of the Presentation at Pittsburgh in 1845.[2] Bishop Hughes brought over Brothers of the Christian Doctrine from Ireland in 1846,[3] while another community of Irish Brothers, a year later, located in Baltimore.[4] None of these foundations, however, was lasting. The failure of such attempts, where sisterhoods that were founded about the same time grew and flourished, argues the existence at the time of conditions making strongly against the establishment and growth of teaching orders of Brothers. A number of the teaching brotherhoods that came to the country during the Immigration Period have grown and prospered; but they have not, generally speaking, kept pace with the growth of the communities of women which were established here at the same time. Vocations to the religious life appear to be more plentiful among women than among men. The disproportion has been less marked in Europe than in the United States, and it is evident that conditions have been operative here which have not obtained, at least to the same extent, in the Old World.

One of these conditions sprang from the rapid growth of the Church, involving, as a consequence, a great need of priests. A somewhat similar condition has been a constant disturbing influence in the public schools. The tendency has been all along for male teachers to drop out of the public schools, because their talents could

[2] Lambing, Hist. of Cath. Ch. in Dioc. of Alleg. and Pittsb., p. 473.
[3] Hassard, Life of Archb. Hughes, p. 284.
[4] U. S. Cath. Mag., VI, p. 105.

command a higher service as well as a higher salary elsewhere. Teaching Brothers who had received a classical training often felt themselves called to the higher life of the priesthood; and bishops, sorely pressed for ministers to break to their people the bread of life, were usually not unwilling to accept anyone who could be properly prepared. All the teaching brotherhoods have suffered severely from this condition, although it is probably less operative to-day than in the past.

Another condition, peculiar to American life, which has had a retarding influence upon the growth of the teaching brotherhoods, is the tendency towards a commingling of the religious or clerical life with the life of people in the world. This condition does not, of course, materially affect the orders of women. The clergy, although subject to its influence, have a safeguard in the character of the holy ministry. The teaching brotherhood, on the other hand, has to withstand this influence, without any countervailing check of the kind. The American teaching brother can not hold himself aloof from the world to the same extent as the nun, or as the teaching Brother in the Old World. In the routine of his daily activities, within and without the class-room, there are a hundred points of contact between the American teaching Brother and the world that are unknown to the more mature religious life in Europe. This condition may pass away, but it has been an important factor in the failures of the teaching brotherhoods referred to above, and its influence has been felt even in the case of those that have grown strong.

There is still another condition that has to be considered. There have not been, at any time, Brothers enough to take charge of the boys in Catholic schools, ardently as this was desired by many of the leading bishops and priests. But even had they been numerous enough, another factor would necessarily have proven a check upon their employment in parish schools. The matter of economy is vital for the Catholic school. Hundreds of Catholic schools keep open because the expense is actually just no more than it is. In debt-ridden parishes, where the problem all the year round is, how "to make ends meet," the school is sometimes felt to be a burden so great that any expedient not inconsistent with the essential purpose of the school which would be calculated to reduce its expense is welcomed. The teaching Brother worked for about one-half the salary of the male teacher in the public school; but the Sister could live on one-half of the Brother's salary. If a school were to be opened, therefore, Sisters were usually employed, as a matter of course. If Brothers were already in the parish, a change was often made, when opportunity offered. Looked at practically, such a policy meant, in many cases, the cutting down of the expense of the school by almost one-half. And in some instances, too, the condition of the parish exchequer left very little choice in the matter.[5]

Still, many parishes employed the Brothers, and even parishes that had to put forth special efforts to make accounts balance, have been known to struggle on and make great sacrifices, in order

[5] See chapter on The Economic Side.

to provide the best teachers possible for the boys. The demand for teaching Brothers has always been greater than the supply, and the demand has grown greater with each succeeding year. The development of the upper grades of the grammar school, and the addition of high school grades to hundreds of schools, has made their services altogether indispensable. On their part, the teaching brotherhoods have clearly recognized this strong academic drift upwards, and they have risen to meet it.[6] While maintaining their elementary schools, wherever possible, they have none the less perceived that their main field of service in the future, in the schools, is to be the upper grades, together with commercial and industrial training. The recognition of this has brought with it a corresponding advance in standards of training. In one instance, a normal training of several years, following upon and distinct from the novitiate, has marked the advance from the old normal course, which was confined to the year of the novitiate alone. Higher or severer normal school standards have, in fact, characterized the growth of all the teaching brotherhoods in recent times.

BROTHERS OF THE CONGREGATION OF THE HOLY CROSS (1841)

The Brothers of the Congregation of the Holy Cross have the honor of being the first of the existing teaching brotherhoods to be established

[6] Cf. chapter on Current Movements and Problems—Catholic High Schools.

in the United States. Early in the Immigration Period, a colony of the Brothers, with Father Sorin at their head, arrived from France, and from Notre Dame as a center they exercised an influence upon the school movement that was widely felt. Founded about the year 1820, and known originally as the "Brothers of St. Joseph," the community united with an association of priests to form the Congregation of the Holy Cross. Both the Sisters of the Holy Cross and the Sisters of Providence of Indiana are closely connected in origin with this congregation.[7]

It was in response to an appeal of Bishop de la Hailandière, of Vincennes, that Father Edward Sorin, with six Brothers, embarked for America in the year 1841, arriving at New York on September 13.[8] After a stay at St. Peter's, near Vincennes, where they taught school for about a year, the community was transferred to the tract of land selected by Father Badin years before for an educational center, the place being named by Father Sorin, Notre Dame du Lac. Here the mother-house was established. A college and a manual labor school were soon opened. With the arrival of more religious from France and of candidates for the novitiate at Notre Dame, the work of the Brothers was extended. Besides several schools in the vicinity of Notre Dame, they also took charge of parish schools at Fort Wayne, Cincinnati, Chicago, Milwaukee and other places in the Middle West. For many

[7] Trahey, The Brothers of Holy Cross.
[8] Cf. The Cath. Sch. Sys. in U. S., pp. 241, 355; Trahey, op. cit., p. 47.

years, too, they had flourishing schools in Philadelphia, Trenton, and Camden, in the East. Most
of these parish schools were eventually relinquished. The chief cause of this was, the scarcity
of vocations to the teaching brotherhood, together
with the remarkable growth of the college at
Notre Dame, which necessitated an ever greater
concentration of the community at home. The
Brothers have continued in charge of a number of
parish schools, however, and of late years, perceiving the trend of Catholic school growth, they
have been quietly preparing to take a larger part
in the work of secondary education. Recently,
they have taken charge of high schools in Fort
Wayne and Chicago.

The concentration of the teaching Brothers at
Notre Dame, while it was a disadvantage to the
school movement, contributed much to the growth
of the institutions at the mother-house, and
especially the college, where the Brothers have
from the beginning had principal charge of the
secondary and commercial classes, and also of
certain administrative positions.[9] It is interesting
to record that the work of Father Sorin and the
six pioneer Brothers, continued in the joint labors
of the Priests and Brothers of the Holy Cross,
have splendidly fulfilled the prophetic plan of
Father Badin for the establishment of a great
Catholic educational center at the old mission-
station of the Potawatomi; and that, with the
recent establishment at Notre Dame of a new normal school for the higher training of the Brothers, the influence of this educational center bids

[9] Trahey, op. cit.; The Cath. Ch. in the U. S. of A.

fair to make itself even more widely felt in the
future in the Catholic school movement, as well
as in the domain of the higher education.

BROTHERS OF THE CHRISTIAN SCHOOLS
(Christian Brothers) (1846)

Long before the first permanent establishment
of the Christian Brothers in the United States, the
efforts made by various American prelates to
secure members of the Order from Europe were
evidence of the high esteem in which the Brothers were held as teachers and of the urgent
need that was felt for them.[10] At length, in
November, 1846, through the agency of the Rev.
Dr. Coskery, rector of the cathedral in Baltimore,
several Brothers arrived in that city from Canada, and opened a school in Calvert Hall.[11]
Almost from the first, candidates for admission
to the Order began to apply. Both an academy
and a free school were conducted.

Two years later a house was founded in New
York, which thenceforward became the chief center of the Order in this country. The New York
band came from France, and was composed
of Brother Styléan, Director, and Brothers
Andronis, Albien, and Pastoris. A school and an
academy were opened in the French parish of St.
Vincent, whose pastor, Father Lafont, had been
largely instrumental in bringing the Brothers to
New York. Brother John Chrysostom, after-

---

[10] Cf. Cath. School System in U. S.
[11] U. S. Cath. Mag., V, p. 686; The Cath. Ch. in the U. S.
of A., I, p. 84.

wards a noted teacher, entered the Order soon after their arrival. Other candidates came also, and the membership rapidly increased. Much had been expected of the Brothers' school work, and the Catholic public was not disappointed. Bishop Hughes, who had long looked for the coming of the community as the culmination of his plans for the advancement of education in the diocese, was an enthusiastic witness to the good results. Placing his own cathedral school under their direction, he did everything in his power to further the progress and spread of their work. Ten schools were opened by the Brothers within the first ten years.[12]

A novitiate and a normal school were opened on Second Street in 1861, the candidates having been sent to Montreal previous to this time. From Second Street, the training schools were removed in turn to Westchester, Amawalk, and, finally, in 1906, to a fine new building erected at Pocantico Hills, on a site commanding a superb view from the Hudson River to the Sound.

As we are concerned here chiefly with the work of the Brothers in the schools, it will suffice to mention the establishment of Manhattan College in 1853, the institution having been begun as an academy. La Salle Academy was started on the first arrival of the Brothers, in St. Vincent's Parish. It was removed from Canal Street to Mulberry Street after some years, and was trans-

[12] The Cath. Ch. in the U. S. of A., I, p. 77; Cath. World, LXXIII, p. 721; Fifth Ann. Rep. of Supts. of Cath. Schools, N. Y.; 1908, p. 85; Considine, Brief Chron. Account; Cath Herald, Jan. 12, 1856; Freeman's Journal, April 20, 1907; Cath. Ed. Rev., I, p. 313.

ferred, in 1856, to its historic site on Second
Street. St. James' Academy, Brooklyn, was
founded in 1851. Two other schools with sec-
ondary as well as grammar grades, St. James and
St. Gabriel's, were opened subsequently in New
York.[13]

Under the energetic administration of Brother
Facile, the work of the Brothers was early extended to other places. A year after their arrival
in New York, a colony was sent to St. Louis.
Academies and parish schools were founded at
Troy, Albany, Syracuse, and Utica. In 1861,
in response to the appeal of Bishop Timon, of
Buffalo, they took charge of St. Joseph's College
there, which became an important center of their
school work in the vicinity. Other schools were
opened throughout New York State in succeeding
years, while new colonies were sent out to more
distant places. The most important of these, perhaps, was the colony sent to San Francisco, in
1868. The work of the Brothers in New England was begun by the founding of the La Salle
Academy, Providence, in 1871. Parochial
schools, academies or high schools have been
opened since then in Fall River, Lynn, and
Waltham, Mass., in Manchester and Dover,
N. H., and in Hartford, Conn. At Detroit, also,
the western limit of the New York Province, a
school was founded.[14]

The establishment in Baltimore continued to
increase, but it was not until the year 1878 that
a novitiate was permanently established there, and

[13] The Cath. Ch. in the U. S. of A., p. 79.
[14] Op. cit.

Baltimore became the head of a new district of the Order. The novitiate and training school were first opened in Calvert Hall. Brother Christian, to whom this result was chiefly due, completed the work by securing a fine property at Ammendale, near the outer suburbs of Washington. Here the novitiate and normal school were transferred, after the erection of a suitable building. The Baltimore District includes New Jersey, Pennsylvania, and the States farther south. The work of the Brothers in Philadelphia was begun as early as 1853, Bishop Neumann, like his predecessor, having earnestly solicited their services. The first Brothers came from Canada, and took charge of the Assumption School. From this, they took charge of other parish schools, an academy being opened at St. Michael's in 1862, and La Salle College, five years later. Parish schools were also taught in the larger cities of New Jersey, as well as in the States to the south. A number of industrial schools were founded, one of these being an institution for colored boys situated at Belmead, Powhatan County, Va. High schools were established at Cumberland, Md., and Augusta, Ga. Several collegiate institutions, in addition to those mentioned, were founded in this district, notable among which is Rock Hill College, near Baltimore, with which the celebrated Brother Azarias was long connected, Calvert Hall College, Baltimore, and St. John's College, Washington.[15]

[15] Op. cit.; Hist. Sketches of the Cath. Chs. in Phila., pp. 177, 186; Memorandum on the founding of the first schools of the Brothers in Phila., in possession of the Rt. Rev. P. R. McDevitt.

Bishop Peter Kenrick, of St. Louis, shared the zeal and enthusiasm of his illustrious brother, the Bishop of Philadelphia, for Catholic schools, and the year following the arrival of the Christian Brothers in New York, he secured a colony of three for his diocese. With the staunch support and encouragement of the bishop, the Christian Brothers College was soon founded by the community, in addition to their taking charge of several parish schools. Under the direction of Brother Patrick, this institution took a leading place among the Catholic colleges of the land, and became the chief center of the influence of the Brothers in the West. So promising was the prospect, that a novitiate was opened in 1866, the bishop donating the old Seminary property at Carondelet for the purpose. The novitiate and normal school were subsequently removed to their present location at Glencoe. Of great importance for Catholic education in the far Southwest was the foundation of St. Michael's College, at Santa Fé, in 1859, the long and dangerous journey across the plains from Missouri being made by wagon. Besides the college at Santa Fé, both secondary and elementary schools have been established at Bernalillo and Las Vegas. Other colleges were established at St. Joseph, Missouri, and Nashville, Tennessee. A series of prosperous secondary schools was also developed in the West. St. Patrick's Commercial Academy, Chicago, dates from the year 1860. Another large secondary school, De La Salle Institute, was opened in Chicago more recently. High schools or commercial colleges were erected at St. Joseph and Kansas City, Mo., and at St. Paul, Minneapolis, and Duluth.[16] The St. Louis District comprises all the territory west of Chicago, as far as the Pacific Coast States.

The work of the Brothers on the Pacific Coast was begun in 1868, when the superior-general, yielding to the requests of Bishop Alemany, sent Brother Justin with seven companions from New York to take charge of the newly founded St. Mary's College, San Francisco, and to form a new district of the Order. The college leaped at once into public recognition and favor. Subsequently, it was transferred to Oakland. In 1897, the normal institute was established near Martinez, on a beautiful site, amid vineyards and olive-groves. Besides St. Mary's College, several parish schools were taken in charge by the Brothers, in San Francisco and other places. The drift of the work of the community in the district, however, has been towards secondary rather than primary education, and a number of large secondary schools have been developed, chief among which are the Sacred Heart College, at San Francisco; St. Joseph's Academy, Berkeley, and the Christian Brothers College, at Sacramento. Farther north, high schools have been established at Portland and Vancouver.[17]

Altogether, in the four districts, there were 1091 Brothers in 1910, with about 31,000 pupils. In the New York District, the community has charge of 45 parochial and 18 complete secondary schools.

[16] The Cath. Ch. in the U. S. of A., p. 86; Cath. World, LXXIII, loc. cit.; Cath. Dir.
[17] Op. cit.

These figures, along with the sketch that has just been given of the expansion of the community, show that, notwithstanding the special difficulties confronting the teaching brotherhoods, the Brothers of the Christian Schools have had a steady and vigorous growth, surpassing, in fact, the growth of most of the congregations of priests. They have had a commanding influence in the development of Catholic high schools. Their organization, like that of the Jesuits and some of the larger sisterhoods, is really country-wide, and each of the four provinces has, together with a distinct field of work, an autonomy and a responsibility of its own.

There are several factors that stand out very prominently when one looks for the causes that have produced these results. One is, the influence of strong, forceful far-seeing, attractive personality. This influence, as has been shown, has been the making of the greater communities of women. Conspicuous among the pioneer builders of the Order's greatness are Brothers Facile and Patrick. The former, being sent over by the superior-general soon after the inauguration of the work in New York, assumed the direction, as provincial, of the community both in Canada and the United States. With an eye that seemed to see clearly into the distant future, and an energy and enthusiasm that could have sprung only from religious fervor, Brother Facile devoted himself for twenty-five years to the work of organization. He mapped out the field, selected the great centers, and sent men to each who appeared to have been born to their tasks. When he withdrew from the work, he left behind him, in Canada and in this country, seventy-six establishments, one thousand Brothers, and upwards of thirty-six thousand pupils.[18]

Brother Patrick was a worthy successor to Brother Facile, as he had been the latter's right hand in the administration for many years before. A brilliant mind and a great teacher, Brother Patrick was, at the same time, a great organizer. He possessed, to a singular degree, the power of attracting the interest and sympathies of men. He not only carried on successfully the great work of his predecessor, but completed and perfected it. It might be said, indeed, that what Brother Facile did for the material growth of the community, Brother Patrick did for its academic development. As the head, first of the college at St. Louis, and afterwards of Manhattan College, New York, he raised the standing of each within a few years to such a degree that they easily rivaled the strongest and oldest Catholic colleges. And in a higher order of activity, subsequently, as superior of the province and as assistant-superior-general, his influence continued to be firm and active in the same direction, his aim being particularly directed towards raising the standard of scholarship in the entire community, by a more thorough and extended training in the normal schools.

An easily discernible factor in the growth of the community has been its organization and spirit. The Institute of the Christian Brothers came to America not only fully organized, but

[18] The Cath. Ch. in the U. S. of A., I, p. 77; circular.

with nearly two centuries of experience behind it.
Its rules and constitutions provided for almost
every contingency. Initiative was needed, but in
the opening of new establishments, the organizing
of new provinces, or in the carrying on of the
daily school-room work, the broad outlines of
what was to be done were to be found already
traced out in the rules. And along with this
highly developed organization, the early Christian
Brothers naturally brought with them the *morale*
which had been derived from the historic achieve-
ments of the Order in the Old World.

A most important element, too, in the growth
and success of the community has been its system
of training the candidates for teaching. In each
of its provinces in this country, there is a normal
school establishment, including three distinct
houses: a preparatory college, a novitiate, and a
normal school proper. In the latter, the candidates, after having already gone over the matter
they are to teach, devote several years to a
thorough pedagogic preparation for teaching, including a review of the matter already seen, a
study of more advanced subjects, a study of educational history, and of the science and art of
teaching. The rules thus provide for a thorough
training of the teacher for his work. It was
adherence to these rules that gave to the Order
in the United States so many brilliant teachers,
and that fitted even the ungifted teacher so well
for the work he was called upon to do as to render
him, generally speaking, both efficient and
faithful.

BROTHERS OF THE SACRED HEART (1847)

One of the results of the educational movement inaugurated by Bishop Portier at Mobile, Alabama, after he became the head of the diocese in 1843, was the establishment in the United States of the Brothers of the Sacred Heart, who had been founded at Lyons in 1820.[19] Through the efforts of the Rev. John S. Bazin, who soon afterward became Bishop of Vincennes, but who was at the time vicar-general of Mobile, a colony of the Brothers was secured for the diocese, where they arrived in 1847, opening a free school in the heart of the city of Mobile. They also took charge of the orphan asylum. The first teachers of the Order in the United States were Brothers Athanasius, Alphonse, David, and Placide. There were urgent calls for the Brothers from other dioceses, and in 1854 a college and school were opened at Bay St. Louis, Miss., in the Diocese of Natchez. In the course of time, schools were opened at Natchez, Vicksburg and Meridian in the Diocese of Natchez, and at New Orleans, Baton Rouge, Donaldsonville, Alexandria, and Mansura in Louisiana.

A broad field of educational service and a promising future was thus opened out to the community in the South when the Civil War came, with all its calamitous effects, and for a time the Brothers experienced the greatest difficulty in carrying on their work. After the war, however, they took

[19] For the work of Bishop Portier, cf. Cath. School System in U. S., p. 296.

up with renewed ardor the task of opening new schools and developing them along lines demanded by the needs of the times, and their work has been of the very greatest utility in the furtherance of Catholic education in the South. From almost the very beginning they have given special attention to secondary education, and they have established a number of important institutions of this class throughout the South. Schools were also opened in the North. Under Bishop de St. Palais, they took charge of a school in Indianapolis; and a number of prosperous schools, both secondary and primary, are conducted by the Brothers in New England. But most of the teachers are engaged in the schools in the South.

A novitiate was established at Mobile in 1857, but at present the novitiate, the postulate, and the mother-house of the community for the United States are located at Metuchen, N. J., in the Diocese of Trenton. In the year 1900, the houses in Canada were erected into a separate province. It is to the Province of Canada that the members of the community engaged in teaching in the dioceses of Manchester and Providence belong.

In 1900, there were 225 Brothers in the United States, with 5 secondary schools, 10 parish schools, and about 2700 pupils.[20]

[20] Records of the mother-house, Metuchen; Shea, IV, pp. 280, 684; Alerding, Hist. Diocese Vincennes, p. 208; Cath. Dir., 1910, p. 762 and passim.

FRANCISCAN BROTHERS (1847)

One of the most zealous and active of the bishops of the Immigration Period in behalf of Catholic schools, Bishop O'Connor, of Pittsburgh, brought a second community of teaching Brothers from Ireland, in the year 1847.[21] The Brothers were from Mount Bellew, in the Archdiocese of Tuam. A college was established at Loretto, and several schools were opened in the diocese. Another college was subsequently established at Spalding, Neb. In the year 1910, there were 67 members belonging to this community in the United States.[22]

Another branch of the same Order was brought by Bishop Loughlin to Brooklyn, in 1858. Two Brothers began the work of teaching, but they were soon joined by new members. Out of the first humble beginnings, St. Francis College has developed, together with St. Leonard's Commercial Academy, also in Brooklyn, and over a dozen parish schools. St. Francis Academy is chartered as the preparatory department of the college. The novitiate is located at Centerport, Long Island. There were 76 Brothers in this community, in 1910, with an enrollment of over 8000 pupils.[23]

[21] Cf. Introduction to present chapter.
[22] Lambing, The Cath. Ch. in the Dioceses of Pittsburgh and Allegheny, p. 474; Cath. Dir.
[23] Cath. Ch. in the U. S. of A., p. 172; Cath. Dir.; Freeman's Journal, Mar. 2, 1907.

BROTHERS OF MARY (1849)

The Brothers of Mary were induced to come
to the United States through the influence of the
Rev. Clement Hammer, pastor of Holy Trinity
Church, Cincinnati, a parish that was one of the
historic school centers of the pioneer West. The
Rev. Leo Meyer and four teaching Brothers,
Andrew Edel, John B. Stintzi, Maximin Zehler,
and Damian Litz, arrived at Cincinnati from
Alsace, December 3, 1849.[24] The Brothers began
at once the work of teaching. Father Meyer, who
was the superior, purchased a large estate near
Dayton, the following year, and here the mother-
house was permanently established. A day school
was first opened, but boarders were afterwards
also received. This was the germ of St. Mary's
Institute, an institution comprising a college and a
preparatory school, and the most important establishment of the Brothers in this country. A normal school and novitiate were also opened at the
mother-house.

The Society of Mary of Paris—the name proper
of the community—is composed of priests and lay
brothers; but the latter far outnumber the former,
and devote themselves by preference to the work
of the primary school. Although this has been
the special aim, the Brothers engaged in elementary teaching have, nevertheless, felt the
strong tide of popular sentiment for the establishment of Catholic secondary schools. The community has borne a leading part in the high school

[24] The Cath. Ch. in the U. S. of A., I, p. 94; Cath. Dir.

movement, principally by the development of high
school grades in connection with its parish schools.
Its influence in this way is shown by the fact that,
out of the forty-three parish schools in charge of
the Brothers, twenty-seven contain one or more
high school grades. In addition, they conduct
several fully equipped secondary schools.[25]

The first mission of the society was at San
Antonio, Texas, and was undertaken in 1852, at
the instance of Bishop Odin. Apart from this,
however, the schools taught by the Brothers
during their first twenty years in America were
nearly all in Ohio, and the work was concentrated
chiefly in Cincinnati and Cleveland. At the
mother-house, the various institutions were developed, vocations were received and trained, and
thus the number of teachers greatly increased.
The four pioneer Brothers were the pillars upon
which the steadily enlarging structure of the community rested. Brother Zehler devoted himself
chiefly to the building up of St. Mary's Institute,
at the mother-house. Brother Edel was the
founder and long the president of the institution
at San Antonio. Brother Stintzi founded and
directed many of the parish schools opened by
the community in Ohio during the first twenty
years. In recognition of his successful school
work, he was appointed inspector of primary instruction, and during the ensuing seventeen years
he labored to raise the standards both of the
schools and of the teaching. Brother Litz is distinguished, in the annals of the Order, by the wide
extension he gave to its educational work. After

[25] Op. cit.

laboring in Wisconsin for a year, he founded St. John's Cathedral School at Cleveland, in 1857. Thence he went to Rochester, in 1864; and after founding a school at New Orleans, he taught at Baltimore, New York City, and Paterson. Brother Litz contributed educational articles to the Catholic press, and was one of the foremost educators the Order has produced.[26]

The period of active expansion, which began in 1869, was continued through the provincialship of the Rev. J. N. Reinbolt, whose twenty-one years of administration were marked by so many new establishments that he is regarded by many as a second founder of the province.[27] The movement of expansion went on during the administrations of Fathers Beck and George Meyer. Schools were founded even in Mexico and Manitoba, and a college and several schools on the Hawaiian Islands. Of the new establishments, SS. Peter and Paul's School, St. Louis, Mo.; St. Louis College, San Antonio; Spalding Institute, Peoria, and St. Mary's School, Dubuque, are institutions of secondary education. In San Antonio, St. Mary's College was reserved for day scholars, with the building of the new St. Louis College, outside of the city, for boarders. In 1907, the western houses of the community were organized into a separate province, the mother-house of which was located at Clayton, Mo., where a normal school was opened.

The high repute of the Brothers of Mary as

---

[26] The Cath. Ch. in the U. S. of A., I, p. 96.
[27] Ib., p. 97.
[28] Ib.

teachers has been due, not only to the careful training the rules provide for in the normal school, but also to the system of inspection and supervision that obtains with reference to those actually engaged in teaching. For the office of inspector of instruction, the ablest and most experienced teachers have been selected, and the work of the inspector has borne abundant fruit in the improvement of methods of teaching. The pioneer, Brother Stintzi, was succeeded in this office by Brother J. B. Kim, whose qualities and experience as a teacher were reinforced by a zeal and energy that never flagged. For a period of almost twenty years, he devoted himself to the duties of the inspectorship, making the round of the numerous schools, in the constant effort to improve the methods and teaching. It is to him, perhaps, more than to anyone else, that the academic advancement of the community is due.[29]

In 1908, the society counted over 400 members in the United States, with an enrolment of upwards of 12,000 pupils.[30]

XAVERIAN BROTHERS (1854)

The community of the Xaverian Brothers was founded with the express purpose of furnishing teaching Brothers to the United States. The founder, Theodore Ryken, a native of Holland, had assisted missionary priests in this country by teaching catechism. Realizing the great lack of religious teachers, he returned to Europe, and, on

[29] The Cath. Ch. in the U. S. of A., I, p. 97.
[30] Ib., p. 98.

June 5, 1839, organized the new community in Belgium. Seven years later, he and twelve other young men made the religious vows. In 1848, a house was established in England.[31]

The first mission of the Brothers in the United States was in the Diocese of Louisville, long known as the Diocese of Bardstown. Under Bishop Flaget, attempts had been made in vain to form a teaching brotherhood.[32] Bishop Spalding, however, meeting the founder of the new society in Bruges, induced him to send a colony of the religious to his diocese. The founder, who had taken the name of Brother Francis Xavier, with a predilection for the land of his earlier missionary labors came himself, accompanied by six Brothers, the party arriving at Louisville, Aug. 11, 1854. Two parish schools were at once opened.

The early years of the community in Europe had been full of trial. An even severer ordeal awaited it in America. The Know-Nothing movement was in full force, and the faith of Louisville Catholics was being tried as by fire. The Brothers were pursued with suspicion, ridicule and insult, and were finally forced to abandon their home. They were thereupon recalled to Europe. Only the founder remained behind, together with Brother Stephen, who had joined the community soon after their arrival, and who is therefore regarded as the pioneer American Brother.[33]   In

[31] The Cath. Ch. in the U. S. of A., p. 283.
[32] Cath. Sch. Sys. in U. S., p. 231.
[33] Brother Stephen died in 1911, after sixty-three years of active service in the community.—Cath. School Journal, Oct., 1911.

1860, a second colony arrived, consisting of six members. Two new schools and a novitiate were now opened. A select school was also begun, which developed into St. Xavier's College, one of the most important Catholic institutions of secondary education in the West.

New members joined the Order in Louisville, and the Brothers were soon able to found other establishments. The first, as well as the most influential of these, was at Baltimore, where they were invited by Bishop Spalding, when he was transferred to that See, and where they took charge of St. Mary's Industrial School. They transferred the novitiate to Baltimore, when America was recognized as a province of the Order in 1875, and, in connection with the novitiate, established Mt. St. Joseph's College, which became the mother-house. Under Brother Alexius, the first provincial, and his successors, Brothers Dominic and Isadore, the work of the Brothers has been successfully extended. They have had an important part in the Catholic high school movement, especially in Virginia, where they conduct secondary schools at Richmond, Norfolk, Fort Monroe, and Newport News. At Danvers, Mass., they opened a preparatory school in 1907. They have also charge of industrial schools in several dioceses, and of a number of parish schools.

There are preparatory training schools for candidates for the community at Louisville, Danvers, and Baltimore. After completing a high school course, these pursue their studies for some time at Mt. St. Joseph's College, whence they enter the novitiate.   During the novitiate, lasting two years, their studies are continued.

In 1910, there were 250 Brothers in the United States, with 6425 pupils.[34]

[34] The Cath. Ch. in the U. S. of A., loc. cit.; Cath. Dir.

CHAPTER V

SCHOOL LIFE AND WORK DURING THE IMMI-GRATION PERIOD

MATERIAL EQUIPMENT

ALL THROUGH the Immigration Period pastors and people struggled hard, in the face of the gravest difficulties, to improve the material equipment of the schools. By the term "equipment" is meant chiefly the school building and its accessories, with the indispensable requisites for the teaching of school, such as benches or seats, desks, blackboards, and the arrangements for heat and light. The curriculum was usually very simple, and there was no thought, in most cases, of many of those material accompaniments to class-room work which we include in the requisite equipment of the school to-day. But earnest efforts were made to improve the necessary school equipment, as it was understood at that time.

At the beginning of the Immigration Period many of the best parish schools in the East were taught in church basements, while in the West log school-houses were still far from uncommon. The total cost of all the Catholic school buildings in the State of New York in the year 1846 was probably less than $50,000, and New York at

this time had become the center of the parish
school movement.[1] It did not cost much to make
school-rooms in the basements of newly erected
churches. Some of the "splendid cathedrals" of
the time were erected at a cost no greater than
that of modest parish churches of to-day. With
the rapid influx of immigrants, and the growth of
the Catholic population, separate school buildings
began to multiply. In the West, this movement
was naturally of slower development. The church
nave was often used for school purposes on week
days, as was the case in Cleveland, where the little
frame building, 60 by 30 feet, erected as a church
in 1848, was made to serve also as a school, the
sanctuary being closed from view by folding
doors.[2] But such an arrangement did not usually
last very long. Separate school buildings came
sooner or later with the growth of the parishes,
and although the first ones were rough-looking
and bare, these gave way in turn, after some years,
to structures that were larger and better adapted
to the work of instructing the young. From the
primitive arrangement, too, of teaching boys and
girls in the same class-rooms or at least in the
same building, there was usually a tendency towards the complete segregation of the sexes, by
the establishment of separate boys' and girls'
schools.

[1] U. S. Cath. Mag., V, p. 170.
[2] Records Amer. Hist. Soc., III, p. 129.

RELIGIOUS ATMOSPHERE

In typical Catholic parish schools, the curriculum during this period consisted of the traditional "three R's"—reading, writing, and arithmetic, together with spelling, grammar, geography and history. In girls' schools, the Sisters taught the pupils to "use the needle as well as the pen; to make and to mend; to darn and to knit, and become useful in the home."[3] The studies in Catholic schools were, generally speaking, the same as those in the public schools about them, with the exception, of course, of catechism.[4] The atmosphere and spirit of the Catholic school was, however, peculiar to itself. This has been the vital point of difference, from the very beginning, between Catholic and non-Catholic schools; and, with the growth of the great teaching communities, and the replacement of lay teachers by religious, this difference became greater and more clearly perceptible.

As typical of the spirit which the religious teacher strove to foster in the school, the following may be quoted from a Teachers' Manual in use at the time. The book was an official directory for a teaching community which occupied a front rank and was establishing schools in almost every part of the country:

"The training of the heart, the head, and the hands must enter into our scheme of education.

[3] Life of Mother Warde, p. 112.
[4] For the scope of these studies at the time, the methods employed in teaching them, and the results achieved, see Johnson, " Old Time Schools and School-books."

In the heart, we should endeavor to cultivate piety and the domestic virtues, as charity, patience, meekness, and self-denial; in the mind, a knowledge of the branches deemed necessary or useful to a woman; and the hands we should train to the distinctively feminine accomplishment, the use of the needle.

"Rule by kindness rather than by severity. Make the class-room attractive. Foster the self-respect of your pupils, and excite emulation and the hope of reward. Deal with the children individually. Corporal punishment is forbidden.

"Endeavor to instil piety into the hearts of your pupils. Teach them how to pray, and show them the example. Once a week, oblige each child in the lower grades to recite alone the principal vocal prayers. In the higher grades, occasionally examine the pupils in the same manner. Explain the offices of the Church, especially the Holy Sacrifice of the Mass, on which you should give an instruction once a week. Each day, in every class, a hymn relating to the mystery or devotion of the time should be sung.

"In speaking of the life of Our Lord, encourage the children to show their love for Him by practising acts of mortification and other virtues. Inspire your pupils with a noble pride in being children of the Catholic Church, and teach them to follow the spirit of the different festivals and seasons of the ecclesiastical year.

"Make pupils self-reliant. Teach them to think and act for themselves. Encourage the dull and timid, rather than urge forward the more gifted children. Require the exact words of the book in the recitation of prayers, catechism, and the rules of grammar and arithmetic; in all other branches encourage the pupils to use their own language.   Reserve the place of honor for the essential branches—reading, writing, spelling, arithmetic, grammar, history, and geography."[5]

It is evident, from the discussion of the methods of teaching these "essential branches" which follows in the Manual, that the better Catholic schools of this period were fully abreast of the best non-Catholic schools of the time in respect to the secular studies.   It will be noted that besides the giving of direct catechetical instruction, which usually occupied half an hour every day, it was sought to foster a strong devotional Catholic atmosphere by the singing of religious hymns, the explanation of the liturgy, and instructions on the life and virtues of Christ.   Leading Catholic educators of the time clearly recognized, too, the importance of making the religious instruction concrete and practical.   Thus, we are told that, in the catechetical method of Mother Warde,

"The children were taught, with much precision, their duties to God, their neighbor, and themselves.   Dry facts were never presented to the pupil.   Every truth was illustrated by some beautiful example or soul-stirring story.   Truth and sincerity were strongly fostered, while every effort was used to stamp out falsehood and deceit.   The children were shown the manner in which the Christian virtues may be practised and the opposite vices uprooted."[6]

[5] From the "Course of Studies" of the Sisters of Notre Dame of Namur, whose mother-house was established in Cincinnati; quoted from "Origin of the Cath. Ch. in Salem" (Mass.), by Rt. Rev. Louis S. Walsh, p. 105 seq.
[6] Mother M. Xavier Warde, p. 110; cf. also the Lives of Mother Caroline Friess and Sister Louise.

But what of the religious instruction in boys' schools? It must be remembered that the religious communities of women—whose system and methods of religious instruction are represented in the above quotations—often had charge also of the younger boys. For the teaching brotherhoods, we may take as typical the work of the Christian Brothers in one of the schools they founded during this period. Writing of his school days in the early '50's, one of the best known priests of our time has left us the following impressions of the religious instruction imparted by the Brothers:

"Their system was intelligent, their discipline strict—almost military, their affection for us deep and religious. But of course I love them best for the Christian-doctrine course they gave me. No word describes it so well as the word 'thorough.' It was given us by men who knew what they taught, and had the gift of teaching intelligently. It embraced a full summary of the whole dogmatic system of Christian truth; a practical, working knowledge of Christian morality; much ecclesiastical history, especially concerning the early and heroic age of the Church and the acts of the martyrs; together with a wonderfully full equipment of controversial matter. When, in after years, I swung off into the world and was beset with its false maxims, the Brothers' maxims held me fast in the true religion. This had more than anything else to do with keeping alive in me the elements of divine faith. I have no hesitation whatever in saying that the fact that I spent those years of my boyhood in the Brothers' school has been the main reason why I have remained a Catholic. . . . If I wished to emphasize any quality in them it would be their manliness. They were courageous, generous, honorable men, and their influence was all bent on making us manly Catholics.[7]

Not all the schools, however, were taught by religious. Some of the secular teachers were but ill prepared to impart religious instruction effectively; yet, in many cases, Catholic secular teachers strove successfully to foster a strongly religious atmosphere, as may be illustrated by the following description of a school taught by a young lady at Littlestown, Pa., in 1867. The school contained 55 boys and 65 girls.

"The school was thoroughly religious. The classes began with prayer, and on Wednesday and Friday afternoon some one of the scholars said the beads, to which the whole school answered. It was usual to have one of the boys read aloud some book on etiquette, or on some entertaining or religious subject while the girls were engaged in sewing."[8]

TEACHERS AND PUPILS

As the pioneer religious from the communities of Continental Europe did not know English, it might be supposed that this would prove a serious drawback to the efficiency of their early work as teachers. A drawback it undoubtedly was; and, since teachers continued to come from abroad,

[7] The Rev. Walter Elliott, C.S.P., in Cath. World, Vol. LXXIII, p. 728, supplemented by letter to the author, Oct. 3, 1909.
[8] Hist. of St. Aloysius' Church, Littlestown, Pa., p. 53.

the condition often lasted for some time. But the difficulty was really not so great. Native postulants were soon received. Catholics were eager to have the Brothers and Sisters in their schools, even though fresh from Germany or France. These, in turn, realizing the opportunity and the need, labored heroically to acquire the language of their adopted country. Often, indeed, they took up the work of teaching in English-speaking schools after being in the country only a few weeks. The Sisters of Notre Dame of Namur, for instance, reached Cincinnati Oct. 30, 1840, and on the 18th of January following they opened school, only one of the band of eight being able to speak English fluently. The case was typical, and it was met by most of the immigrant communities in much the same way. The various branches of study were distributed among the Sisters in Cincinnati, we are told, according to the degree in which each excelled in them, one teaching writing, another painting, one music, and another needle-work. The Sister who could speak English went from class to class in order to help, until the teachers had acquired enough of English to talk with their pupils. The pupils, on their part, were eager to help out.

"Sometimes a Sister would leave the room and, returning with a slate, read from it what she wished to say. Many were their amusing blunders; as, for instance, when one wished to tell her pupils to erase something from the blackboard, she said, 'Raise that from the board!' Having been told of her error, she resolved to use the simpler words, 'Rub it out!' The following day she said, with some assurance, 'Rip that out from the board!' and one mischievous child took a pair of scissors and pretended to obey. Daily the pupils were told to 'get into their desks.' " [9]

Even Catholic children, in seeing the Sisters for the first time, gazed with awe upon them, as though beings come from some superior world. A pupil of the pioneer school of the School Sisters of Notre Dame in Milwaukee, has left us a picture of her first religious teacher, with a recollection of her first impressions:

"Her large rosary cross, as it swung by her side, was the first thing to attract our attention. With timid, silent wonder we regarded the stately Sister, as, bright and smiling, she stood before us. Perceiving our curiosity, she presently remarked: 'Yes, dear children, take a good look at me, with eyes and mouths open.' Somewhat abashed, the elder pupils cast down their eyes, but the little ones persisted in scrutinizing their first School Sister, in her black robe with wide sleeves, her strange head-dress and large rosary cross." [10]

This was a German school, with German Sisters, and there was here, of course, no difficulty about the language. In Milwaukee, however, as in other cities at the time, the Know-Nothing agitation made it unsafe for the Sisters to appear in their religious garb on the street. In this school,

"A dark corner was partitioned off, to serve as a little dressing-room for the Sisters. At that

[9] Memoirs of Sister Louise, pp. 46, 56.
[10] Mother Caroline Friess, p. 121.

time they could not even cross the street in their religious dress. Here, too, they partook of their meager dinner of soup and vegetables brought from the convent in a tin pail." [11]

The communities which came from Ireland possessed a great advantage, in their knowledge of English, over the communities from the continent of Europe, and the schools of the Sisters of Mercy reached a high degree of efficiency from the very beginning. It is interesting to note the importance attached by these well trained Sisters to object-teaching, in even those pioneer days. Their first school in Chicago, founded in 1846, at the corner of Michigan and Madison Streets, soon boasted of quite a collection of home-made apparatus to accompany class and recitation-work. On parchment, which was sent by friends in Ireland, the Sisters sketched maps of the different countries, in a series adapted to the different grades or classes. For globes they made sphere-frames of willow branches, and over this material they fastened parchment upon which was sketched the map-work of the hemispheres. Blackboards were made of planed timber formed in squares, which were fastened to the wall and painted. Numeral-frames were formed of delicate elm framework, with strings of wire stretched horizontally, on which were strung small spools painted in the primary colors. In this old wooden building in pioneer Chicago, we are told that

"The community-room, with its rough board walls, was a veritable ware-house of school sup-

[11] Mother Caroline Friess, p. 125.

plies. In variety and design to suit all wants might be seen hand-made maps and charts, solar systems and globes, ball-frames and color plans; squares, cubes, cones, cylinders, and all the necessaries for teaching form; collections of minerals, sponges, coral, etc., and specimens of the vegetable kingdom for object-lessons; cardboard, paints, brushes, mucilage, scrap-books, and other school paraphernalia." [12]

In view of the advanced methods employed by these Sisters, and the careful training they had received, it is not surprising that Mother Warde was pressed with demands from all sides to open schools. Yet, among their first pupils in Chicago were "children of trappers, border-men, hardy settlers, and sea-faring men," while a class of Indians was formed for instruction in Christian doctrine.[13]

School-teaching, even in the cities, was a trying occupation in those days. In the smaller towns and country districts, it often involved hardships comparable with those endured by the sturdy pioneers who formed the first infant settlements in the West. Where the school-teacher was a Sister, this was especially apt to be the case, because to poverty and privation there was added a social isolation which would have rendered the life unendurable, except for the transforming influence of the religious spirit. Usually, two or three Sisters were sent to the smaller places. Some glimpses of the teacher's life under such circumstances may be had from a description of

[12] Mother M. Xavier Warde, p. 141.
[13] Ibid.

school-teaching at New Diggins, Wis., in the '60's and '70's, by a Sister of St. Dominic. The place was practically a Catholic settlement; and the teachers, although religious, were paid by the state.

"It was a small mining town of one short street and a wide prairie full of mineral holes. Our abode was a cottage of four rooms, and our furniture was all that the heart of an anchorite could desire. A fervent zeal and an enthusiasm so ardent that it still glows and often bursts into flame carried me through the first three months of the school year, and then I had to summon up all the courage I had inherited from my Puritan forefathers, for from the farms round about the little town there came to me the stalwart youths who worked in summer and went to school in winter.

"Poor little me! How they towered above me! How big and strong and invincible they seemed; but how gentle, simple, and submissive they proved to be. How eager they were to learn, and how respectful they were, because I was a woman, but more because I wore the religious garb.

"And so Sister and I ploughed our way, on the bitter winter mornings, through the old fashioned depth of snow, to the queer, roughly built schoolhouse, and did our best for our simple hearted charges. At noon we ploughed our way back to our icy cold cottage, built a fire in our tiny stove, made a cup of tea, consumed it and a goodly slice of bread and butter with an appetite that regarded quantity rather than quality. I remember that we had only one knife and one teaspoon, but were quite rich in the possession of two forks and two small cups and saucers (one pink and the other blue), also three plates and a few other odds and ends of table furnishings.

"Lonely? Never! We were too busy, and then, in the little frame church, so very near to us, was the Blessed Sacrament.

"It is amazing how attached I became to that seemingly desolate place. To be busy about the things of God is a wonderful heart tonic. Our boys and girls claimed our attention all day, and some of the boys came to the cottage in the evening to do extra work in bookkeeping and business arithmetic.

"My hardy masculine pupils came long distances, over almost impassable country roads, and they were boots—'boots'—capitalized and emphasized. To the sturdy calfskin footgear, with the hob-nailed soles, the yellow clay of the locality clung in heavy masses and was finally plastered over the great rough planks of our schoolroom floor." [14]

Whether engaged in teaching in cities, towns or country places, the Sister's life was, then and now, a life of intense activity—far more so than that of the lay teacher; for besides school work, there were, in the case of the former, religious exercises and various other duties and observances incident to the community life. Vacation brought its own round of activities, less irksome and monotonous, and enlivened by a larger companionship, for vacation was generally spent at the mother-house, but with little opportunity for idle hours. Writing from the famous academy at Emmitsburg, in

[14] Sister Charles Borromeo, O.S.D., Little Essays for Friendly Readers, p. 207; The Cath. School Journal, Jan., 1907, p. 236.

1848, a Sister of Charity has left us a description
of her life as a teacher which may be taken as a
fair illustration of the activity of the average
religious teacher, whether engaged in academy or
school work:

"At one time school is commencing and everything has to be arranged in 'apple-pie order,' as
regards studies and classes, etc., etc., and as soon
as the way is clear, come the preparations for
Mother's Day and the Play—which important
events fairly over, the Distribution compositions
claim all my leisure, then preparations for Distribution, then the Distribution itself, then the vacations, then the Retreat, and then the routine com-
mences again. In reading this you might suppose
the vacations to be, as the name implies, free time
—but never were you more mistaken than you
would be in such a supposition, for it is the busiest
time of all, since every long or odd job is put off
to be done in vacation. These various duties,
with my regular classes, my painting, sleep, meals,
and religious exercises—last but by no means least
—fill up my time so completely, that it seems
sometimes that before I have time to realize the
arrival of one month, the next has taken its place.
As for days and weeks, they are nothing." [15]

TEXT-BOOKS

From the time of the Revolution Catholics in
the English-speaking States appear to have made
free use of the text-books which were in common
circulation in non-Catholic schools—a tendency

[15] Letters of Sister Ignatia, p. 26 (Georgetown Univ. Lib.).

which has continued down even to the present time. A desire was indeed felt all along for distinctively Catholic text-books, and this desire gave rise to a formal decree of the Second Provincial Council of Baltimore.[16] The ideal, however, has never been fully realized, although, as time went on, the number and circulation of Catholic text-books greatly increased.

Father Molyneux, of Philadelphia, writing in 1785, said he was having printed *a Spelling Primer for children with a Catholic Catechism annexed*—a work which he had had printed some years before, and which was an abridgment of Bell's. About the time Father Molyneux was getting out his first Catholic English school-book, Noah Webster was preparing his *Speller, Grammar* and *Reader*. Webster's *Speller* became a standard text-book in Catholic as well as non-Catholic schools. Not long afterward, Pike's *Arithmetic* and Murray's *Grammar* made their appearance. The latter book, published first in England, came to be, for several decades, the most popular grammar in this country, and was widely used in Catholic schools. The first geography appeared in 1800. Text-books soon multiplied in these common branches. Catholics generally made use of those that were regarded as the best school-books of the time.[17]

Bishop Carroll's catechism, adopted from England, came to be generally and permanently accepted in Catholic schools, although others have

[16] Cath. Sch. Sys. in U. S., p. 250.
[17] Ib. p. 134; Balt. Archives, Case 5, Letter K, Carroll Administration; cf. Johnson, Old Time Schools and School-books; Reeder, The Hist. Devel. of School Readers.

been put forth from time to time.[18]   Father Molyneux had Bishop Challoner's *The Catholic Christian Instructed* reprinted in this country, and this
work as well as Reeve's *History of the Old and
New Testament,* in two volumes, served as readers in the post-Revolution schools.[19]   The series
of text-books compiled and published by Father
Richard in Detroit had a considerable circulation
in Catholic schools in the West.[20]   In 1833, we
find Father Mazzuchelli getting out a Winnebago
version of the catechism which Father Baraga
had prepared for the instruction of the Ottawa
Indians.[21]

Early Catholic educators in both East and West
had thus labored to meet the wants of Catholic
schools in the matter of text-books.   The Immigration movement, with the multiplication of
Catholic schools and the coming of the religious
orders, greatly stimulated the production of distinctively Catholic text-books.   Catholic book-
stores and publishing houses, too, were opened in
several of the larger cities.   Prominent among
these may be mentioned the establishment of
James Ryan, who kept a "Classical and Mathematical Book-store" at 322 Broadway, New
York, in 1826, and who announced at this time
that he was publishing *The Mathematical Diary,
containing new researches and Improvements in
the Mathematics, with collections of Questions.*[22]

[18] Cf. Cath. Sch. Sys. in U. S., p. 250.   A copy of the 1804
edition of this catechism exists in the Congressional Library.
[19] Records Amer. Cath. Hist. Soc., X, p. 225; XI, p. 69.
[20] Cf. The Cath. Sch. Sys. in U. S., p. 190; Ann. Prop. Foi,
VI, (1833-4), pp. 166, 171; VIII, p. 323.
[21] Wisconsin Hist. Coll.. XIV, p. 159.
[22] Amer. Cath. Hist. Researches, New Series, II, p. 335.

The following year, he published *An elementary treatise on arithmetic*. He had previously published *an elementary treatise on algebra,* and *The new American grammar of astronomy*.[23]

Another publisher who contributed to the growing Catholic school movement was Eugene Cummiskey, of Philadelphia. Early in 1843, he announced the publication of the *First and Second Book of Reading Lessons*. Before the end of the year, the *Third Book* was announcced, and three years later *The Literary Class Book, or Fourth Series of Select Reading Lessons, in prose and verse* made its appearance.[24] These books were reprints of readers prepared by the Brothers of the Christian Schools in Ireland. The publication of the entire series evidences the existing demand for Catholic school books, as well as the efforts that were being made to carry out the decree of the Second Provincial Council of Baltimore.

A young man who was teaching in a Catholic school in Baltimore at this time saw the great and growing need of Catholic text-books, and set to work courageously to supply the need himself. This was Martin J. Kerney, a nephew of the Rev. Nicholas Kerney, pastor of St. Patrick's Church, in the same city. Martin was born at Lewistown, Md., in the year 1819, and went to Mt. St. Mary's when only eleven years old, working his way through the college by various employments until his graduation-year. It was expected that he would be a priest, but he married and studied law. Before graduating in law, his uncle prevailed on

[23] Rep. Comm. of Ed., 1897-8, p. 829.
[24] U. S. Cath. Mag., 1843, Jan., Oct.; 1846, July.

him to open a school. In the early '50's, after graduating in the law, he was elected to the legislature, where he introduced and championed a bill providing for the distribution to Catholic schools of their *pro rata* share of the school tax. This action proved the death of his political prospects. He devoted himself chiefly to literary work from this time until his death in 1861. He was editor of the *Metropolitan* magazine, and also of the *Catholic Almanac,* and he edited and published the *Child's Youth's Magazine.* His most lasting and influential work was, however, the writing and editing of text-books for Catholic schools. His interest in the Catholic school movement of the time was intense—an interest which was doubtless due in part to his admiration for Bishop Bruté, a close friend of the family.[25] Many of his text-books became standard works in Catholic schools and academies, and several of them, with repeated revisions, have continued to be used down to the present day.

In the year 1845 he brought out his *Compendium of Ancient and Modern History,* which ran through thirty editions in twenty-two years.[26] His *Abridgment of Murray's English Grammar,* which was announced in 1846, was long a standard text in Catholic schools. The same was true of the *Columbian Arithmetic,* which appeared two

[25] These details were communicated to the author by the Rev. John Barry, Catonsville, Baltimore Co., who is related to the Kerney family. For an account of the educational work of Bishop Bruté, cf. Cath. Sch. System in U. S.

[26] This work, of 431 pages, in 1867, was revised and enlarged by John O'Kane Murray, in 1880 (599 pages). Its latest revision and enlargement was by Prof. Charles H. McCarthy, in 1909 (737 pages).

years later. In 1850, he published the *First Class Book of History*, designed for beginners, and the *Catechism of the History of the United States*. The former of these two works reached its twenty-second edition in 1868, and, like the *Compendium*, is still widely used.[27] The *Catechism* was designed to accompany Irving's Series of Catechisms, and was also very popular. The success of this work induced Kerney to bring out new and revised editions, for Catholic schools and colleges, of the other texts in Irving's Series. This task occupied him during the four following years. The series included a text-book in each of the following subjects: astronomy, botany, Grecian antiquities, Jewish antiquities, Roman antiquities, practical chemistry, and the history of England. He also edited Burke's text of Lingard's History of England.[28] Subsequently, he was engaged in editing the *Metropolitan* magazine (1853-1858).

Many of Kerney's texts were brought out by John Murphy & Co. of Baltimore, publishers of the *Catholic Almanac* and *The United States Catholic Magazine*, the leading Catholic periodical of the time. This firm rendered a great service to the cause of Catholic education by the publication of Catholic text-books. In addition to the works already mentioned, the following list of Catholic school books, advertised by Murphy & Co., in 1846, will show the rapid progress that had been made in this direction

[27] A book of 175 pages in the original edition, it has now, after a number of revisions and enlargements, 437 pages (edition of 1900).
[28] Cf. Bibliography, in Cong. Library, Wash.

within a few years. The subjoined prices of the books will not be without interest: [29]

Manual of Catholic Melodies, Hymns, Psalms, etc.	$1.00
Short Introduction to the Art of Singing	.12
Compendium of Ancient and Modern History, by J. M. Kerney	1.00
Butler's Larger Catechism	.04
Butler's Smaller Catechism	.02
Catholic School Book, containing easy and familiar lessons	.15
English Reading Lesson	.31
Modern History, by P. Fredet, D. D.	.87
Models of English Literature	.75
Reading Lessons, by the Christian Bros., 1st book, paper	.06
Reading Lessons, by the Christian Bros., 2d book, one-half bound	.12
Reading Lessons, by the Christian Bros., 3d book, bound	.50
Universal Reading Book, muslin	.31

Father Peter Fredet (1801-1856), was professor of history at St. Mary's College, Baltimore. His histories, *Ancient* and *Modern*, became very popular in Catholic colleges and academies, and ran through many editions. The *Modern History* appeared in 1842, and the other volume some years later.[30]

Singing-books were in demand, and much attention was paid in many of the schools to instruc-

---

[29] U. S. Cath. Mag., V, no. 11.

[30] From a volume of 353 pages as first published, the *Modern History* has been expanded until, in its latest revision by Prof. McCarthy (1910), it was enlarged to 783 pages.

tion in singing. The above list was not, it need scarcely be said, exhaustive. Text-books had been published by other Catholic firms, and some had been brought out by Murphy & Co. that do not appear in this list. Moreover, besides distinctively Catholic works, the firm handled the leading non-Catholic text-books, and the long list of these appearing in the advertising columns of the *United States Catholic Magazine* shows the extent to which non-Catholic works continued to be used in Catholic schools, notwithstanding the comparative activity of Catholic authors and publishers of school books.[31]

Another Catholic publishing house of the time was that of D. & J. Sadlier & Co., of New York. In the early '40's this firm began to bring out new Catholic text-books, as well as revised editions of standard non-Catholic works. Many of the Catholic books were prepared by the Christian Brothers. The Sadliers' publications covered almost every subject in the grades of both the elementary schools and the academies. One of their most notable works was the *Metropolitan Readers,* compiled by Mother Angela, of the Sisters of the Holy Cross. The series consisted of six readers, the last of which appeared only after the Civil War. Although rather gloomy-looking, with few and but poorly executed illustrations, and with lessons that perhaps dealt too often with the more serious subjects, the *Metropolitan Readers,* for all this, did very excellent service.

Bishop Gilmour's series of readers, which were brought out by Benziger Brothers during the

[31] U. S. Cath. Mag., VI, no. 5.

'70's, represented a real advance.[32] There was an abundance of illustrations, and these were not simply incidental, but were made use of in order to convey the ideas of the text to the mind of the child. Bishop Gilmour's *Readers* formed a transition from the dry and formal text-books of earlier times to the bright and attractive school books of to-day. The bishop had a clear perception of certain psychological principles whose adoption by the teachers of our time has brought about a far greater change in the methods and spirit of teaching than even the change that has taken place in the form of the text-books.

In the matter of improvement in text-books in more recent times, Catholics may be said to have kept fairly abreast of the general educational movement. In the '80's, the Catholic Publication Society brought out a new series of readers, under the editorship of the Rev. John Lancaster Spalding, afterwards Bishop of Peoria. Benziger Brothers, who have, during recent decades, assumed the lead in the publication of Catholic school books, deserve credit for the continual efforts made to produce Catholic text-books embodying the results of the best educational thought and practice. Distinctively Catholic text-books are, however, still confined mostly to the classes in English and Christian doctrine. In

---

[32] Bishop Gilmour was a sturdy champion of Catholic schools. He spoke and lectured often in their behalf. His deep personal interest in the welfare of the schools and his keen insight into their vital needs were evidenced again, later on, by the educational organization he established in the Diocese of Cleveland, after the Third Plenary Council. See chapter on Organization and Administration.

other subjects, with perhaps the exception of singing, Catholic educators employ freely to-day, as
they have done from the beginning, the works of
non-Catholic authors.

CHAPTER VI

IN THE FAR WESTERN STATES

PLAN AND SCOPE

IN KEEPING with the general plan of this work, as a study of the origin and development of the Catholic school system, it is the intention to deal with only the earlier period of Catholic school growth throughout the Far Western States in the present chapter. In a previous volume, the foundation of the school system in the States lying east of the Mississippi and immediately to the west of it, was described, and also the early Spanish missionary schools in California and the Southwest.[1] It remains to describe the Catholic school movement in the Far West. The plan of the work forbids the attempt to enter into the history of the schools in each diocese fully or in detail; and the general educational influences and conditions that were felt in each diocese, in the Far Western States as elsewhere, will be considered in the chapters that follow. These general influences took the form of school legislation and organization, school economics, discussions respecting the character and rights of the Catholic school and its relations to the state, the prac-

[1] The Cath. School System in the U. S.: Its Principles, Origin, and Establishment.

tical efforts made to adjust those relations more
satisfactorily, and other educational movements.
The study of these general features involves the
history of Catholic school development throughout all the States and dioceses. The movement
was everywhere one, not only in spirit and purpose, but also in its external trend and phenomena.
At the period we have now reached, therefore,
it is only these larger and more universally felt
influences with which, in view of our purpose, we
have mainly to deal.

Something has already been said of the first
Catholic schools in the States lying immediately
west of the Mississippi River. In Missouri, the
early schools have been dealt with at considerable
length, not only because Catholic educational history began very early in Missouri, but also because the State became the cradle of Catholic
educational activity throughout the Far West.[2] In
the other States east of the Rocky Mountains,
the development of the school system was mainly
due to the immigration movement, whose general
educational characteristics and influence have just
been studied; in this group of States, therefore,
we shall content ourselves with noting the circumstances relating to the founding of the earliest
schools. In the States lying farther west, where
special influences were at work, attention will be
directed to the character of these special influences, so far as the general scope of the work may
permit, as well as to the circumstances surround-
ing the earliest Catholic schools.

[2] The Cath. School System in the U. S.: Its Principles, Origin, and Establishment, ch. VIII, p. 297 seq.

IOWA, MINNESOTA, THE DAKOTAS, NEBRASKA, KANSAS

Although public schools probably antedated Catholic schools in IOWA, Catholic schools were, nevertheless, established there at a very early period. The first public school was founded in 1830, and when Iowa was admitted to the Union as a State, in 1846, there were but one hundred public schools, all built of logs.[3] Several Catholic schools appear to have been established in the Territory previous to 1840 by Father Mazzuchelli, the pioneer Dominican missionary. In that year, he built the new St. Paul's Church, in Burlington, with a basement to be used as a school.[4] Davenport had also a church, with a schoolroom attached. About the same date, Bishop Loras, who had been appointed to the See of Dubuque three years before, opened a boys' school in a room in his own house.[5] Priests taught school quite commonly in Iowa in the pioneer days, but with the arrival of the Sisters of Charity of the Blessed Virgin in Dubuque, in 1843, the history of organized educational work in the diocese really begins.[6] Efforts were made to establish teaching brotherhoods for boys in the diocese, the Brothers of St. Joseph being brought from Notre Dame, Ind., in 1844, and Brothers of the Christian Doctrine from Europe, in 1851; but in neither case were the establishments permanent.[7]

[3] Dexter, Hist. of Ed. in the U. S., p. 116.
[4] Laurent, in Iowa Cath. Messenger, Jan. 27, 1894.
[5] Ib.; cf. also Cath. Almanac, 1840.
[6] See Ch. II, Srs. of Charity of the Blessed Virgin.
[7] Shea, Hist. Cath. Ch. in U. S., IV, pp. 244, 247.

The first Catholic school within the State of MINNESOTA appears to have been the Indian school which was taught by Father Francis Pierz, at Grand Portage, in 1838.[8] Father Pierz and Bishop Baraga established several Indian missions in northeastern Minnesota. It was the custom of these two scholarly missionaries to teach the Indians, especially the young, not only Christian doctrine, but also to read and write their own language, and it is probable that there were other Indian schools in the State, in addition to the one at Grand Portage. These schools, however, were not of a permanent character. The history of organized Catholic education in Minnesota begins with the arrival of the Rt. Rev. Joseph Cretin at St. Paul, in July, 1851, as the first bishop of the diocese. Bishop Cretin, as vicar-general at Dubuque, had been associated with Bishop Loras in the educational activity that marked his administration of the diocese. Bishop Cretin set to work immediately, in his new field, to lay the ground-work of a system of Catholic schools. Minnesota (including the present States of North and South Dakota) had been made a Territory only two years before. At the time of Bishop Cretin's arrival, the population of the Territory was but 5000, and that of the village of St. Paul, 1200; but immigration was beginning to swell these numbers. The bishop could count but 7 priests in all his vast diocese.[9] The first non-Catholic school was only four years old. Soon

[8] Verwyst, Life of Bishop Baraga, p. 384.
[9] The Diocese of St. Paul: The Golden Jubilee, p. 59; Shea, op. cit., IV, p. 260.

after his arrival, Bishop Cretin brought four Sisters of St. Joseph, from Carondelet, Missouri, with Sister St. John Fournier as superioress, and on Nov. 10, 1851, the Sisters opened their first school in the log-building erected a few years before as St. Paul's first church. A special school building was begun the following spring. Other Sisters came from Carondelet. A strong central establishment, including an academy, was built up, and parish schools were taken in charge by the Sisters in St. Paul and Minneapolis and other places throughout the diocese.[10] Bishop Cretin also brought a colony of Benedictine Sisters, under Mother Benedicta Riepp, from the parent establishment of St. Mary's, Pa., and established them at St. Cloud, Minn., in 1857. Several years later, they transferred the mother-house to St. Joseph's, in Stearns County, and from here as a center the Sisters opened parish schools in many places throughout the State. Both of these communities have contributed greatly to the development of education throughout Minnesota and the Northwest.[11]

The first school in NORTH DAKOTA was a Catholic school established at Pembina, in the year 1818.[12] The beginning of systematic Catholic school organization in North Dakota dates from the year 1880, when a colony of Presentation Nuns from Dublin, Ireland, arrived at Fargo,

[10] Records of the mother-house, St. Louis; Most Rev. John Ireland: Sermon on Occasion of Fiftieth Anniversary of Sisters of St. Joseph, p. 2; Ravoux, Memoires, Reminiscences, etc., p. 80; Shea, op. cit., IV, p. 258 seq.
[11] The Cath. Ch. in the U. S. of A., I, p. 296; cf. also Chapter III supra, The Benedictine Sisters.
[12] Cf. The Cath. Sch. System in the U. S., p. 319.

and opened a school and academy. This was six years before the admission of the Territory into the Union as two States.[13] A branch establishment was founded at Aberdeen, in SOUTH DAKOTA, in 1886, and a number of other schools were opened later on by the Sisters from here. The Benedictine Sisters from St. Joseph's, Minn., opened schools in several places in North Dakota. A convent of Benedictine Sisters from Missouri was also established at Yankton, S. Dak., in 1888, and this community has opened numerous schools in both of these States. Another community known as the Sisters of Mary of the Presentation, which was exiled from France during the recent persecution of the religious orders there, has taken charge of a number of schools in North Dakota. In many of the country districts in the Dakotas, as also in other western States, the district schools are practically Catholic, the settlers being mostly Catholics, and the religious instruction of the children being cared for by the Catholic lay teachers, under the supervision of the pastors.[14]

Catholics were among the pioneers in educational work in KANSAS, although they may not be able to claim the credit of having founded the first school. Father De Smet, the celebrated Jesuit missionary, in 1838, established a mission among the Potawatomi Indians, who had been shortly before transferred from Northern Indiana and Southern Michigan to Kansas.[15] A school was probably opened at the same time. Three years

[13] Cath. Directory, 1910, p. 789.
[14] Ib., p. 359.
[15] De Smet, Western Missions, p. 343.

later, there were two schools connected with the
mission center of St. Mary's, on the Kansas River,
one school being for boys and the other for girls.
The girls' school at this time was taken in charge
by the Ladies of the Sacred Heart.   Both were
boarding schools of an industrial character, as was
generally the case with Catholic schools for the
Indians, and both were highly successful.[16] Schools
were also opened among the Osage Indians, on
the Neosho River, in 1847, and were attended
with like success.   Here also there were separate
schools for boys and girls, and special attention
was given to the industrial arts.   The girls' school
was conducted by the Sisters of Loretto, from
Kentucky.[17] With the opening of Kansas to white
settlers in 1854, the history of Catholic education
in the State, on a permanent organized basis, begins. Benedictines from St. Vincent's, Pa., arrived
the following year, and in 1860, the energetic
Father Wirth founded St. Benedict's Abbey at
Atchison, where a college was also begun.   Three
years later, Bishop Miège brought Benedictine
Sisters from St. Joseph's, Minn., who founded a
new mother-house at Atchison, and from here
the Sisters were sent to take charge of schools
in various parishes of Kansas and the neighboring
States.[18] A colony of the Kentucky Sisters of
Charity, from Nashville, Tenn., was established
at Lawrence, in 1859, where the Sisters opened an

[16] De Smet, Western Missions, pp. 348, 527; Chittenden and
Richardson, Life, Letters and Travels of Father Pierre Jean
De Smet, S.J., Vol. II, p. 720; and Vol. III, p. 1199.
[17] Records of Sisters of Loretto: cf. Cath. Sch. System in
U. S., p. 235; De Smet, op. cit., pp. 355, 358, 361, 387; Shea,
loc. cit.; Hodge, Handbook of Amer. Indians, p. 885.
[18] Cath. Directory; Shea, p. 658.

academy. Soon afterward, they founded another
academy at Leavenworth, which became the
mother-house of this independent branch of the
Order. A number of schools were opened by the
Sisters in Kansas, and the community became in
time one of the largest and most important teaching bodies in the West.[19]

It is probable that a school was opened by Fathers Verreydt and De Smet, the Jesuit missionaries,
when they established a mission among a tribe of
the Potawatomi Indians at Council Bluffs, near
Omaha, in 1838. The Indians were, however,
some years later removed to Kansas.[20] In 1859,
there were but two priests in NEBRASKA, with a
Catholic population of about 300 families, scattered along the River Counties.[21] Omaha at this
time was a mere village. Immigrants, however,
were pouring into the Territory, and among them
were many Catholics. The first Catholic church
in Omaha was built in 1856, and about two years
later a large frame schoolhouse was erected for a
boys' school. This was the first Catholic school
for white children in Nebraska of which we have
historic record. Lay teachers were employed. A
vicar-apostolic, in the person of the Rt. Rev.
James M. O'Gorman, was appointed in 1859, and
in 1863 this prelate erected a convent in Omaha
which was occupied the same year by seven Sisters
of Mercy, from Manchester, N. H.[22] The Sisters
opened an academy and schools. A school was

[19] Cath. Dir.; Shea, p. 659; Palladino, Indian and White in
the Northwest, p. 293, seq.
[20] Creighton University: Reminiscences, p. 25.
[21] Records Amer. Cath. Hist. Soc., III, p. 111.
[22] Ib.; Shea, IV, p. 655; Creighton Univ., p. 35.

also established at Nebraska City.   Bishop James
O'Connor took charge of the diocese in 1876,
and under his administration there was constant
and rapid educational progress, a number of
teaching orders being brought to the State, among
which were the Sisters of St. Francis from Lafayette, Ind.[23]

MONTANA, COLORADO, UTAH, WYOMING

The history of the Jesuit missions in MONTANA
begins with the founding of St. Mary's Mission,
not far from the present city of Missoula, by
Father De Smet, in 1841.   Other missions were
founded by the Jesuits among various Indian
tribes in Montana in succeeding years, and it is
probable that there was some formal teaching of
the Indian youth at all these stations.   This was
certainly the case in respect to agriculture and
other industrial arts.   Catholics were, in this sense
and to this extent at least, the pioneers in educational work in Montana.   About 1855, a school
which was to be supported by government funds
was opened at the second of the missions, known
as St. Ignatius, but it had soon to be closed for lack
of means.[24]   In 1863, however, school buildings
were begun, and in the Fall of the following year
four Sisters of Providence, from Montreal, with
Sister Mary of the Infant Jesus at their head,
arrived to take charge of the work.   This was the
first boarding school for Indians in the Far Northwest.[25]   As usual in Catholic Indian schools, the

[23] Creighton Univ., p. 40; Hist. of the Cath. Ch. in U. S. of
A., p. 345.
[26] Palladino, Indian and White in the Northwest, p. 74.
[25] Ib., pp. 80, 122.

teaching of the elementary academic branches was accompanied by training in the common industrial arts. The Sisters conducted a separate school for boys. Several other schools were opened later on by the same community. When the Rt. Rev. J. B. Brondel was appointed to take charge of the Church in Montana, in 1883, one of his first acts was to secure a colony of Ursuline Sisters from the Diocese of Cleveland. Six members of the Order, with Mother Amadeus as superior, arrived at Miles City, in 1884, and immediately opened a school among the Cheyenne Indians.[26] The mother-house of the order was subsequently established at St. Peter's Mission, among the Blackfeet Indians. From this place as a center, the Sisters went forth to take charge of most of the schools which were established at the missions.[27] The educational work of the Sisters in Montana has continually called for a high degree of self-sacrifice—often indeed of real heroism, while their influence for the uplift of the Indian tribes has been second only to that of the devoted missionary priests. Montana was made a Territory in 1864, shortly after the opening of its gold mines, and settlements of whites were rapidly formed. Five Sisters of Charity from Leavenworth, under Sister Julia, reached Helena in 1869, and established St. Vincent's Academy. They also conducted day schools for both boys and girls, and founded secondary as well as primary schools in other important settlements.[28]

[26] Palladino, Indian and White in the Northwest, p. 208.
[27] Ib., passim.
[28] Ib., p. 289; The Cath. Ch. in Montana, in Amer. Cath. Q. Rev., XII, p. 504.

The building of schools and the Catholic educational development in Montana, from this time forward, followed the influx of settlers, and kept pace with the growth of the Catholic population. The Rt. Rev. John P. Carroll, who became Bishop of Helena in 1904, has labored to perfect the diocesan system by the establishment of a college and a series of strong secondary schools.

When COLORADO was organized as a Territory by Congress, in 1861, it contained 25,329 inhabitants. It had previously been part of Kansas, and only three years before the above date white settlers from the east had begun to stream into it, attracted by the reported discoveries of gold. The first school was opened at Denver, in 1859.[29] Catholics were among the first to be on the ground. Father Joseph P. Machebeuf, who subsequently became Bishop of Denver, was sent from Santa Fé the following year to assume spiritual charge of Colorado; and this apostolic man, whose enlightened zeal in the cause of education recalls that of the great priests who were exiled to this country by the French Revolution, directed his attention at once to the problem of providing schools for the little ones among his widely scattered flock. In 1863, he was able to open a Catholic school, in charge of a lay teacher, beside the newly finished church in Denver.[30] The following year, he succeeded in bringing four Sisters of Loretto, from Kentucky, to Denver, to open an academy and schools.[31] This was the

---

[29] Hall, Hist. of Colo., p. 219.
[30] Howlett, Life of Rt. Rev. Joseph P. Machebeuf, p. 311.
[31] Cf. Cath. Sch. System in U. S., Sisters of Loretto, p. 224.

beginning of St. Mary's Academy, which has developed into one of the most important institutions of the kind in the West. His efforts to secure teaching orders of men were not so successful, and it was only in 1884 that he was able to establish a college for boys, by inducing the Jesuits to transfer their college at Las Vegas, New Mexico, to Colorado.[32] At the time he was raised to the episcopal dignity, in 1868, there were, outside of Denver, but three priests in his immense diocese, including both Colorado and Utah; yet, with a sublime faith in the future, he endeavored to plant schools alongside the churches in the growing towns. More Sisters of Loretto arrived; an academy and school were opened at Pueblo in 1875; and schools in other places in subsequent years.[33] Additional teaching communities were brought into the diocese: the Sisters of Charity, from Mt. St. Joseph, Ohio, in 1869; the Leavenworth Sisters of Charity, in 1874; the Sisters of St. Joseph, from St. Louis, in 1877; the Sisters of Mercy, in 1882; besides others in later years. The Benedictine Fathers, who came to the diocese from St. Vincent's, Pa., in 1887, established a boarding school for boys at Pueblo.[34]

Although the Mormons settled in UTAH as early as 1847, it was long before Catholics were there in number sufficient for the establishment of their own schools. Notwithstanding the sparseness of the Catholic population, the Sisters

---

[32] Howlett, op. cit., p. 396.
[33] Ib., p. 384 seq.
[34] Ib., pp. 368, 382, 392; Cath. Dir., 1910, p. 329.

of the Holy Cross sent thirteen Sisters, in 1875, to establish St. Mary's Academy at Salt Lake City, and to open a school. This academy took rank as one of the leading institutions for the education of girls in the West. Three years later, the Sisters founded an academy and school at Ogden, and in subsequent years schools were also opened at Park City and Eureka.[35] The Catholic population of the Diocese of Salt Lake, which includes the larger part of Nevada, is at present about 11,000.[36]

In WYOMING, as in Utah, Catholic education has been very slow of development, because the total population has continued small, and Catholics have been scattered. The pioneer teaching order of women in the State is that of the Sisters of Charity, of Leavenworth, Kansas, which opened a parish school in Laramie, in 1878, the school being continued until about 1901.[37] The Sisters of the Holy Child Jesus, from Sharon Hill, Pa., established an academy and school in Cheyenne in 1884.[38] The Sisters of St. Francis, from Glen Riddle, Pa., have charge of St. Stephen's Indian Boarding School, in Fremont County. The Catholic population of Wyoming at present is about 10,000.[39]

[35] Records of the mother-house, at St. Mary's, Notre Dame, Indiana.
[36] Cath. Dir., 1910, p. 602.
[37] Records of the mother-house, Leavenworth.
[38] Records of the mother-house, Sharon Hill.
[39] Cath. Dir., 1910, p. 281.

OREGON, WASHINGTON, IDAHO

Catholic education in OREGON was Canadian in origin, as well as in the influences that presided over its earlier development. Father Francis Norbert Blanchet, the future Archbishop of Oregon, arrived there from Montreal, in 1838, having come chiefly for the purpose of ministering to the Canadians in the Willamette Valley and at Fort Vancouver, on the Columbia, who were in the employ of the Hudson Bay Company. Oregon, or the "Oregon Country," comprised at the time, not only the present State of that name, but also Washington, Idaho, and part of Montana. Father Blanchet showed the importance he attached to Christian education and outlined, as it were, his future policy, when, on Oct. 17, 1843, with only about a thousand Catholic whites in Oregon, he founded St. Joseph's College at St. Paul, in the Willamette Valley, placing Father Langlois in charge, assisted by two laymen. The school opened with an attendance of thirty boarders. At the same place, and at some distance west of the college, a frame structure, 30x60 feet, was erected for a girls' academy, to be conducted by Sisters.[40] In 1842, Father De Smet journeyed from Montana to visit Father Blanchet, and, two years later, returning from Europe, after a long and dangerous

[40] Blanchet, Historical Sketches of the Cath. Ch. in Oregon, pp. 30, 83; O'Hara, Francis Norbert Blanchet, in Cath. Univ. Bull., XVI, p. 754; Shea, op. cit., IV, p. 316; Gleanings of Fifty Years—The Sisters of the Holy Names in the Northwest, p. 47.

voyage around Cape Horn, the famous Jesuit missionary arrived at Fort Vancouver, bringing with him six Sisters of Notre Dame from Namur. The academy was opened without delay, and there was a good attendance. The building, however, had been left in a partly unfinished condition, owing to the scarcity of mechanics, and the Sisters, it is related, "were soon initiated into the requirements of pioneer life: one might be seen handling the plane, another glazing, and still others painting the windows and doors." [41]   In 1844, Father Blanchet was appointed bishop and vicar-apostolic, and two years later the country of Oregon was divided into several bishoprics, and he was named archbishop. Returning from Europe in 1847, he brought with him, besides a number of priests, seven additional Sisters of Notre Dame. [42]   Archbishop Blanchet was the apostle of Catholic education, as he was also of Catholicity, in the Far Northwest. From the very beginning, he planned the establishment of a complete educational system; and, at the cost of incessant personal labor and hardship, and of a great financial burden and risk, he laid its foundations broad and deep. His educational work in Oregon during those early years, and his development of that work subsequently, stamps him as one worthy of a place among the great Catholic educational pioneers.

The college and academy, with the schools connected with them, were prospering, and in

[41] O'Hara, loc. cit.; Blanchet, Hist. Sketches, p. 143.
[42] Blanchet, op. cit., p. 158.

1849, the Sisters opened another academy and school at Oregon City, the archiepiscopal residence, on land donated by Dr. John McLaughlin, the "Father of Oregon." [43] The discovery of gold in California, with the tide of emigration from Oregon that followed, seriously imperilled the future of Catholic education in the Territory. Not only many of the laity left the country, but members of the clergy and all the members of the sisterhood newly implanted in the diocese went to California, to take up religious or educational work there. St. Joseph's College was closed, and the Archbishop was left practically without Catholic teachers. But the spirit of the intrepid pioneer and apostle rose superior to the crisis. After journeying to South America, on a collecting tour, to relieve his serious financial embarrassments, he hastened to Montreal, to secure, if possible, new religious teachers for his schools. Meanwhile, with an undaunted faith in the future, he purchased a large unfinished frame building in the rising city of Portland, to be used as an academy and school.[44]

The Archbishop's appeal for teachers was responded to by the Sisters of the Holy Names of Jesus and Mary, a teaching community that had been founded in Canada only a few years before; and on October 21, 1859, twelve of the Sisters reached Portland, after a journey by way of the Isthmus of Panama. Sister Mary Alphonse was named superior. The young sisterhood entered upon its pioneer educational work in the Far

[43] Gleanings, p. 54.
[44] Gleanings, p. 56 seq.

Northwest with the enthusiasm and zeal characteristic of a new religious organization. St.
Mary's Academy was at once opened in the
building at Portland, with a school in connection
with it. The schools at Oregon City and St. Paul
were reopened, and another school started in the
more central part of Portland. The academy
also had soon to be enlarged. In 1863, twelve
more Sisters arrived. An academy and school
were now opened at Salem, the capital, and similar institutions soon after at The Dalles. In
1866, St. Mary's Academy was chartered by the
State.[45]

With the erection of a novitiate in Oregon,
and the gradual growth of the community, the
educational activity of the Sisters was still further
broadened. Academies and schools were opened
at Jacksonville, in southern Oregon, at Baker
City, and at other places. St. Mary's Academy
in Portland was further enlarged and its faculty
increased, and, with the steady growth of the
curriculum, it came to be recognized, even by non-
Catholics, as one of the leading educational institutions in the Northwest. In 1866, its charter
was revised, and under the name of St. Mary's
Academy and College, it was empowered to confer collegiate degrees.[46]

St. Michael's College for boys was begun by
Archbishop Blanchet in 1872.[47] Other teaching
orders were, in time, introduced into the diocese,
notably the Benedictines, the Christian Brothers,

[45] Gleanings, pp. 14-106.
[46] Ib., pp. 110-191.
[47] Ib., p. 116.

and the Congregation of the Holy Cross for the education of boys—the last mentioned having established Columbia University at Portland; and the Benedictine Sisters, the Sisters of Mercy, the Dominican and Franciscan Sisters, and the Sisters-Servants of the Immaculate Heart of Mary, for the education of girls. The Sisterhood of St. Mary was established at Beaverton, in 1886.[48] An event of historical interest was the dedication at Oregon City, in October, 1907, of McLaughlin Institute, a grammar and high school, near the spot where lie the mortal remains of the "Father of Oregon," the earliest benefactor, as he was ever the firm friend, of Catholic education in the State.[49]

The progressive spirit of Catholic educators in Oregon was shown by the formation, in 1906, of the Catholic Educational Association of Oregon. The Association has brought about uniformity in text-books and courses of study throughout the archdiocese, and secured recognition by the State of the Catholic school system. By the school laws of 1910, " a representative of the Catholic Educational Association of Oregon" is given a place on the Board of Standardization.

WASHINGTON was organized as a separate Territory in 1863, but for a score of years afterward its growth was very slow. The history of Catholic education in the Territory begins properly with the establishment of the See of Walla Walla, and the appointment of the Rev. Augustine M. A. Blanchet, of Montreal, as its first

[48] Cath. Dir., 1910, p. 784.
[49] The Portland Cath. Sentinel, Oct. 10, 1907.

bishop, in 1846.[50]   The new bishop was a brother
of the first archbishop of Oregon, and shared in
his educational zeal.   In December, 1856, in
answer to his request, five Sisters of Charity of
Providence, with Mother Joseph of the Sacred
Heart as superioress, arrived from Montreal by
way of the Isthmus of Panama, and established
themselves at Fort Vancouver, where, in the following February, they opened a school.[51]   Other
Sisters came in subsequent years, and with their
arrival, and the establishment of a novitiate, the
work of the community was extended.   A school
was opened at Steilacoom in 1863, and an academy
at Walla Walla the following year.   They took
charge, also, of several Indian schools.   Academies were subsequently established at North
Yakima, Olympia, and Sprague, their central
house remaining at Vancouver.[52]

Another important development came with the
establishment of the Sisters of the Holy Names
in Seattle in 1880.   The community had grown
strong in Oregon, and, with the rise of Seattle and
the increase of immigrants in Washington, it
was decided to extend their work to that State.
The unpretentious academy which was made the
center of their labors in Seattle has expanded
with the growth of the population, until to-day,
with a magnificent structure on Capitol Hill, it is
justly regarded as one of the most efficient schools
for girls in the country.   Several other academies

[50] Shea, op. cit., pp. 319, 324.
[51] O'Hara, Pioneer Cath. Hist. of Oregon, c. XVIII; Gleanings, pp. 58, 69.
[52] O'Hara, loc. cit.; Cath. Northwestern Progress, Apr. 3,
1908; Cath. Dir., 1910, p. 627.

and schools were also established by the Sisters in Seattle. An academy which was founded at Spokane in 1888 has developed into an institution whose efficiency is recognized far and near. The work of the Sisters in the State has been concentrated in Seattle and Spokane, and a worthy tribute to their merit and an evidence of the esteem in which they are regarded as educators by all classes of the population, is the fact that the normal school departments of the Holy Names academies in both these places have secured recognition from the State and been placed on the same footing as the State normal schools.[53]

The development of Catholic education in Washington, especially in the earlier period, with which we are here chiefly concerned, centered largely about the work of these two communities; but other teaching bodies have also had important influence. Among these may be mentioned the Benedictine Fathers, the Christian Brothers, and the Brothers of Our Lady of Lourdes, who established either colleges or secondary and elementary schools for boys; and the Benedictine Sisters (two branches), the Sisters of St. Dominic (two branches), the Franciscan Sisters, the Ladies of the Sacred Heart, the Visitation Nuns, and the Sisters-Servants of the Immaculate Heart, who opened either academies for girls or schools for both girls and boys.[54]

In IDAHO, the first Catholic school was established at Idaho City, by Holy Name Sisters from

---

[53] Gleanings, pp. 147-163.
[54] Cath. Dir.; Records of the mother-house, Sisters of St. Francis, Glen Riddle, Pa.

Oregon, in August, 1867.[55] In January of the
same year, through the influence of Father Tous-
saint Mesplié, the pioneer secular priest of
Idaho, and other leading Catholics, the territorial legislature passed, by a close vote, a bill
providing for the support of Catholic schools
from the public funds. The bill was, however,
vetoed by the Governor. Father Lootens, who
was made bishop the following year, was anxious
to provide schools for the diocese, but the population, consisting chiefly of miners, was very
small. In consequence of an exodus of the settlers, the school at Idaho City was closed in
1869.[56] The population increased but slowly.
In 1889, the Sisters of the Holy Cross came to
the diocese, and opened St. Teresa's Academy
and school at Boise, and since then Catholic education has made notable progress. Another school
was begun by the Sisters at Pocatello, in 1892.[57]
Benedictine Sisters from Switzerland established
a convent and school at Cottonwood in 1906,
and have also taken charge of several other
schools.[58] The Rt. Rev. A. J. Glorieux, who was
made bishop in 1885, has labored strenuously in
behalf of the educational development of the
diocese, and besides the teaching bodies already
mentioned there have been introduced into Idaho
the Brothers of Christian Education from Canada, who have charge of a school at De Smet,
at the Coeur d' Alène Indian Mission; the Sis-

[55] Gleanings, p. 113.
[56] Founders of the Church in Idaho, in Amer. Eccl. Rev.,
V. 32, p. 6 seq.
[57] Records of the mother-house.
[58] Cath. Dir., 1910, pp. 247, 766.

ters of Charity of Providence, from Missoula; the Sisters of St. Joseph, from Tipton, Ind.; the Sisters-Servants of the Immaculate Heart, from Scranton; and the Ursuline Sisters from Toledo, O. There are two schools for boys in the diocese, six academies for girls, and eight parish schools, with a Catholic population of about 15,000.[59]

CALIFORNIA AND NEVADA

The second period in the educational history of CALIFORNIA[60] begins with the arrival, towards the end of the year 1850, of its newly consecrated bishop, Rt. Rev. Joseph S. Alemany, a Spanish Dominican, who had been at the head of his Order in Ohio.[61] California had become a part of the United States, and since the recent discovery of gold, immigrants were pouring into the country, many of them being Irish Catholics. There was urgent need of priests, and, in the eyes of the new bishop, true to the traditions of the Dominican Order, and in the eyes of the pioneer clergy, there was hardly less urgent need of schools. As evidence of this conviction, it may be stated that the first church in San Francisco, "a little wooden shanty" erected in 1849 on the site of the St. Francis' Church of later times, had been made to serve also as a school.[62] In 1851, the State legislature passed an act which legalized municipal support of denominational

[59] Cath. Dir., p. 247.
[60] For an account of the early mission schools, cf. The Cath. Sch. System in the U. S., p. 51.
[61] Shea, op. cit., pp. 356, 704.
[62] Gleeson, Hist. of the Cath. Ch. in Cal., p. 270.

schools. Teachers in Catholic schools, whether lay or religious, were accordingly paid by the municipal authorities. But the bright hopes which this legislation engendered in the minds of Catholics were short-lived. After four years, the act was repealed, and the denominational schools ruthlessly abandoned to their fate.[63] The spirit of Bishop Alemany and his clergy and people was, however, equal to the emergency. From Europe he had brought with him Sister Mary Goemare, a Dominican Nun from Paris, who at once opened a school at Monterey. Sister Goemare was joined, in the spring of the same year, by Sisters Francis and Aloysia from the Dominican convent in Ohio, and a novitiate was opened. An academy and school was founded at Monterey the same year, and later on at San Francisco and other places in the State. The mother-house of the community was afterwards established at San Rafael, where a Dominican college was founded.[64] In 1851, the Sisters of Notre Dame of Namur who had been brought to Oregon some years before by Father De Smet, were induced to come to labor in California; and, being joined by four members of the Order from Cincinnati, they established an academy and parish school at San José.[65] From here as the mother-house, the Sisters opened academies and schools at Marysville (1856), San Francisco (1866), Santa Clara (1872), and other places.[66]

[63] Gleeson, Hist. of the Cath. Ch. in Cal., p. 273.
[64] Records of the mother-house, San Rafael.
[65] Records of mother-house, Cincinnati; cf. Chapter II, Sisters of Notre Dame of Namur.
[66] Records.

At the same time, a strong central institution was
built up, the Notre Dame College at San José
becoming recognized as one of the leading colleges for girls in the West. Sisters of Charity
from Emmittsburg were brought by the bishop
to the diocese in 1852, and assumed charge
of several schools.[67]

Bishop Alemany was transferred from the See
of Monterey and named as the first archbishop
of San Francisco in 1853, the northeastern section of the State being subsequently erected as
the Diocese of Sacramento. The archbishop
struggled zealously to provide schools and teachers for the towns and cities that were springing
up around him as though by magic. He sent the
Rev. H. P. Gallagher to Europe, and he secured
in Ireland a colony of Presentation Nuns and
another of the Sisters of Mercy, who arrived in
California in 1854.[68] Sisters of the Holy Names
were brought from Montreal, in 1868, and
from Oakland as a center they have established
both schools and academies, the most noted of
which is the College of the Holy Names, at the
same place.[69] Among the other teaching communities which were brought into the diocese subsequently were, the Sisters of St. Joseph of Carondelet, Mo.; the Sisters of the Holy Cross;
the Dominican Sisters, from Brooklyn; the Sisters of Charity, from Dubuque; the Ladies of
the Sacred Heart, and the Ursulines.[70]

[67] Shea, p. 705; Gleeson, op. cit., p. 210.
[68] Gleeson, p. 217.
[69] Gleanings, p. 100; Cath. Dir., p. 208.
[70] Cath. Dir., p. 209.

Nor was the education of boys neglected. Rev.
John Nobili, S. J., who had come from Oregon
two years before, opened a small school for boys
at Santa Clara, in March, 1851, which was the
beginning of Santa Clara College.[71] Three years
later, Father Maraschi, S. J., laid the foundations of the present College of St. Ignatius, at
San Francisco.[72] An establishment for boys,
capable of accommodating two hundred pupils,
was also erected in the suburbs of San Francisco.
The teachers at first were secular priests and laymen, but when Archbishop Alemany secured the
Christian Brothers in 1868, the institution,
known as St. Mary's College, was turned over
to them.[73] Other schools, both secondary and
elementary, were opened by the Brothers in the
city as well as in other places. Their most
important foundation was St. Mary's College,
Oakland, which later became a new provincial
center of the order.[74] The Brothers of Mary,
from Dayton, O., established St. Mary's College,
Stockton, and schools at San Francisco and San
José.[75]

Bishop Alemany was succeeded at Monterey
and Los Angeles by the Rt. Rev. Thaddeus
Amat, who labored with no less zeal than his
predecessor in the cause of the schools. Sisters
of Charity were secured from Emmittsburg and

[71] Doyle, J. T., Address at Santa Clara College, Aug. 9, 1870;
Bryan J. Clinch, The Jesuits in Amer. California, in Rec.
Amer. Cath. Hist. Soc., XVII, p. 135 seq.
[72] Clinch, op. cit., p. 142.
[73] Gleeson, op. cit., p. 276.
[74] Cath. Dir.; cf. Chapter IV supra, The Christian Brothers.
[75] Cath. Dir.

France, and Sisters of the Immaculate Heart
were established in the diocese, with their
mother-house at Los Angeles; but it was to the
communities already settled in the Archdiocese
of San Francisco that Bishop Amat and his successors naturally looked first in order to provide
teachers for the schools. Several of these, including the Christian Brothers, extended their
work to the diocese. The Sisters of St. Joseph,
of Carondelet, have taken charge of many of
the schools, having founded a new provincial
center of the work of the Order at Los Angeles.[76]

The Rt. Rev. Eugene O'Connell, after being
consecrated, in 1861, as bishop and vicar-apostolic of the northeastern portion of California,
subsequently known as the Diocese of Sacramento, also turned to the communities in the
Archdiocese of San Francisco to obtain religious
teachers. A number of these established schools
in this part of the State, and several communities were secured from eastern centers.

An important event, historically as well as
practically, in the educational annals of California, was the decision of the Hague Arbitra-
tion Tribunal, in 1902, which, at the instance of
the United States Government, obligated Mexico to the payment annually of the sum of
$43,050.99 (Mexican), as the interest on the
Pious Fund, to the Archbishop of San Francisco
and the Bishop of Monterey, with the immediate
payment of the sum of $1,420,682.67 (Mexi-
can), as accumulated arrears. The Pious Fund
consisted originally of property donated by pious

[76] Cath. Dir.

persons to the Society of Jesus for the benefit of
the missions, including the mission schools.[77]

The western section of NEVADA is attached to
the See of Sacramento, and in the early mining
settlements of this part of ·the State several
Catholic schools were established under the administration of Bishop O'Connell. Through the
efforts of the Rev. P. Manogue, who afterwards
became Bishop of Sacramento, the Sisters of
Charity opened a school at Nevada City and an
academy and school at Virginia City, in the year
1864,[78] but neither of these establishments has
been permanent. An academy and a school at
Reno were founded by Dominican Sisters from
New Orleans.

TEXAS, NEW MEXICO, ARIZONA, OKLAHOMA

The Franciscan missions and schools in TEXAS
were suppressed by the Spanish Government in
1812.[79] The Rev. John M. Odin, a Lazarist
from Missouri, who was laboring as a missionary in Texas, was named bishop and vicar-apostolic in 1842, Texas having become an independent republic. It contained at the time only
four priests.[80] Bishop Odin, like his fellow-Laz-
arist, Bishop Rosatti, of St. Louis, was not only
a saintly man, but a man of unbounded faith in
the virtue of a truly Christian education. He

[77] Recueil des Actes et Protocoles concernant le Litige du
"Fonds Pieux de Californies," p. 110 (State Dept. Lib.);
Darby, Modern Pacific Settlements, p. 135; Shea, p. 710.
[78] Cath. Encyc., Nevada.
[79] For the early mission schools in Texas, see Cath. Sch. System in U. S., p. 46.
[80] Cath. Encyclopedia, Galveston; Shea, op. cit., IV, p. 288.

induced the Ursuline Sisters at New Orleans to send a colony to Texas; and in 1847 they founded an academy and school at Galveston, and, four years later, a similar establishment at San Antonio.[81] From Lyons, France, he brought the Sisters of the Incarnate Word, who established an academy and school at Brownsville, in 1853. Other colonies of these religious came later, and founded schools in many places.[82] The Brothers of Mary, from Ohio, were also brought to Texas, where they opened a school in San Antonio, in 1852. The work of the Brothers has developed with the growth of the State, several important colleges being founded, as well as a number of schools.[83] The Oblate Fathers, in 1854, took charge of the college and seminary which the bishop established.[84] In 1858, a law was passed by the legislature of Texas, which practically provided for the support of denominational schools from the public funds; but this law was subsequently repealed.[85]

When Bishop Odin was promoted to the archiepiscopal see of New Orleans, in 1861, he was succeeded in Texas by Bishop C. M. Dubuis, a prelate who shared not only his predecessor's indefatigable missionary zeal but also his enthusiasm in the cause of education. Under Bishop Dubuis, the development of Catholic education was carried steadily onward. The teaching

[81] Records of the mother-house, New Orleans.
[82] For the development of the work of these Sisters, see Chapter III, Sisters of the Incarnate Word.
[83] See Chapter IV, Brothers of Mary.
[84] Cath. Encyclopedia; Shea, op. cit., p. 689.
[85] Shea, p. 691.

orders already in Texas extended their work, forming new schools and strengthening those already existing, while other communities were likewise introduced. Chief among these were the Sisters of Divine Providence, who were brought from Lorraine, France, to Austin, in 1866, their central establishment being transferred to Castroville two years later, where they opened an academy and school. The community, as it increased in number, took charge of schools and academies in many places, not only in Texas, but also in other dioceses throughout the Southwest and the South. In 1896, the mother-house was transferred to San Antonio.[86]

Out of the Diocese of Galveston, the dioceses of San Antonio and Dallas and the Vicariate of Brownsville have been formed. These new sees have drawn the teachers for their schools largely from the communities existing in the original Diocese of Galveston, especially the sisterhoods of the Incarnate Word and Divine Providence, although other communities have likewise been introduced into the State. Among these may be mentioned the Dominican Sisters from Ohio, the Sisters of the Holy Cross, the School Sisters of Notre Dame, and the Sisters of St. Mary, from Lockport, N. Y. The Congregation of the Holy Cross, the Basilian Fathers and the Marist Brothers have established schools for boys.[87]

The territory included in NEW MEXICO, when ceded to the United States in 1848, embraced,

[86] Cath. Dir.
[87] Cath. Dir.

besides the State of that name today, Utah, Nevada, and a large part of Arizona and Colorado. The civilized inhabitants were, however, mostly confined to the present limits of New Mexico. The population had declined, and so also had religion; and although schools were taught at the larger missions, at least from time to time, there was little of the old Franciscan zeal for education left.[88] The repeated efforts of Bishop Tamaron, of Durango, about the middle of the eighteenth century, to establish schools in all the missions of New Mexico, did not meet with much response.[89] Governor Gavino Perez's attempt to establish schools, in 1837, was the occasion of an insurrection which cost him his life.[90] When an American bishop was appointed in 1850, the inhabitants numbered about 70,000, mostly Mexicans and Indians, with some Europeans in the large towns. They were generally Catholics, at least in the observance of the outward forms of worship, but the spirit of religion appeared to be almost extinct. There were but fifteen priests, six of these being incapacitated for work by old age.[91] Some bright spots appeared, nevertheless, in the dark picture. The Rev. Antonio José Martinez, pastor at Taos, a secular priest and a man of learning, opened a school soon after his arrival there, in 1826, he himself being the principal teacher, and the school

---

[88] For the early mission schools, see Cath. Sch. Sys. in U. S., p. 39.
[89] Shea, op. cit., IV, p. 296.
[90] Ib., p. 305.
[91] Ib., loc. cit.; Howlett, Life of Bishop Machebeuf, pp. 155, 164.

being taught in his own house. He also established a printing-office, and from this, the first printing-office in New Mexico, came its first newspaper, as well as school books and catechisms. Father Martinez had no sympathy for America or things American, though he does not appear to have been directly involved in the uprising that led to the massacre of Governor Bent and others, in 1847.[92]

The man selected for this unpromising harvest-field was great enough to set his hand courageously to the work, although he realized fully the difficulties, and realized too that he had to confront them almost single-handed. Before being made Bishop and Vicar-Apostolic of Santa Fé, the Rt. Rev. John B. Lamy had labored in the Diocese of Cincinnati. A native of Lempides, France, he had distinguished himself in the pioneer missions of Ohio by a rare degree of priestly zeal, prudence, and endurance. His attitude towards education was shown by his opening a school for boys in his own house at Santa Fé soon after his arrival. Father Machebeuf, a brother-priest in Ohio, who later became Bishop of Denver, joined himself to Bishop Lamy for the work in New Mexico, and, writing at the time of the educational views which they shared, he said:

"As the source of evil here is the profound ignorance of the people, the first remedy must be instruction, and for this we need Christian schools for the youth of both sexes, but especially

[92] Howlett, p. 228; Haines, Hist. of N. Mex., p. 186 seq.; Prince, Hist. Sketches of N. Mex.

for young girls. The means of forming them to
virtue and to good example, which is rare in
New Mexico, is the establishment of religious
houses conducted by persons devoted to their
calling, and filled with the spirit of self-sacrifice.
To this end the bishop has already opened a
school for boys in our house, and he has knocked
at many a door in the United States in order to
secure Sisters for the girls."[93]

The bishop had gone to attend the First Plenary
Council of Baltimore, but before leaving, he directed Father Machebeuf to purchase a large
house for an academy and convent—the home of
the hoped-for sisterhood.

The Sisters of Loretto, in Kentucky, responded
to Bishop Lamy's appeal, and in January, 1853,
four Sisters, with Sister Mary Magdalen Hay-
den as superior, opened the Academy of Our
Lady of Light in Santa Fé.[94] Their arrival
heralded the dawning of a new era in New Mexico. The attendance at the academy and school
far exceeded expectations. A novitiate was established, and more Sisters came from Loretto.
Schools were soon opened by the Sisters at Taos
and Mora, and later on, academies and schools
at Las Vegas, Socorro, Bernalillo, Las Cruces,
and other places.[95] The Sisters of Mercy, too,
established a new mother-house at Silver City,
and founded an academy and school there and at
Mesilla.[96]

[93] Howlett, op. cit., p. 181.
[94] Records of the mother-house, Loretto; Cath. School System in U. S., Sisters of Loretto, p. 231.
[95] Howlett, p. 187 seq.
[96] Cath. Dir.

To secure religious teachers for boys was even more difficult, but in 1859, after repeated failures in the attempt, the bishop succeeded in obtaining four Christian Brothers from France, who, under Brother Hilarien, opened a school in Santa Fé which was the beginning of the present St. Michael's College.[97] The Brothers also established schools at Bernalillo and Las Vegas.

Among other communities which came to the diocese later, may be mentioned the Sisters of Charity, from Mt. St. Joseph, O., and the Sisters of St. Francis, from Lafayette.[98]

Although there are only about two dozen distinctively Catholic educational institutions in the State, for a Catholic population of 127,000, yet in many of the country missions, the inhabitants being entirely Catholic, the teachers are Catholic, and the schools virtually so.[99]

In the above account, the foundation of Catholic education in ARIZONA, which was erected into a vicariate-apostolic in 1868, under the Rt. Rev. J. B. Salpointe, has also been, to some extent, included. The Sisters of Loretto from New Mexico founded academies and schools at Las Cruces, Flagstaff, and Bisbee. The Sisters of St. Joseph, from St. Louis, came to the diocese in 1870, and opened academies and schools at Tucson, Yuma, Prescott, Florence, and on the Gila River Reservation.[100] Sisters of the Precious Blood from Mariastein, Ohio, established a school at Phoenix, while Sisters of the Blessed

[97] Shea, p. 663.
[98] Cath. Dir.
[99] Cath. Dir.
[100] Records of the mother-house.

Sacrament took charge of the Indian school at St. Michael's Mission.[101]

Before OKLAHOMA was organized as a Territory, in 1890, the Benedictine Fathers had been laboring there, a college having been established at Sacred Heart in 1880. In 1884, at the invitation of the Benedictines, Sisters of Mercy came from the Diocese of Peoria, and opened a school for the Potawatomi Indians at Sacred Heart. Later on they established their mother-house at Oklahoma City, opening an academy there and at Ardmore, besides parish schools in a number of places.[102] The year after its formation as a Territory, Oklahoma was erected into a vicariate-apostolic, under the Rt. Rev. Theophile Meerschaert. Benedictine Sisters came from Iowa the same year, and founded an academy at Guthrie; they also conduct several parish schools.[103] The Sisters of Divine Providence, of San Antonio, have a most promising field of work in Oklahoma, having begun labor in the diocese in the year 1900, by the opening of St. Joseph's Institute, at Perry. They have since taken charge of a large number of parish schools.[104] The Sisters of St. Francis, from Glen Riddle, Pa., began work in the diocese in 1887, and are at present engaged as teachers in four Indian schools.[105] A college and school for boys has been established by the Brothers of the Sacred Heart at Muskogee.[106]

[101] Cath. Dir.
[102] Records of the mother-house, Oklahoma City.
[103] Cath. Dir.
[104] Records of the mother-house, San Antonio.
[105] Records of the mother-house.
[106] Cath. Dir.

With a Catholic population in 1910 of about 33,000, the State of Oklahoma has 36 parish schools for whites, with an enrollment of 3120 pupils.[107]

[107] Cath. Dir., 1910.

CHAPTER VII

SCHOOL LEGISLATION

FIRST PROVINCIAL COUNCIL OF BALTIMORE

WHILE elementary education was not made the object of any formal legislation at the First Synod of Baltimore, which was held in 1791, the matter was evidently discussed, for in his pastoral letter the following year Bishop Carroll emphasized "the necessity of a pious and Catholic education of the young," and expressed the hope that young men trained at the newly founded college at Georgetown might, on returning to their homes, become teachers in the local Catholic schools.[1] The first important legislation on the subject dates from the holding of the First Provincial Council of Baltimore in 1829. Between these two assemblies, Catholic education had gone forward with steady strides. Seminaries, colleges, academies, and schools had been established, and it was hoped that educational opportunities might be provided, under Catholic auspices, proportionate to the Catholic population. It was in this hope and spirit that the following canon was framed in the First Provincial Council:

[1] Shea, Life of Archb. Carroll, p. 399.

"Since it is evident that very many of the young, the children of Catholic parents, especially the poor, have been exposed and are still exposed, in many places of this Province, to great danger of the loss of faith or the corruption of morals, on account of the lack of such teachers as could safely be entrusted with so great an office, we judge it absolutely necessary that schools should be established, in which the young may be taught the principles of faith and morality, while being instructed in letters." [2]

In framing this canon, the members of the Council were but enacting into a general law what each of the bishops had already labored to put in practice within his own jurisdiction, by the foundation of schools.[3] Uniform Catholic text-books were also an ideal in the minds of the Fathers. A standard catechism was to be published, and non-Catholic text-books were to be subjected to revision before being employed in Catholic schools.[4] The Second Provincial Council, held in 1833, attempted to give practical effect to this decree, by appointing a permanent standing committee to supervise the preparation of text-books for Catholic schools. No book was to be allowed in the schools which did not gain the approval of the majority of the committee, and the Fathers of the Council promised to do their utmost to secure the adoption by Catholic colleges and schools of the text-books approved.[5] These decrees on text-books, how-

[2] Decreta Conc. Prov. et Plen. Balt., n. 34.
[3] Cf. Cath. Sch. Sys. in U. S., p. 249.
[4] Decreta, n. 35.
[5] Decreta, n. 9.

ever, were never fully or effectively carried out,
the chief difficulty being the lack of Catholic
books in sufficient number and variety to meet
the needs of the schools. The legislation is,
nevertheless, instructive. It points to what has
always been cherished as an ideal, and it shows
how this ideal may be realized in time, through
the authority of the Councils of the Church.
Efforts to bring about uniformity even in the use
of the catechism were not successful, although
the work of the Provincial Councils of Baltimore
in this respect was seconded by several diocesan
synods at other places. The time, in fact, was
not yet ripe for such legislation. The crying
need was still—and it continued to be so for
many decades—the building up of Catholic
schools. And the legislation of the First Provincial Council on this more fundamental point
came to be regarded by many members of the
heirarchy, in the course of time, as leaving much
to be desired.

FIRST PLENARY COUNCIL

In the seven Provincial Councils of Baltimore
held between the years 1829 and 1852, there was
little legislation about the schools, after that of
the first two Councils, referred to above.[6] But
in the First Plenary Council of Baltimore, held
the latter year, while an overwhelming tide of
Catholic immigration was pouring into the coun-

[6] In the Fourth Council, held in 1840, pastors were directed
to prevent Catholic pupils in the public schools from being
made to join in the use of the Protestant bible and Protestant
hymns and prayers.—*Decreta Conc. Prov. et Plen.*, n. 54.

try, the problem of providing Catholic schools in sufficient number was taken up anew, and a solution was suggested for the financial difficulties involved. The decree adopted read:

"We exhort the bishops, and, in view of the very grave evils which usually result from the defective education of youth, we beseech them through the bowels of the mercy of God, to see that schools be established in connection with all the churches of their dioceses; and, if it be necessary and circumstances permit, to provide, from the revenues of the church to which the school is attached, for the support of competent teachers." [7]

The Council also made an effort to secure the adoption of a standard English as well as a German catechism. [8]

PROVINCIAL COUNCILS OF CINCINNATI

The feeling that there should be stricter legislation about the establishment of parish schools and their attendance by Catholic children found formal authoritative expression first in the West. In the great growing commonwealths lying beyond the Alleghanies, German parishes were numerous, and the Germans, both clergy and laity, were deeply impressed with a conviction of the necessity of the parish school. [9] The Fathers of one of the Provincial Councils of Cincinnati, in exhorting pastors to establish Catholic schools,

[7] In Decreta Conc. Prov. et Plen. Balt., 1829-1852 n. 13, p. 47.
[8] Ib., p. 29.
[9] Cf. Cath. Sch. Sys. in U. S.

held up the zeal of the German parishes in this respect as a model:

"Our excellent German congregations leave us nothing to desire on this subject. The children attend at mass every morning, they sing with one accord the praises of God, they go from the church to the school. They are accustomed to cleanliness and neatness of dress, to punctuality and order, to diligence and affectionate respect for their parents, the Reverend Clergy, and their teachers. We have nothing more at heart than that the pupils of our English schools should imitate these examples." [10]

"In the minds of the Fathers of the Cincinnati Councils," it has been said, "the question of religious education was the test of fidelity or infidelity to God." [11] Among the Fathers of the First Provincial Council of Cincinnati, which met in 1855, Archbishop Purcell, of Cincinnati, and Bishops Rappe, of Cleveland, Baraga, of Upper Michigan, and Spalding, of Louisville, were conspicuous for their championship of Catholic schools, which were made the subject of the following decree:

"We admonish pastors of souls again and again to strive by all the means in their power to prevent the boys and girls entrusted to them from frequenting those schools which they cannot attend without grave danger to their faith and morals; and at the same time we exhort

[10] Pastoral Letter, in Acta et Decreta Quatuor Conc. Prov. Cin., p. 93.
[11] Rt. Rev. J. L. Spalding, in Life of Archb. Spalding, p. 202.

parents to aid and sustain parochial and other schools which are under Catholic direction." [12]

Bishop Rappe had consistently obliged his parish priests, wherever possible, to establish parochial schools, and at the Fourth Synod of Cleveland, held in 1857, he embodied this obligation in the statutes of the diocese.[13] At the Second Provincial Council of Cincinnati, held the following year, the same attitude was adopted and made binding upon all the bishops of the province:

"It is the judgment of the Fathers that all pastors of souls are bound, under pain of mortal sin, to provide a Catholic school in every parish or congregation subject to them, where this can be done; and in order that each Ordinary may know what are the parishes in which this obligation exists, they decree that the Tridentine Law, s. XXII, c. IX, is to be practically enforced, by which rectors of churches are required each year to render an exact account to their Ordinaries of all the revenues accruing to their churches in any way, which they therefore strictly enjoin as to be observed by the aforesaid rectors." [14]

The Province of Cincinnati at the time extended from the Alleghanies to the Mississippi; and if Catholics throughout this section have steadily maintained an attitude of more uncompromising fidelity to the principle of the Catholic school for the Catholic child than those of any other section of the country, it has been due very

[12] Decreta, XIV.
[13] Shea, Hist. Cath. Ch. in U. S., IV, p. 557.
[14] Decreta, VI.

largely to the spirit of the great schoolmen which found permanent expression in these decrees. Their educational attitude and legislation had its influence, too, in the framing of the school decrees of the Third Plenary Council of Baltimore.

SECOND PLENARY COUNCIL OF BALTIMORE

The Second Plenary Council was attended by seven archbishops, thirty-eight bishops, three mitred abbots, and over one hundred and twenty theologians,—at the time, the largest conciliary assemblage, it has been said, since the Council of Trent.[15] The legislative enactments of the Council covered a wide range, and constitute a body of laws so fully developed, so admirably adapted to the needs of the Church in this country, and so precisely and clearly expressed that the last Plenary Council had little or nothing to add to many of them. This was less true, however, in the matter of education than in most of the other matters dealt with. Comparatively little, in fact, was done by the Second Plenary Council in the way of educational legislation. The Civil Was was just over. Catholic education had been seriously affected by it, many of the Sisters having been transferred from the class-room to the military hospital, to serve as nurses.[16] Recruitment and practical reorganization of the educational forces, rather than further development, was felt to be the need of the hour. Hence the Council

[15] Spalding, Life of Archb. Spalding, p. 304.
[16] Cf. Chapter II, Mother Angela and the Sisters of the Holy Cross, and c. III, The Sisters of Charity of Cincinnati.

did little more than re-state the decrees of the
previous Baltimore Councils.

After alluding to the dangers incident to the
attendance of Catholic children at the public
schools, and citing former decrees, the Fathers
pointed to the remedy in the following words:

"The best, nay the only remedy that remains,
in order to meet these very grave evils and incon-
veniences, seems to lie in this, that in every
diocese schools—each close to the church—
should be erected, in which the Catholic youth
may be instructed in letters and the noble arts as
well as in religion and sound morals.

"Following, therefore, in the footsteps of our
predecessors, we urgently bid pastors of souls to
devote their energy as far as they can to the
erection of parochial schools, wherever this is
possible. In these schools, carried on under the
eyes of the pastors, the dangers which we have
just said inhere in the public schools will be
avoided; the pupils will be kept free from that
indifferentism which is now so rampant; they
will learn to walk in the Catholic way, and to
bear the yoke of the Lord from their youth." [17]

The multiplication of religious communities
and the employment of their members as teachers
in the schools was warmly commended; [18] and
where religious teachers could not be had, the
greatest care, the Fathers declared, should be
taken to select lay teachers distinguished by their
faith and character, as well as knowledge. [19]

[17] Decreta, 430, 431.
[18] Ib., n. 432.
[19] Ib., n. 433.

Parents were bidden to co-operate with their pastors, and contribute generously of their means for the erection and maintenance of parochial schools.[20] It was recognized that it was scarcely possible, as yet, to have a Catholic school in each parish. Every precaution was therefore to be taken to render as slight as possible the detriment to those Catholic children who had to attend the public schools, and they were to be gathered in the church on Sundays and festivals, and even oftener, for catechetical instruction.[21]

INSTRUCTION OF THE PROPAGANDA

The legislation of the Second Council of Cincinnati went beyond that of the Second Plenary Council, in obliging pastors to establish and maintain parish schools. Many of the bishops continued to urge stricter legislation. The matter was carried to the Propaganda, the Roman Congregation which had jurisdiction in American affairs, and in the year 1875, this Congregation issued an "Instruction to the Bishops of the United States concerning the Public Schools," [22] which was approved and confirmed by the Pope. After enumerating the dangers to the faith and morals of Catholic children from the public schools as actually constituted and conducted, as had been ascertained by the Congregation from American bishops themselves, the general prin-

[20] Decreta, n. 434.
[21] Ib., n. 435.
[22] In Con. Plen. Balt. III Acta et Decreta, Append., p. 279. The extracts here quoted are from the translation in *The Pastor*, IV, p. 232 seq.

ciple was laid down that both the natural and the divine law forbid the frequentation of such schools, unless these dangers could be rendered remote. The obvious remedy for Catholics, both for their own sake and for that of the vital interests of the American Republic, was to establish their own schools:

"All are agreed that there is nothing so needful to this end as the establishment of Catholic schools in every place,—and schools no whit inferior to the public ones. Every effort, then, must be directed towards starting Catholic schools where they are not, and, where they are, towards enlarging them and providing them with better accommodations and equipment until they have nothing to suffer, as regards teachers or furniture, by comparison with the public schools."

That Catholics in some places, however, owing to circumstances, would still have just cause to send their children to the public schools, was clearly recognized and provided for:

"The Sacred Congregation is not unaware that circumstances may be sometimes such as to permit parents conscientiously to send their children to the public schools. Of sourse they cannot do so without having sufficient cause. Whether there be sufficient cause in any particular case is to be left to the conscience and judgment of the bishop. Generally speaking, such cause will exist where there is no Catholic school in the place, or the one that is there cannot be considered suitable to the condition and circumstances in life of the pupils."

After emphasizing the responsibility of parents in the matter, the Instruction concludes as follows:

"Parents who neglect to give this necessary Christian training and instruction to their children, or who permit them to go to schools in which the ruin of their souls is inevitable, or, finally, who send them to the public school without sufficient cause and without taking the necessary precautions to render the danger of perversion remote, and do so while there is a good and well-equipped Catholic school in the place, or the parents have the means to send them elsewhere to be educated,—that such parents, if obstinate, cannot be absolved, is evident from the moral teaching of the Church."

THIRD PLENARY COUNCIL

The Instruction of the Propaganda of 1875 has importance not only as an authoritative utterance sanctioned by the supreme authority in the Church, but also because it formed the basis of much of the school legislation of the Third Plenary Council, which convened at Baltimore in the Fall of 1884. The Council was attended by eleven archbishops, sixty bishops, several abbots, the superiors of seminaries and of the various religious orders, and a large number of theologians. The question of education was recognized as involving one of the chief tasks before the assembly. This was shown by the fact that about one-fourth of all the decrees adopted were devoted to the subject of education. It was dealt with in all its regular departments—schools, col-

leges, seminaries. One of the most noteworthy
acts of the Council was the establishment of the
Catholic University at Washington.

Since the time of the Second Plenary Council,
the feeling had been growing that stricter and
more explicit school legislation was needed. The
school had become a burning question among
Catholics long before the assembling of the Third
Plenary Council. In some dioceses, attendance
at parochial schools was made practically "a test
of fidelity or infidelity to God," and parents were
excluded from the sacraments who sent their children to the public schools. In others, parents
were left to do as they pleased. There was much
discussion of the matter in both public and private; and the general expectation, coupled with
the previous Instruction of the Propaganda,
placed upon the Council the duty of defining
clearly and fully the rights and obligations of
both pastors and parents in respect to the Catholic school.

The Committee on Schools in the Plenary
Council, consisted of Archbishop Feehan, of Chicago, as chairman, with Bishops Spalding, of
Peoria, Flasch, of La Crosse, and Cosgrove, of
Davenport, together with a secretary and nine
theologians. Recalling the chief points of the
school legislation of previous Baltimore Councils,
the Fathers of the Third Plenary Council declared themselves as firmly convinced as had been
their predecessors, that religious indifferentism
was the actual and the necessary fruit of the
public schools as conducted.[23] "To shut religion

[23] Decreta, 197.

out of the school," they declared, "and to keep it for home and the church, is, logically, to train up a generation that will consider religion good for home and the church, but not for the practical business of real life. But a more false and pernicious notion could not be imagined." [24] They lay it down, therefore, as a general law, that parents are bound to protect their children from the dangers of this sort of education, by sending them to Catholic schools:

"Therefore we not only exhort Catholic parents with paternal love but we also command them with all the authority in our power, to procure for their beloved offspring, given to them by God, re-born in Christ in baptism, and destined for heaven, a truly Christian and Catholic education, and to defend and safeguard them from the dangers of an education merely secular during the entire period of childhood and youth; and therefore to send them to parochial schools or others truly Catholic, unless perchance the Ordinary, in a particular case, should judge that it might be permitted otherwise." [25]

In the Instruction of the Propaganda, the right of Catholic parents to send their children to the public schools, under certain circumstances, was, as has been shown, clearly recognized. This right was explicitly conceded by the Fathers of the Third Plenary Council, as it had been by the councils before them, and they sought to prevent interference in the future with its legitimate exercise:

[24] Pastoral Letter, Conc. Plen. Balt. III, p. lxxxiv.
[25] Decreta, 196.

"Since, therefore, for a sufficient cause, approved by the Ordinary, parents may wish to send their children to the public schools, providing the proximate dangers are removed by the necessary cautions, we strictly enjoin that no one, whether bishop or priest,—and this the Pope through the Sacred Congregation expressly forbids—should dare to repel such parents from the sacraments as unworthy, either by threat or act. And much more is this to be understood concerning the children themselves. Wherefore let pastors of souls, while they warn the faithful committed to them of the dangers of these schools, take great care lest, led by an immoderate zeal, they may violate, by word or deed, the most wise counsels and precepts of the Holy See." [26]

Having thus defined the respective duties and rights of Catholic parents with reference to both the Catholic and the public school, the Council proceeded to remedy the causes which were operating to justify the attendance of Catholic children at the public schools. The causes were two —the frequent lack of Catholic schools, and, in many instances, their inferior academic standing. "Two objects," they declared, "we have in view, viz., to multiply our schools, and to perfect them. We must multiply them, till every Catholic child in the land shall have the means of education within its reach. . . . We must also perfect our schools. We repudiate the idea that the Catholic school need be in any respect inferior to any other school whatsoever." [27] To effect the

[26] Decreta, 198.
[27] Pastoral Letter, p. lxxxv.

first object, the multiplication of schools, the following decree was adopted:

"All these things having been well considered, we decide and decree that:

"I. Near each church, where it does not yet exist, a parochial school is to be erected within two years from the promulgation of this Council, and is to be maintained *in perpetuum,* unless the bishop, on account of grave difficulties, judge that a postponement be allowed.

"II. A priest who, by his grave negligence, prevents the erection of a school within this time, or its maintenance, or who, after repeated admonitions of the bishop, does not attend to the matter, deserves removal from that church.

"III. A mission or a parish which so neglects to assist a priest in erecting or maintaining a school, that by reason of this supine negligence the school is rendered impossible, should be reprehended by the bishop and, by the most efficacious and prudent means possible, induced to contribute the necessary support.

"IV. All Catholic parents are bound to send their children to the parochial schools, unless either at home or in other Catholic schools they may sufficiently and evidently provide for the Christian education of their children, or unless it be lawful to send them to other schools on account of a sufficient cause, approved by the bishop, and with opportune cautions and remedies. As to what is a Catholic school, it is left to the judgment of the Ordinary to define." [28]

Touching their second object, the perfecting of the schools, the Fathers devoted a special section

[28] Decreta, n. 199.

of the decrees to the consideration of ways and means to secure the result. The more important of these will be referred to more explicitly in treating of the organization of the schools. For the present, it will suffice to say that the plan of the Council, as expressed in these decrees, comprised the following specific elements: special instruction to candidates for the priesthood, while in the seminaries, in the principles of educational science, especially as regards the teaching of catechism and bible history; a close personal relationship of the pastor to the school; the conversion of the parish schools into "free schools"; the concession of certain rights and privileges to the laity in respect to the schools; the requirement of a teaching-diploma, to be won by examination, for all diocesan teachers, whether secular or religious; the naming of "school committees" in each diocese, for the visitation and examination of schools; and the establishment of normal schools, strictly so called, in religious communities where such did not yet exist. The hope of the Council was that the parochial schools, through the application of these means, might continue to grow more efficient, and prove to be "the honor and ornament, the hope and strength, not only of the Church but also of the republic." [29]

[29] Decreta, n. 200-207.

CHAPTER VIII

GROWTH OF SCHOOL ORGANIZATION

THE PARISH

IN THE organization and administration of the parish school, three elements of authority meet which are, practically speaking at least, sharply distinct,—the diocese, the community, and the parish. Each has authority over the school; but, following the law of the division of labor, the rôle of each has gradually so shaped itself as to be confined chiefly to a special sphere. The diocesan authority, in the first place, exercises a general supervision over all the schools of the diocese, comparable with that of the state superintendent over the public schools of the State; but besides this, the diocesan supervision extends to individual schools also. The immediate religious superior, again, controls the actual carrying on of the work of the school, much after the manner of the public school principal; while the higher religious superiors, controlling, as they do, the teachers as well as the teaching in a large number of schools, possess a practical power over the school which is comparable, in some respects, with that of the diocesan authority. The parish priest, finally, is the ordinary and immediate representative of the diocese in the management of the school. He is by right the school principal, but he does not usually exercise this right, except to a limited extent. He carefully supervises the teaching of. Christian Doctrine, if he does not teach the class himself, or have his assistant do so. The measure of actual school responsibility which the pastor has to bear is not small, however, for upon his shoulders falls the full burden of providing for the material and moral support of the school.

This last responsibility is sufficient of itself to exhaust the time and energy that the parish priest is ordinarily able to devote to the school. Archbishop Hughes would have the parish priests "reserve to themselves, as altogether a part of their duty, the care of the parish school, and not rely entirely upon the zeal and devotedness of the teachers, howsoever well proved." [1] Doubtless, if the pastor is to be made to feel—as is altogether desirable—that one of his most important works is education, it is necessary that he be closely and practically interested in the school.[2] But in a city parish, with its large school, and its many other large and varied responsibilities, it is practically impossible for the pastor to fulfil the duties of the active principalship of the school. In smaller places it might, perhaps, be done. In city parishes, one of the curates is usually named "principal of the school," but even then, much of the work of the

[1] Conc. Prov. Neo-Eb. III, d. I.
[2] Rev. F. W. Howard, address to teachers, Columbus, Ohio, 1909.

school principal is left to the religious superior to do. Comparatively few among the clergy have had the advantage of any professional pedagogical training. Only of late years has pedagogy begun to make its way into the seminaries. However desirable it may be, therefore, that the clergy should be brought into closer practical touch with the school, there has evidently been, in general, a feeling on their part that, under existing conditions, it were best to leave the burden of the active supervision of the school to the religious superior immediately in charge.

THE DIOCESE

EARLY ATTEMPTS AT ORGANIZATION

Up till near the end of the Immigration Period, little had been done towards the effective and systematic organization of Catholic school work in the various dioceses. Whatever of organization existed was due to the religious orders in charge of the schools, each working within its own sphere. The first noteworthy diocesan effort in this direction was made by the Rt. Rev. John Nepomucene Neumann, of Philadelphia, in the year 1852. A "Central Board of Education" was formed, composed of the pastor and two lay delegates from each of the parishes in the city, and presided over by the bishop. One of the chief objects was to secure means for the opening of new parochial schools; but it was also planned to endow the Board with a general supervisory control of the schools. The Board's duties were to be: "1. General applications for aid.

2. Recommendation of a general plan of instruction for all the parochial schools. 3. The distribution, under the direction of the bishop, of such funds as they may receive. 4. And all such other powers as may be added hereto by the unanimous action of the board." [3]

The time, however, was not yet ripe for the carrying out of the project in full. The Know-Nothing movement and the Civil War checked the advance of Catholic education, and it was not until a quarter of a century after the attempt of Bishop Neumann that the movement towards better organization was again well under way. On Feb. 9, 1879, the Rt. Rev. Joseph Dwenger, Bishop of Fort Wayne, Indiana, issued a pastoral letter, establishing a system of diocesan supervision by which all the schools of the diocese were brought under the general control of a school board, consisting of eleven members and a secretary, all priests. The board had power to prescribe studies, text-books, the qualifications of teachers, and, in general, to take any action that was calculated to make for the betterment of the schools. Teachers were to be examined by the board, and to each member were assigned a certain number of schools in his vicinity, which he was to visit annually and examine. The board, in its First Annual Report, issued in July of the same year, furnished much statistical information about the condition of education in the diocese, and expressed the hope of being able, in time, to create a "diocesan school system." [4] The essen-

[3] Cath. Herald, May, 1852.
[4] First Annual Report, p. 5.

tial feature of the plan was thus, a central board, having authority over all the schools of the diocese, with a divisional responsibility of inspection and examination.

The cry for better organization of existing educational agencies was being heard on every side, and when the Fourth Provincial Council of Cincinnati, which had jurisdiction over the Middle Western States, met in 1882, it adopted the Fort Wayne plan of a central board of control, with the additional provision, however, that, in the case of cities, there should be also a subordinate local school board. The decree ran as follows:

"In every diocese, there shall be named by the Ordinary a committee of studies, to which, besides others, the rural deans *ex officio* will belong. This committee shall have authority over everything pertaining to Catholic parochial schools. In cities, moreover, where there are several churches, there shall be a special committee of studies, under the entire direction of the diocesan committee." [5]

THE THIRD PLENARY COUNCIL'S PLAN

The Third Plenary Council of Baltimore, which met two years later, gave careful consideration to the matter of organization, in studying the question of ways and means to promote the efficiency of the parish schools. The need of greater unity of purpose and action was recognized, and it was clearly seen that this could be

[5] Acta et Decreta, p. 224.

brought about only through a greater centralization of the directing educational agencies. At the
same time, it was realized that the progress of
the schools was also dependent upon the more
thorough preparation of the teacher. Both of
these views were embodied in the decrees
adopted, which provided for a central school
board in each diocese, together with subordinate
local boards, after the plan of the Council of
Cincinnati. The chief function of the central
board was to be, to examine and watch over the
qualifications of teachers. It was prescribed that

"Within a year from the promulgation of the
Council, the bishops shall name one or more
priests who are most conversant with school
affairs to constitute a Diocesan Board of Examination. It shall be the office of this board to
examine all teachers, whether they are religious
belonging to a diocesan congregation or seculars
who wish to employ themselves in teaching in the
parochial schools in the future, and, if they find
them worthy, to grant them a testimonial or
diploma of merit. Without this, no priest may
lawfully engage any teacher for his school, unless
they have taught before the celebration of the
Council. The diploma shall be valid for five
years. After this period, another and final examination will be required of the teachers.

"Besides this board for the examination of
teachers for the whole diocese, the bishops, in
accordance with the diversity of place and language, shall appoint several school boards, composed of one or several priests, to examine the
schools in cities or rural districts. The duty of
these boards shall be to visit and examine each

school in their district once or even twice a year, and to transmit to the President of the diocesan board, for the information and guidance of the bishop, an accurate account of the state of the schools." [6]

The laity were also to be admitted to certain educational rights and privileges, which were to be defined more precisely by diocesan statutes.[7]

It is to be noted that only lay teachers and teachers belonging to diocesan communities were bound by the above statute. In point of fact, very many of the teachers belonged to communities that were not diocesan. And even in the case of diocesan communities, the demand for teachers was so great that it was frequently found to be practically impossible to enforce immediately the high standard of pedagogical efficiency which the Council had in mind. The scheme of a "Diocesan Board of Examination" did not, for these reasons, accomplish as much directly as was expected of it. But the central board found plenty of work to do. The material equipment, curriculum, text-books, reports of the examinations and visitations of individual schools,—these and other matters offered abundant opportunity for the exercise of the authority of the board.

The Third Plenary Council, it is true, speaks only of a central "examination" board, and the decree says nothing of its exercising any wider authority. But this was, nevertheless, contemplated and expected. The Provincial Council of Cincinnati, in its decree on the same sub-

[6] Conc. Plen. Balt. III Acta et Decreta, n. 203, 204.
[7] Ib., n. 202.

ject two years before, had conferred upon the central board "authority over everything pertaining to Catholic parochial schools." The Third Plenary Council, while decreeing the institution of a central board in each diocese, and prescribing its most important function, left the determination of the amplitude of the powers of the board to the bishop. The result was, generally speaking, as had been anticipated, that the full control of diocesan educational interests was vested by the bishops in the central boards.

The larger and more fully developed dioceses took up at once the work of school organization, as decreed by the Plenary Council. Even before the Council, a number of dioceses had followed the example of Fort Wayne. After the Council, the board system became the accepted norm of diocesan school organization. Bishop Gilmour, of Cleveland, a leader of Catholic educational thought, as well as a practical educator, issued, in the spring of 1887, a "Constitution and By-Laws for the Government of the Parochial Schools" of his diocese, which may be taken as typical of the efforts made by the bishops to give practical effect to the above decree of the Plenary Council. By this "Constitution" two boards were created, "one central, embracing the schools and general system of education throughout the diocese; the other local, embracing, under the direction of the central or Diocesan Board, the schools and system of education within the districts designated for the work of the local Boards." The central board was to consist of seven members, who were to be examiners of all candidates for teaching, and also to act as inspectors of schools in the districts respectively assigned to them, being required to visit at least once a year each school within their districts. Full control of the schools, in all practical matters, was vested in the central board, under the authority of the bishop. The local boards were to consist of three, five, or seven members, to be selected from the priests within the district over which the local board presided. The local boards were likewise to visit and examine each school within their districts at least once a year.[8]

The effect of the introduction of this system was everywhere, in addition to the betterment of the teaching, which will be referred to farther on, the awakening of a fresh interest in the schools and in everything pertaining to them, as well as a movement towards greater unification and co-ordination of Catholic educational work.

THE SUPERINTENDENT SYSTEM

The board system brought a real center of organization into Catholic school work. Enthusiasm was quickened, and the teaching was lifted up to a higher plane of efficiency. Catholic educators eagerly looked forward to further progress. But the advance that had been made also opened up new problems. The central board was found to be an admirable institution for the settlement of educational questions of a practical character, but these questions had to be brought

[8] Constitution and By-Laws for the Government of the Parochial Schools of the Diocese of Cleveland.

before it. The members were not primarily educators, but pastors. They had little time to give
to the study of educational problems, even if
they had had the requisite training for it. They
visited the schools, but the inspection was more
often characterized by a spirit of kindly, paternal
interest than by practical pedagogical insight. It
soon became evident that the central board
needed to be supplemented by a man who, to a
scientific training in pedagogy, should add those
qualities of zeal, discretion, and large-minded-
ness which would fit him to act as the executive
officer of the board.

The school board in New York was the first
to recognize the need, and in 1888 the Rev. William J. Degnan, D. D., was appointed inspector
of schools. The title was later changed to that
of superintendent. Dr. Degnan resigned after a
year, on account of ill health. The Rev. Michael
J. Considine was selected to succeed him, and
continued in the position during the ensuing
eleven years. Father Considine labored successfully to raise the standards of the schools, and
in this he was warmly supported by the school
board as well as by Archbishop Corrigan. Other
dioceses were quick to notice the beneficial effects
of the work of the superintendent in New York.
The Rev. Stephen F. Carroll was appointed inspector of schools for the Diocese of Omaha, in
1891, and the plan was soon adopted in other
places.[9]

In 1894, Rev. J. H. Shanahan, subsequently
Bishop of Harrisburg, was appointed by the

[9] Letters; Cath. World, Oct., 1911.

Philadelphia school board, with the approval of
Archbishop Ryan, as superintendent of schools
for the archdiocese. Father Shanahan was emi-
nently qualified for the work, and a brief experience enabled him to introduce a very important
modification into the system. Perceiving that
recommendations that had to be made to religious orders touching the teachers would be more
effective if made through the medium of an executive of the same Order, appointed for this purpose, he was led to the institution of the office of
community inspector of schools. The community inspector was given supervisory authority
over all the schools of the Order in the diocese,
with no other duties. At stated times, these inspectors were called together by the diocesan
superintendent, who made known to them, collectively or singly, according to the nature of the
matter, the impressions and suggestions gathered
during his annual visitation of the diocese regarding the condition of the schools. These meetings also afforded opportunity for the discussion
of current educational topics and problems. As
thus developed, the system comprised a central
board of control; the superintendent of instruction, as the board's executive officer; and a
board of assistants to the superintendent, made
up of representatives of the various teaching
orders, each being over the schools of his or her
own Order.[10]

Under the able and energetic direction of the
successor of Bishop Shanahan in Philadelphia, the

[10] For the functions of the community inspector, see paper of
Bro. Anthony, in Rep. Cath. Ed. Assn., 1907.

Rt. Rev. Philip R. McDevitt, who became superintendent in 1899, the system reached a degree of
practical perfection which drew general attention
to it. The following regulations, adopted by the
Pittsburg Diocese, show the practical relations
of school board, superintendent, and community
inspectors under the Philadelphia system:

"Each teaching community in the diocese shall
have a Community Supervisor of Schools, who
shall be under the direction of the Diocesan
Superintendent of Parish Schools; the Supervisors for Communities having charge of five or
more schools to be free from all other assign-
ments to duty.

"The duties and powers of the Diocesan
Superintendent of Parish Schools shall be as follows:

"1. The Superintendent, being the Executive
Officer of the School Board, shall act under the
advice and direction of the Diocesan Board. He
shall have the general supervision of the parish
schools.

"2. He shall observe the work and discipline
of the teachers employed in the schools, and shall
report to the Pastor and the Executive Committee of the School Board when he shall find any
teacher deficient or incompetent in the discharge
of any school duties, or who is not provided with
a Diocesan Certificate.

"3. The Superintendent shall attend the meetings of the Executive Committee of the Diocesan
School Board, and shall submit to the Executive
Committee and the Board such matters as he
may deem important. After the close of the

school year he shall prepare, as soon as possible, an annual detailed report for publication.

"4. He shall pay special attention to the grading of the schools, and shall see that the textbooks adopted by the Diocesan School Board are used.

"5. As Executive Officer of the Board, he shall be accountable for the general good condition of the parish schools, and shall in every way practicable advise and stimulate the teachers in the performance of their duties.

"6. He shall have power to call meetings of the Community Supervisors, of the Acting Principals, and of the teachers, for lectures and instructions on school work.

"7. He shall have power to ask at any time for specimens of the pupils' work in any of the grades, and may ask the teachers for their methods of presenting the subject-matter proper to the grade. He shall also be privileged to suggest better methods than those in use whenever in his judgment an improvement can be made."

The Philadelphia system has been gradually extended to other dioceses. At present, sixteen have adopted it, and it is, in all probability, destined to become the norm of diocesan educational government. Thirty-seven dioceses have the simple School Board system, and thirty-six are still without any formal diocesan educational organization.[11] Most of the latter, however, are either newly formed or are educationally weak. The membership of the diocesan school boards varies from two to eighteen. In most cases, under the School Board system, the members visit

[11] Cath. Directory, 1910.

and examine the schools themselves. But many dioceses have, in addition to the central board, district boards, as recommended by the Third Plenary Council; while several have also a special board for the examination of teachers.[12]

THE TEACHING COMMUNITY

CHARACTER OF THE TEACHING COMMUNITY

THE third element of organization in the Catholic school system is, as has been said, the religious community. The religious community is not, primarily, a teaching body. Its principal end is the spiritual advancement and advantage of its members. But inasmuch as this purpose is, in the case of teaching communities, linked to the office of teaching, the community may be rightly regarded, practically speaking, as an organization of teachers. It is only as such, at any rate, that it will call for consideration here.[13] As a religious order, with its rules, constitutions, and traditions, the ideal of the community is to avoid change; as a teaching organization, its ideal must be that of continual progress, through better equipment, better methods of instruction, and the more thorough preparation of teachers. This distinction lies at the base of the legislation of the Third Plenary Council for the betterment of the teaching in Catholic schools.

The statute concerning the examination of teachers, it will be remembered, affected only

[12] Cath. Directory, 1910.
[13] Cf. Amer. Eccl. Rev., XLI, pp. 31, 235, 483, for a discussion of the question as to whether and how far the community may be regarded in this light.

diocesan communities.   Under the Philadelphia plan, all communities, those whose rules have the approval of Rome as well as those which are diocesan, are brought within the system of a centralized diocesan control through the community inspectorship. Where this system does not obtain, the non-diocesan communities are less directly under diocesan control. The bishop may, according to the Third Plenary Council, make suggestions and enter into agreements with the superiors of these Orders about the teaching or the teachers, but the ultimate control over them lies, not with the bishop, but with the Congregation of Religious in Rome.[14]

THE THIRD PLENARY COUNCIL ON NORMAL SCHOOLS

The Third Plenary Council probably went as far as it could well go in the direction of centralizing the control of Catholic education for each diocese. A work of not less importance or fruitfulness was its legislation on normal schools. Every novitiate of a teaching order is, to a certain extent, a normal school.[15] Previous to the Council, however, the normal course was characterized by two defects which reacted fatally, in many instances, against the efficiency of the Catholic teacher, as compared with the teacher in the public schools: the course was too brief, and it was lacking on the side of scientific pedagogical instruction and training.

[14] Conc. Balt. Plen. III, n. 203.
[15] Cf. Cath. Sch. Sys. in U. S., p. 201.

The novitiate usually lasted only a year. Much of the time during this year was, of course, given up to religious exercises. Previous to the novitiate, the young candidates, according to the rules of the various religious institutes, were to be given several years—two, at least—of instruction and training for their work. But the demand for teachers too often led the superiors to yield to the temptation of cutting down this precious time of preparation by a year or more, unless prevented by the candidate's age. In this way, young girls were often clothed with the religious habit, and sent out to teach in parish schools whose upper scholars were fully their equals in knowledge if not in age. Care was taken, naturally, to place such immature teachers where their lack of knowledge and training would be least liable to be noticed or to work ill. But the schools suffered, and it was but rarely that opportunity was given afterwards to make up for the years of study and training that had been missed.

Again, the science of pedagogy had gained but a slight foothold in the curriculum of the training-schools of the communities, previous to the Council. Their plan of study comprehended the thorough going over again of the courses that had been already made in school, but there was little besides. The old idea, that any one could teach well any subject that he had thoroughly mastered himself, still obtained very widely. Catholic training-schools were notably behind the public normal schools in this respect.

The legislation of the Third Plenary Council

on the subject was as concise as it was clear and decisive. Normal schools were to be erected, the authority of Rome even being invoked to this end, should it be necessary in any particular case. The curriculum was to be made to embrace both the branches that the candidate would have to teach later on in the parish schools, and the science and art of pedagogy. And sufficient time was to be allowed for the completion of the course.

"In order that," the decree runs, "there may be always ready a sufficient number of Catholic teachers, each thoroughly equipped for the holy and sublime work of the education of youth, we would have the bishops concerned to confer with the superiors of congregations dedicated to the work of teaching in the schools, either directly on their own authority or, if need be, invoking the authority of the Sacred Congregation, for the establishment of normal schools where they do not yet exist and there is need for them. These are to be in suitable establishments, in which the young may be trained by skillful and capable teachers, during a sufficient period of time and with a truly religious diligence, in the various studies and sciences, in method and pedagogy, and other branches pertaining to a sound training for teaching." [16]

The authority of the Council was sufficient to induce an almost immediate reform in the conduct of the training-schools. The religious superiors had always favored a full course, and they had yielded only against their will to the

[16] Acta et Decreta, n. 205.

expedient of shortening or omitting altogether
the postulate, or pre-novitiate part. The stronger
and more progressive communities eliminated the
abuse at once, and held all candidates to the completion of a three years' normal course—two
years in the postulate and one in the novitiate.
The smaller and weaker communities had to
struggle hard before being able to enforce this
reform. In a general way, it may be said that
the decree of the Council has had the desired
effect, so far as regards the establishment of normal schools by the communities, and the length
of their curricula. It must be said, however, that
the mind of the Council respecting the study of
pedagogy has not been carried out to the same
extent. The curricula of the normal schools of
the larger and more flourishing communities
leave nothing to be desired, and would, undoubtedly, compare favorably with the curricula of
the best public normal schools. But many communities have continued to make the work of
their normal schools consist too exclusively of the
study of the branches to be taught in the schools.
There is much to be done still, in the case of
many, before the decree of the Council in respect
to the study of the science and art of teaching in
the normal schools can be said to be effectively
carried out.[17]

Much of the credit for the legislation of the
Council on education is due to the Rt. Rev. John
Lancaster Spalding, Bishop of Peoria. His in-
fluence, in the matter of parish school education,

[17] Cf. Educational Briefs, "The Training of the Teacher," by
the author, p. 26.

was directed chiefly towards the perfecting of the training of the teacher. Both within and without the Council, he labored unceasingly to impress upon all his own lofty ideals in this respect. In a notable article on "Normal Schools," in the *Catholic World,* April, 1890, he broached the project of a "central normal school, a sort of educational university," to be established for the higher training of teachers, somewhat after the pattern of Teachers' College, at Columbia University.[18]

SUMMER INSTITUTES

The legislation of the Third Plenary Council has had much to do with the development of a feature of normal school work which has been of very great importance. Practically all the teaching orders now have summer schools or institutes. The course is from four to six weeks in length, and from two to four hours a day. The work covers the ground of the curriculum of the average normal school, there being regular classwork in the school branches, and, in addition, general lectures in courses of pedagogy. These summer schools are held at the mother-houses of the Orders, and noted teachers and lecturers are brought from without, and often from a distance. In some dioceses also a summer institute is held, at which all the religious and lay teachers in the diocese are gathered for a week or two, or even more. The program of these diocesan

[18] The year 1911 witnessed the foundation of such a higher normal school for Sisters at the Catholic University at Washington.

institutes is much like that of the ordinary public school teachers' institute. The community summer schools, on the other hand, with their regular class-work and prolonged curriculum, are able to cover, in quite a satisfactory way, the ground of the regular normal course. Many communities have endeavored to make up in this way for the shortcomings of their normal school work in the past.

NUMBER AND DISTRIBUTION OF TEACHERS

With an enrollment of 1,237,251 pupils in the parish schools of the United States in 1910, the number of teachers may be estimated at about 31,000, on the basis of an average of forty pupils to a teacher. About nine-tenths of the teachers are religious. Male teachers are probably less than one-fifteenth of the total number.

There are two hundred and seventy-five distinct teaching communities, including single independent houses as well as congregations. The teaching brotherhoods number eleven. Many of these teaching communities have a common origin, as has been shown, in the little colonies of religious that came across the seas during the Immigration Period.[19] At present, only forty-nine of the teaching communities are connected with mother-houses outside of the United States, and of these eighteen appertain to Canada.

[19] See chapters on Teaching Communities.

CHAPTER IX

CATHOLIC SCHOOLS AND THE STATE—DISCUSSION OF PRINCIPLES

THE QUESTION

THE question of the relation of the Catholic school to the state is bound up with the larger question of the function of education in general, and this again involves a consideration of the respective relations which the child bears to the church, to the family, and to the state. The treatment of the question proposed will, however, be confined within a limited range, since it is the purpose to present only its historical side, in showing the influence which the discussion of it has had upon the development of the Catholic school system.

In general, it may be said that it is of the lack of the relation that ought to exist between the Catholic school and the state, rather than of the existence of any undue relation, that Catholics have had to complain. The acknowledgment made by the Second Plenary Council of Baltimore, that "the General and State Governments of our country, except in some brief intervals of excitement and delusion, have not interfered with our ecclesiastical organization or civil

rights," [1] holds good also as regards the attitude
of the state towards Catholic schools.   Attempts
have been made, it is true, at various times and
in various States of the Union, to interfere with
the liberty of the schools.   Even aside from the
acts of violence and manifest illegality which
characterized the Native-American and Know-
Nothing movements, deliberate and carefully
planned attacks upon the liberty of teaching,
under a semblance of legality, have not been
wanting. Efforts were made in 1888 to have the
legislature of Massachusetts pass a law granting
an absolute right of inspection and supervision of
private schools to the local school boards, and
proscribing all schools not approved by the board,
or those in which the English language was not
used exclusively. Text-books, curriculum, etc.,
were likewise to be passed upon by the same
authority.[2] The Wisconsin Bennett Law, framed
the following year, was along the same general
lines, but did not go so far.[3] California enacted
a law in 1874 which made it a penal offense for a
parent or guardian to send a child to a private
school, without having first obtained the permis-
sion of the public board of education to do so.[4]
The same idea was involved, to some extent, in
the compulsory education laws of certain States.[5]

[1] Pastoral Letter, p. cix.
[2] Amer. Cath. Q. Rev., XIII, 545.
[3] Cf. Rep. Comm. of Ed., 1894-5, p. 1647; Ed. Rev., I, p. 48 seq.
[4] Montgomery, the School Question from a Parental and Non-Sectarian Standpoint, p. 19.
[5] For the history of compulsory ed. laws in the U. S., cf. Rep. Comm. of Ed. for 1888-9, p. 470 seq.; also, Report to National Ed. Assn. for 1891, p. 403 seq.

According to the Compulsory Education Law of Ohio, for instance, which was sustained by the Supreme Court of the State, in a decision rendered in 1892, a Catholic school principal was obliged to furnish the names, ages, and residences of his school children to the public board of education.[6] New York appears to have set its face strongly against the view that private schools are things with which the State has nothing to do, and its Board of Regents exercises a limited supervision over private educational institutions of every class and grade. Other States, too, are following in the wake of New York. Still, the main principle involved in liberty of teaching has remained, both in New York and elsewhere, untouched.

DIVERGENCE OF CATHOLIC AND NON-CATHOLIC VIEWS

It has been clearly perceived all along, by Catholics at least, that the principles at stake in this matter of liberty of teaching involve ultimately the continuance or the discontinuance of the Catholic system of schools. Up to about the year 1840, Catholics and non-Catholics were in agreement in regarding the parent as the principle of responsibility in respect to the education of the child. This view sprang primarily from the Christian faith, and was quite in accord, too,

---

[6] This case attracted wide attention. For the learned argument of Judge Edmund F. Dunne against compulsory education, before the three courts which passed upon the case, cf. Compulsory Education: The State of Ohio vs. The Rev. Patrick Francis Quigley, D.D.

with the democratic spirit and institutions of the land. But with the educational movement which is generally associated with the name of Horace Mann, there gradually came about a change. The leaders in the "Great Awakening" had made a careful study of certain of the educational systems of Europe, and they came back full of admiration for these, and especially for the school-system of Prussia. The germ of a new doctrine about the relation of the child to the state, as Cardinal Manning has observed,[7] was embodied in the educational ideas which were imported at this time from the Old World.

The germ required some time for its full development. It was, at any rate, only after the disappearance of religious teaching and the religious atmosphere from the public schools that it came to be quietly accepted by the many that, since the work of the school was entirely secular and aimed to fit for citizenship and no more, responsibility for the education of the child pertained primarily to the state, rather than the parent. As a corollary of this conclusion, Catholic schools, even though they fulfilled the same function as the public schools, came to be regarded as in the position of a private enterprise, inasmuch as the state had not founded them and had not chosen to make them its own. This new view of the relation of the school and consequently of the child to the state, which has now become a fixed attitude of the non-Catholic mind, may be expressed here in the words of one who

[7] Cf. The Bible in the Public Schools, The Forum, Mar., 1889, p. 57.

was by no means an extremist in the advocacy of the claims of the state:

"While the state is warranted in making provision for the elementary education of all classes, rich and poor alike, it would be unjust and tyrannical to force any particular portion of the community to avail themselves of this provision when they prefer other methods of unobjectionable instruction. If persons choose to send their children to private or parochial schools, without seeking to evade their share of the burden incident to the governmental system of universal instruction, their right to enjoy this luxury is beyond dispute. If the burden thus imposed is heavy, and to some may appear unjust, the reply is that no system, designed to promote the general good, can be so happily devised as to work with absolute equality and to avoid the necessity for some concession and compromise. It is no doubt a hardship that those who never patronize our public schools should be taxed, equally with those who do, for their support. A proper estimate, however, of the value of these schools as related to our national welfare, will make the yoke of this hardship light and easy to bear." [8]

It is worthy of note that each of the three Plenary Councils of Baltimore was followed by a period of active discussion of the "school question," not only by Catholics, but by non-Catholics as well. There was, doubtless, something of mere coincidence in this. The First Council was

[8] Rev. J. R. Kendrick, in Forum, Sept., 1889, p. 75. For a discussion of certain socialistic tendencies in the public schools, which have sprung from this anti-parental attitude, cf. Coler, Socialism in the Schools (1911); also, The Cath. Ed. Review, Vol. I, p. 353.

held during the Know-Nothing movement, which was largely directed against Catholic schools. The Second was followed by a period of controversy respecting the Bible in the schools. In the years 1869-70, the press of the land, secular and religious, teemed with discussions of the "school question," the burning topic being the exclusion of the Bible from the schools. But the Council of 1866 was not responsible for this discussion. The exclusion of the Bible came as the climax of a movement that had long been in progress. The action of the board of education in Cincinnati in ejecting the Bible from the schools was followed by other school-boards, and the action was sustained by court decisions in various parts of the country. The Third Plenary Council, however, which met in 1884, enacted legislation which undoubtedly gave rise to much of the educational discussion that held the public attention during succeeding years.

CATHOLIC VIEW—THE CHURCH'S RIGHT

In opposition to the view that responsibility for the education of the child pertains primarily to the state, the teaching of Catholics has been that the right and duty of educating belongs primarily to the parent; and, since education in the proper sense of the word is essentially a spiritual function, the control of the education of her own children rests ultimately with the Church. This does not mean that the state has not the right to establish schools. But there is a great difference between establishing schools and educating, between erecting buildings, paying salaries and even compelling children to attend school, and the actual work of education. This distinction lies at the root of the Catholic view concerning the respective rights of church, parent, and state in regard to the education of the child. The distinction has been clearly drawn by Dr. Brownson, one of the profoundest minds, perhaps, that America has produced:

"We deny, of course, as Catholics, the right of the civil government to educate, for education is a function of the spiritual society, as much so as preaching and the administration of the sacraments; but we do not deny to the state the right to establish and maintain public schools. The state, if it chooses, may even endow religion or pay the ministers of religion a salary for their support; but its endowments of religion, when made, are made to God, are sacred and under the sole control and management of the spiritual authority, and the state has no further function in regard to them but to protect the spirituality in the free and full possession and enjoyment of them. We do not deny the same or an equal right in regard to schools and school-teachers. It may found and endow schools and pay the teachers, but it cannot dictate or interfere with the education or discipline of the school. That would imply a union of church and state, or, rather, the subjection of the spiritual order to the secular, which the Catholic Church and the American system of government both alike repudiate.

"All education, as all life, should be religious, and all education divorced from religion is an

evil, not a good, and is sure in the long run to be
ruinous to the secular order; but as a part of
religious education, and included in it, secular
education has its place and even its necessity.
. . . We deny the competency of the state to
educate even for its own order, its right to establish purely secular schools, from which all religion is excluded, as Mr. Webster ably contended
in his argument in the Girard will case; but we
do not deny, we assert rather, its right to establish public schools under the internal control and
management of the spiritual society, and to exact
that a certain amount of secular instruction be
given along with the religious education that
society gives." [9]

THE PARENT'S RIGHT

Education, being thus essentially a function of
the spiritual society, its direction and control
must rest ultimately with that society. The
parent, however, is charged by natural and divine
law with responsibility for the well-being of his
child, in temporal things, and also in spiritual
things. Upon the parent, therefore, devolves
the right and the duty of educating. His responsibility is prior to that of the state, whose
province it is simply to encourage and aid education—leaving out of consideration for the
moment the rights that may devolve on the state
when there is default of the parent's duty. In
the order of nature, the parent's responsibility
is prior also to that of the spiritual society. In

[9] Orestes A. Brownson, in Brownson's Views, p. 64 seq. Cf.
also the argument of Judge Dunne before the Supreme Court
of Ohio, referred to supra, p. 219.

the supernatural order, the Church has, of course, supreme authority to teach directly religious and moral truth. Both children and parents are subject to this authority. But, practically speaking, a certain priority of responsibility devolves upon the parent even here, such as is clearly implied in the following words, addressed to parents by the First Plenary Council of Baltimore:

"To you, Christian parents, God has committed these His children, whom He permits you to regard as yours; and your natural affection towards whom must ever be subordinated to the will of Him 'from whom all paternity in heaven and on earth is named.' Remember that if for them you are the representatives of God, the source of their existence, you are to be for them depositories of His authority, teachers of His law, and models by imitating which they may be perfect, even as their Father in heaven is perfect. You are to watch over the purity of their faith and morals with jealous vigilance, and to instil into their young hearts principles of virtue and perfection." [10]

The priority of the parent's responsibility to that of the state was set forth by Cardinal Manning in an article which was written for an American magazine in 1889. Regarding the parental right in education, he maintained that—

"By the law of nature, fathers and mothers have by right the guardianship of their own chil-

[10] Pastoral Letter of the First National Council of the U. S., p. 10.

dren. Parents have the right to control the education of their children. They are bound to select such schools and instructors as they believe to be safest and best for their children. They are bound also in duty to watch over the associations of their children, and to control them with entire independence."

And he held that parents have this priority of obligation and authority, because—

"The society of mankind springs from the unity, authority, and obedience of homes, and is perpetuated by the parental care and by the domestic life of the people. Filial duty is the root of civil obedience. Home is the school divinely founded for the first and deepest formation of men. The natural society of mankind is ordered and perpetuated by a natural faith in God, and by a natural law of manifold and divine obligations." [11]

RIGHT OF THE STATE

But what of the right of the state? What is the foundation of its right to teach, and what are the limitations of this right? Three limitations are placed by Cardinal Manning upon the liberty of the state in matters of education: the rights of parents, the rights of children, and the duty

[11] *The Forum*, Mar., 1889, pp. 52, 56. This article, under the heading, "A Word from America to the Board Schools of England," was included in the little volume published by Cardinal Manning in 1889, entitled *National Education*. Cf. also the argument of Judge Dunne, referred to supra.

so to provide for the instruction of the people in secular matters as not to interfere with the religious education of children,[12]—all of which follow from the principles enunciated above as to the rights of the Church and of the parent respectively in education. The right of the state to educate is based, according to the Cardinal, on parental duty:

"The right of the state is founded upon the natural right and duty of parents to educate their offspring. So long as they discharge this duty the state has no right to intervene. Parental rights are in possession, and by the law of nature, which is the law of God, they are anterior to state rights and are supreme. If parents neglect their duty they suspend, or even may abdicate, their rights. . . . What the High Court of Justice does in protecting the heirlooms of its wards, the state does in protecting the education of children. They have rights of which they may not be defrauded. But the intervention of the state *in loco parentis* charges the state with the duty of doing what the parents were bound to do. The children, therefore, of Christian parents have a right to Christian education." [13]

An acute American Catholic apologist, dealing with the question from the standpoint of the American Republic and its institutions, has based the right of the state to educate upon the principle of self-preservation:

[12] The Education Commission and the School Rate, p. 28.
[13] Ib., p. 26.

"In no country of the world is the necessity of education more deeply felt than in our own, for in no country do the people enjoy so large a share in the government. Universal suffrage demands universal education, else it might prove to be a curse rather than a blessing. Ignorant voters become an easy prey to demagogues. In order, then, that those who are growing up in this country may be able in the future to exercise intelligently the right of suffrage and the other duties of citizenship, at least a certain amount of elementary education is necessary. We therefore willingly grant that it is both the right and the duty of the state to see that such an education is given. We say not only the right but also the duty, for the duty of self-preservation binds the state as well as the individual, and therefore the state is as much bound to take all lawful means to secure its permanence and well-being as a man is to preserve his life and health. It is through a realization of this duty that our government has established our present system of public instruction. Its aim in this institution is to furnish to each and all of the children under its jurisdiction such elementary knowledge as is necessary and sufficient to make them good citizens of the republic. Now, if this end be attained, the state need have no concern as to the peculiar method by which, or the persons by whom, such instruction is imparted. Provided the end be compassed, the means of its accomplishment must be to the state an altogether secondary consideration. If, then, persons come forward who offer to give such education, and who guarantee that their instruction shall be all that the state requires, that it shall be quite as satisfactory as that now given in the public schools and at less cost, we maintain that the state is bound, in the interest of its citizens, to accept their offer. Such an offer is made by the Catholics of the United States." [14]

[14] The Amer. Side of the School Question, in Cath. World, XXX, Jan., 1880. The article, which is unsigned, was probably written by the editor, Father Hecker. For a critical discussion of the value of this argument of 'self-preservation,' cf. Compulsory Education: The State of Ohio vs. The Rev. Patrick Francis Quigley, D.D., pp. 212 and 343 seq.

Among the public controversial discussions of the school question between Catholics and non-Catholics, the following deserve mention for the light thrown upon their respective positions with regard to the fundamental points involved: Bishop Hughes' controversy in New York, in 1840-1; the controversy of Bishop Spalding with the editor of the *Louisville Journal*, in 1859 (cf. Spalding's Life of Archb. Spalding, pp. 205-215); and the discussion on Denominational Schools before the National Education Association at Nashville, in 1889, the participants being Cardinal Gibbons and Bishop Keane, on the one side, and Edwin D. Mead and John Jay, on the other.

Out of the large number of controversial writings on the school question which have appeared since the days of Bishop Hughes, the following pamphlets or booklets may be mentioned, in addition to those already referred to or to be referred to later in this chapter, as important for the study of the Catholic attitude regarding the respective rights of parent, state, and church: *Common Schools in the U. S. compared with those in Europe*, by Bishop Spalding (from Brownson's Rev., 1858); *The School Question in the U. S.*, by Hon. John J. Monell (1867); *Letters on Public Schools*, by Hon. Chas. R. Smythe (1870); *Christian Free Schools*, by Bishop McQuaid (1871); *Our Public Schools*, by Hon. Edmund F. Dunne (1875); *The School Question from a Parental and non-Sectarian Standpoint*, by Zach. Montgomery (1879?), 133 pp.; *Catholics and Protestants agreeing on the School Question*, by Rev. I. T. Hecker (Cath. World, 1881); *The Judges of Faith: Christian vs. Godless Schools*, by Thos. J. Jenkins (1886); *The Respective Rights and Duties of Family, State, and Church in regard to Ed.*, by Rev. James Conway, S.J. (Amer. Cath. Quart. Rev. IX, 1890); *The Rights of our Little Ones, or First Principles on Ed. in Catechetical Form*, by same author; *Christian Education discussed by Leading Thinkers of the Clergy and Laity* (1891); *The Educational Fact*, by Rev. Timothy Brosnahan, S.J. (Amer. Cath. Q. Rev., 1905); *Pastoral Letter on Christian Ed.*, by Bishop Stang

DIVERGENT CATHOLIC VIEWS

While Catholics have agreed in attributing to the parent priority of right in respect to education, and to the Church the controlling influence over the education of her own children, there have been differences of opinion as to the extent and basis of the state's right in education. Has the state the right to educate, even outside of the exigency imposed on it by the default of parents? Connected with this theoretical question, there has existed a practical question as to the attitude of Catholics towards the public schools: May the teaching of religion be separated from the teaching of the secular branches, and the latter turned over to the state? or, in other words, may Catholics recognize and accept the public schools, provided they be allowed to teach religion before or after school hours? The two questions, although not necessarily connected, have frequently been so in fact. As a matter of convenience, however, as well as for the sake of clearness and continuity, the consideration of the practical question will be postponed to the following chapter.

The enforcement of the decrees of the Third

(1907); *The Christian School,* Pastoral Letter of Bishop McFaul (1907).

Among magazine articles, the following may be mentioned: Cath. World: *The School Question,* XI, 91; *Schools in Relation to State and Religion,* XXII, 433; *Public Schools, are they Free?* XVIII, 1; Tracy, *Church, State, and School,* L, 530; Jenkins, *Amer. Christian State Schools,* LII, 646. Amer. Cath. Quarterly Rev.: Bayma, *The Liberalistic View of the Public School Question,* I, 1, 240; Becker (Rt. Rev.), *Secular Education,* XVII, 176.

For other references, cf. the Bouquillon Controversy.

Plenary Council, requiring pastors to establish
parish schools and parents to send their children
to Catholic schools, raised the interest of Catholics in educational questions to a high pitch. The
great body of the faithful were heartily in sympathy with the spirit of the legislation, and, on
the part of both clergy and people, there was,
in general, a zealous effort to carry out the new
decrees where they had not been already anticipated. A mighty impetus was thus given to the
Catholic school movement, which showed itself in
the erection of new schools as well as in efforts
to raise the standard of efficiency throughout the
entire school-system. The instances in which
the penalties decreed by the Council were invoked
by bishops against members of either the clergy
or laity were, comparatively speaking, few. But
these cases seldom failed to attract the attention
of the press; and although the public discussion
of them exaggerated the importance of the opposition to the decrees, especially to non-Catholics,
it served to intensify the interest of Catholics in
the religious, philosophical and educational questions involved.

DR. BOUQUILLON'S VIEWS

Such was the situation when, in December,
1891, the Rev. Thomas Bouquillon, D. D., Professor of Moral Theology at the newly founded
Catholic University, at Washington, published a
32-page pamphlet entitled, *Education: to Whom
does it Belong?*[15]

[15] Education: to whom does it belong? with a Rejoinder to

The special object he had in view was, he stated, to show that "education belongs to men taken individually and collectively in legitimate association, to the family, to the state, to the Church, to all four together, and not to any one of these four factors separately"; and that " education is one of those mixed matters in which many powers concur, and which is to be regulated amicably by the parties interested." [16]   In reality, however, while not failing to give attention to every element of this general thesis, he dealt principally, both in the original pamphlet and in the *Rejoinder to Critics,* with the question of the right of the state in education, as being the matter about which the divergence of views existing among Catholics chiefly centered.   It is on this point, consequently, that his views are of special interest here.

Starting with the principle that the "right of educating" belongs naturally to every physical and moral person, although the right in this case is but vague, general and dependent, being essentially subordinate to the action of legitimate authority, civil and religious, he passes to the consideration of the parent, for whom he vindicates

Critics. Second edition: John Murphy Co., 1892. The Rev. Thomas Bouquillon was born at Warneton, Belgium, May 16, 1842. He studied philosophy and theology at Roulers, Bruges, and at Rome, where he was made a Doctor of Theology in 1867. After teaching at Bruges, and at the Catholic University of Lille, France, he was appointed to the Chair of Moral Theology at the Catholic University of America, at Washington, in 1889, a position which he occupied until his death in 1903. He published several important theological works, and was a frequent contributor to theological periodical literature.   Cf. Cath. Univ. Bull, IX, p. 158.

[16] Ib., Rejoinder, p. 1.

a *special and proper* right to educate, a right
which gives to the parent inadmissible control of
the education of his child; although here, too,
the right is not independent, but subjected to the
control of authority, religious and civil, within
the proper sphere of each.[17] Coming thence to
the main question, he asks whether the state also
has the *special and proper* right of teaching
human knowledge—the teaching of religion
being, of course, reserved to the spiritual
authority.

"We say *special and proper* right," he con-
tinues, "for there can be no question of a vague
and general right: it were unreasonable to refuse
to the state that which is granted to every legitimate association. Let us add that teaching, as
far as the state is concerned therein, means establishing schools, appointing teachers, prescribing
methods and programs of study: the state teaches
in the same way as it governs and judges, viz.,
through delegates fitted for such functions.
Finally, we are inquiring what is the right of the
state considered in itself, omitting the consideration of the conditions and circumstances under
which it may prudently and legitimately use the
right.

"These considerations being premised to obvi-
ate all equivocation, we affirm unhesitatingly, and
in accord, as we think, with the principles of
sound theology and philosophy, and with the
testimony of the tradition of the Church, that it
must be admitted, as the larger number of theologians do admit, that the state has the right to
educate. The following reason, drawn from the

[17] Education: to whom does it belong? p. 10.

very nature of things, and, in our judgment, thoroughly apodictical, will suffice. Civil authority has the right to use all legitimate temporal means it judges necessary for the attainment of the temporal common welfare, which is the end of civil society. Now, among the most necessary means for the attainment of the temporal welfare of the commonwealth is the diffusion of human knowledge. Therefore civil authority has the right to use the means necessary for the diffusion of such knowledge, that is to say, to teach it, or rather to have it taught by capable agents." [18]

There is discernible in Dr. Bouquillon's views a tendency towards the attribution of more to the state in the matter of the right to educate than American Catholics had been generally willing to allow, and in several passages this tendency appeared in explicit statements. Thus, he was the first to proclaim that the state has the *special and proper* right to educate. He does indeed vindicate for the parent also a special and proper right, and even concedes to the parent the priority of right; but the priority he concedes to the parent appears to be in the order of time, rather than in the moral order, although on this latter point his meaning may be open to question. At any rate, the right of the state to educate, he held, is not simply a right *in loco parentis*, springing from the parent's default, but a right arising

<hr>

[18] Education: to whom does it belong? p. 11. For a critical analysis of this argument, cf. the plea of Judge Edmund F. Dunne before the Supreme Court of Ohio, in the case of The State of Ohio vs. The Rev. Patrick Francis Quigley, D.D., p. 391 seq.

from the very nature of things, a right necessary, or at least useful, to the attainment of the state's end and co-existent with the parental right.[19]

Again, in basing the state's right to educate upon the end for which the state was instituted,—the attainment of the temporal welfare of the commonwealth, Dr. Bouquillon was advancing to new ground, as compared with previous American Catholic apologists. One of these had, as has been shown, claimed for the state the right of prescribing universal elementary education to the degree required for the intelligent discharge of the common duties of citizenship, and this on the ground of its being necessary to the state's self-preservation.[20] But the principle laid down by Dr. Bouquillon as the basis of the state's right is much broader than this. The "temporal welfare of the commonwealth" is more comprehensive than the "self-preservation of the state";[21] and the "diffusion of human knowledge" means much more than "a certain amount of elementary education."[22] Not only was a new position taken, therefore, with regard to the right of the state to educate, but the position taken was made to rest upon a principle that was also new to Catholic school apologists in this country, whatever acceptation this principle may have achieved in the Old World.

From the principles thus laid down, Dr. Bouquillon concluded logically that the state has the power of exacting "ordinary and reasonable con-

[19] Cf. quotation supra; also p. 20.
[20] Cf. p. 228 supra; also, Cath World, Apr., 1870, p. 99.
[21] Education, to whom does it belong? p. 15.
[22] Ib.

ditions of qualification" from those who wish to teach,[23] and also that it may prescribe compulsory education.   Although he was not the first Catholic apologist in this country to ascribe to the state the right of compulsory education,[24] the following expression of his opinion as to how far the state may go in this direction will not be without interest:

"If the state may coerce parents who neglect the education of their children, so also may it determine a minimum of instruction and make it obligatory.   Who admits the former must admit the latter.   The consequence seems to us logically necessary, and we are surprised that all do not see it.   Consider, when are parents called negligent?   Evidently, when they do not give their children a minimum of education.   If then you grant the state power over cases of neglect, you at once give it power to define what is the minimum of education, and to exact that minimum by way of prevention and of general precept.[25]

"In granting to the state the power of making obligatory a minimum of instruction, we do not grant the power of prescribing a standard arbitrarily set up.   This minimum is naturally determined by public opinion, it will comprehend everywhere reading, writing, and the elements of

[23] Op. cit., p. 24.
[24] Cf. Cath. World, Apr., 1870, and Jan., 1880.   Cf. also Amer. Eccl. Rev., Vols. III and VI, for a learned discussion of the subject of compulsory education, by the Rev. Dr. Messmer, later Archbishop of Milwaukee, who would restrict the power of the state in the matter within very narrow limits, although he admits that, in respect to compulsory education, "the Church allows free scope of opinion."—Amer. Eccl. Rev., VI, p. III.
[25] Education: to whom does it belong? p. 26.

arithmetic—the three R's. In certain countries and under certain conditions, the standard may be higher. 'For,' as Taparelli very well says, 'the words, elementary studies, higher sciences, are terms relative to the condition of each society, to the progress of the sciences that are taught in it, to the century in which it lives. A science which today is classed among the elementary, might have been simply marvellous in the middle ages.' While granting to the state the power to force the father to give to the child a minimum of education, we do not grant to the state the power to force the father to *send the child to a certain determined school, if the father chooses to give the prescribed minimum at home, or in any school of his choice.* Compulsory state schools are not logically included in compulsion of education. In a word, to recognize in the state a power is not to recognize in the state the moral right to abuse the power, however much the possibility of the abuse may be admitted.

"If the state may exact on the part of teachers evidences of capability, on the part of the children a minimum of instruction, if it may punish negligent parents, it follows that it may also prescribe the teaching of this or that branch, the knowledge of which, considering the circumstances, is deemed necessary to the majority of the citizens. No more difficulty in the one case than in the other. Moreover, it is not needed that we should remark that the state has over all schools the authority of inspection as to hygiene and public morality." [26]

[26] Education: to whom does it belong? pp. 27, 28.

THE CONTROVERSY

Dr. Bouquillon's pamphlet precipitated an educational controversy among Catholics which was without parallel in American Catholic history, in point of extent, intensity, and bitterness of feeling. He dealt, it is true, only with questions considered in the abstract, and he had no intention, he declared, of derogating from aught that had been laid down in the authoritative decrees of councils as to the necessity, under actual circumstances, of a distinctively Catholic system of schools.[27] But the Poughkeepsie and Faribault plans had excited heated discussion among Catholics, and, while the decision of Rome was awaited,[28] advocates of these measures seized upon Dr. Bouquillon's arguments as affording a basis of sound theoretical principles for the support of such compromises with the state. The distinguished position of the author, too, and his reputation as a theologian, compelled respect for his views. It is not too much to say that the attention of the whole Catholic world was, within a few weeks, fixed upon the school controversy which the publication of the pamphlet aroused.

A few days after the appearance of the pamphlet, the Rev. R. I. Holaind, S.J., in a treatise of some 34 pages, sounded a vigorous call to the defense of what he regarded as the traditional Catholic principles in respect to the right of education.[29] Although his work bore

[27] Education: to whom does it belong? p. 15; Rejoinder, p. 4.
[28] Cf. the chapter which follows.
[29] The Parent First, an Answer to "Education: to whom does it belong?"

the ear-marks of hasty composition, this distinguished Catholic professor and publicist, with a
clear view of the nature and scope of the fundamental principles at stake, denied to the state
the right of compulsory education and the "special and proper right to teach," holding that
necessity, rather than common utility, is the basis
of the state's right to teach, such as it is:

"The parent has the priority both in concept
and in fact. The church has the supreme direction, because she has the noblest end and the
most sacred mission. By her side stands the state,
aiming at the public good without interfering
with private or domestic rights, but ready to
answer the call of the humblest member of
society, ever watching over that order on which
depend the peace and happiness of nations." [30]

Father Holaind's pamphlet was, unfortunately, not free from a certain asperity of tone,
a polemical blemish that attached in greater or
less degree to most of the other writings pertaining to this controversy, including Dr. Bouquillon's *Rejoinder to Critics,* which appeared within
a month of the publication of his original pamphlet, and was directed chiefly against Father
Holaind.

Dr. Bouquillon's views were greeted with a
storm of criticism which clearly showed that,
although he was by no means alone in their
advocacy, and although they found favor even
with some members of the hierarchy, they were,
nevertheless, out of harmony with the views held
by most American Catholics at the time. Catho-

[30] Education: to whom does it belong? p. 21.

lic newspapers and Catholic magazines alike joined in the attack. A voice here and there was raised in his defense, but these were almost lost in the opposing din. The secular press, too, gave evidence that the general public was deeply interested.[31] Perhaps the most notable of the many critical discussions of Dr. Bouquillon's views which appeared was a 116-page booklet by the Rev. James Conway, S.J., entitled, *The State Last,* containing a *Supplement* reviewing the *Rejoinder to Critics.* Besides attacking the soundness of Dr. Bouquillon's views, Father Conway sought to shatter the argument of authority which he had employed, by showing that his views were really in opposition to the teaching of recognized Catholic philosophers and theologians.[32]

[31] Dr. Bouquillon himself contributed an article to the Ed. Review, Apr., 1892, in reply to a previous article by John A. Mooney, entitled, "The Catholic Controversy about Education."

[32] For a study of the Bouquillon Controversy, cf. the Catholic newspapers during the year 1892. Of special interest are the series of "Conversations" contributed to the *N. Y. Freeman's Journal* during Feb. and Mar., by the Rt. Rev. J. de Concilio, and republished in pamphlet form; the articles in the *Catholic News* in Jan., by the Rev. E. A. Higgins, S.J.; and the articles in the *Northwestern Chronicle.*

Of more permanent interest and importance are the following magazine articles: Amer. Eccl. Review, 1892, Feb.: Chatard (Rt. Rev.), *Dr. Bouquillon on the School Question;* Messmer, *The Right of Instruction;* Loughlin, *The School Controversy in the U. S.;* The Editor, *The Rejoinder to the Critics;* April: *State Control and Relative Rights in the School;* O'Sullivan, *Is it Opportune?* May: Schroeder (Rt. Rev.), *Amer. Catholics and European School Legislation;* June: Holaind, *A Last Word;* Nov.: Montgomery, *Contemplated Ed. Alliance between Church and State;* Dec.: Editor, *Recent Decision of the Holy See in case of Faribault and Stillwater Schools* (Supplement). Catholic World, 1892, Jan.: Jenkins, *The Amenities of the School Adjustment;* Feb.: *Dr. Bouquillon's Rejoinder.* Cf. also *Cath. Schools and State Control* (pamphlet), by Janus, 1892.

An important feature of the controversy was the attack made upon Dr. Bouquillon's views by Father Brandi, S.J., editor of the Civilta Cattolica, Rome. On Jan. 2, 1892, the pamphlet was reviewed in the pages of this journal, and severely criticised.[33] To this Dr. Bouquillon replied in his *Rejoinder to the Civilta Cattolica,* which appeared the following month.[34] Father Brandi's reply to this *Rejoinder* was re-published in pamphlet form in March, and dealt largely with the question of the authorities cited by Dr. Bouquillon in support of his views.[35]

Dr. Bouquillon's pamphlet appears to have played an important part in the decision of the Supreme Court of Ohio sustaining the State's Compulsory Education Act.[36] The test-case of "The State of Ohio vs. The Rev. Patrick Francis Quigley, D. D.," was before the Supreme Court, on appeal, when the pamphlet appeared. Copies of it were given to the judges, and the views of the author entered largely into the arguments of the case. Judge Dunne, counsel for the defense, in his able and exhaustive argument against compulsory education, devoted no less than fifty pages to a critical discussion of Dr. Bouquillon's views.[37]

[33] *La Civilta Cattolica,* 1892, Vol. I, p. 82. This article appeared in an English translation in several Catholic papers, and was also reprinted in pamphlet form by Benziger Bros.

[34] Education, to whom does it Belong? A Rejoinder to the *Civilta Cattolica,*—this being Dr. Bouquillon's third pamphlet.

[35] La Santa Sede e La Questione Scolastica negli Stati Uniti, 5 Marzo, 1892, Vol. II, p. 385.

[36] See page 219.

[37] Cf. Compulsory Education: The State of Ohio vs. The Rev. Patrick Francis Quigley, D.D., pp. 354-403.

PROPOSITIONS OF CARDINAL SATOLLI

The decision of the Holy See in the Faribault school case, in the spring of 1892, combined with other causes, brought a lull in the storm. The matter continued to be agitated, however, and when, in the fall of that year, the Most Rev. Francis Satolli came to represent the Holy See at the Columbian Exposition and to examine into the affairs of the Church, he announced to the Archbishops, assembled for their annual meeting in New York, Nov. 16, that he had been commissioned by the Holy Father to speak to them, in his name, on the question of Catholic education, the recent discussion of which in the United States had attracted the attention of the Catholic world. He then read and explained fourteen propositions, which he laid before them for the purpose of finally settling the school question. These propositions reaffirmed the decrees of the Third Plenary Council touching the establishment and maintenance of parish schools, and the duty of parents to send their children to them, while, at the same time, they dealt more explicitly with the question of the attendance of Catholic children at the public schools. Their historical interest naturally centers about this last point. Several of the original propositions, which were in Latin, were regarded by some of the prelates as involving a departure from the legislation of the Third Plenary Council, inasmuch as they were thought to have a tendency to excuse too readily the sending of Catholic children to the public schools. Alterations were made in these, and in the official English translation, only the propositions as amended appear. The quotations that follow are from the English version. The attitude of the Church towards the public schools is set forth in several propositions:

"The Catholic church in general, and especially the Holy See, far from condemning or treating with indifference the public schools, desires rather that, by the joint action of civil and ecclesiastical authorities, there should be public schools in every State, according as the circumstances of the people require, for the cultivation of the useful arts and natural sciences; but the Catholic Church shrinks from those features of public schools which are opposed to the truth of Christianity and to morality; and since, in the interest of society itself, these objectionable features are removable, therefore, not only the bishops, but the citizens at large should labor to remove them, in virtue of their own right and in the cause of morality." [38]

Were these "objectionable features" removed, it was declared to be lawful for Catholics to send their children to the public schools:

"Wherefore, if it be clear that in a given locality, owing to the wiser dispositions of public authorities, or the watchful prudence of school board, teachers and parents, the above named dangers to faith and morals disappear, then it is lawful for Catholic parents to send their children to these schools, to acquire the elements of let-

[38] Prop. VII, original translation; cf. Rep. Comm. of Ed., 1894-5, p. 1667, where the Propositions are found in full.

ters and arts, provided the parents themselves
do not neglect their most serious duty, and the
pastors of souls put forth every effort, to instruct
the children and train them in all that pertains
to Catholic worship and life." [39]

And again:

" It is greatly to be desired, and will be a most
happy arrangement, if the bishop agree with the
civil authorities or with the members of the
school board, to conduct the school with mutual
attention and due consideration for their respective rights." [40]

The reference which then follows to the recent
letter of the Pope to the Archbishop of New
York and the bishops of the Province, in which
appeal is made for the recognition by the state
of the just rights of Catholics in respect to the
education of their children at the common expense, shows that the ultimate ideal which the
author had in mind was that of distinctively
Catholic schools, recognized and supported by
the state.

In regard to supplying religious instruction to
Catholic children actually attending the public
schools, several plans were suggested:

"The first consists in an agreement between
the bishop and the members of the school board,
whereby they, in a spirit of fairness and good
will, allow the Catholic children to be assembled
during free time and taught the catechism; it
would also be of the greatest advantage if this

[39] Prop. VIII.
[40] Prop. XI.

plan were not confined to the primary schools, but were extended likewise to the high schools and colleges, in the form of a free lecture." [41]

This was, in fact, the arrangement carried out in the Faribault plan. The propositions also urged, as was done by the Third Plenary Council, that the parish schools be maintained on a plane of efficiency not inferior to that of the public schools:

"It is left to the judgment and the wisdom of the Ordinaries to decide whether, in a certain part of their respective dioceses, a parochial school can be built and kept up in a fitting condition, not inferior to the public schools, taking into consideration the temporal condition of the parents, while graver needs for procuring their spiritual welfare and the decent support of the Church are pressing." [42]

In this connection, it was suggested that teachers in Catholic schools secure, not only the certificate or diploma of the diocesan board, but also a teacher's diploma from the educational authorities representing the state. [43]

THE POPE'S LETTER ON THE SCHOOL QUESTION

The fourteen propositions of Archbishop Satolli, who, soon after the meeting of the Archbishops in New York, was named Apostolic Delegate to the United States, instead of settling

[41] Prop. XII.
[42] Prop. IX.
[43] Prop. XIII.

the school controversy, only led to its breaking
out afresh. Contrary to the intention of the
Holy See, the propositions were made public, and
interpretations were put upon their meaning
which threatened to foster even more serious dissension among Catholics than had been mani-
fested by the Bouquillon controversy. Those who
had favored the views of Dr. Bouquillon, or at
least a more tolerant attitude towards the public
schools, were disposed to see in these propositions a justification of their attitude. On the
other hand, the opponents of Dr. Bouquillon and
of the Faribault plan, while maintaining that the
propositions were never intended to bear some
of the meanings drawn from them, felt that Catholic educational interests were jeopardized anew.
The discussion of the school question was, in
fact, begun all over again. At this point, however, Rome opportunely intervened. Inviting an
expression of opinion from each of the archbishops, the Holy See ascertained that while some
found in the propositions no reason for apprehension, "to others it seemed that the propositions partially abrogated the disciplinary law
concerning schools enacted by the Council of
Baltimore, and they feared that the diversity of
interpretations put upon them would engender
sad dissensions, which would prove detrimental
to the Catholic schools." [44] Such interpretations,
the Supreme Pontiff declared, were totally alien
from the meaning of the Delegate, inasmuch as
the principal propositions offered by him were

[44] Letter of Pope Leo XIII, dated May 31, 1893, to James
Cardinal Gibbons, in Amer. Cath. Quart. Rev., XVIII, p. 648.

drawn from the decrees of the Third Plenary
Council. His latter propositions were, therefore, not to be understood so as to make them
disagree with these decrees. To leave no room
for further doubt, the decrees of the Baltimore
Councils, together with the decrees of the Holy
See, were explicitly declared to be the supreme
norm, determining the Catholic attitude towards
both parish and public schools:

"In order that, in a matter of so grave importance, there may remain no further room for
doubt or for dissension of opinions, as we have
already declared in our letter of the 23d of May
of last year to our venerable brethren, the Archbishop and the Bishops of the Province of New
York, so we again, as far as need be, declare
that the decrees which the Baltimore Councils,
agreeably to the directions of the Holy See, have
enacted concerning parochial schools, and whatever else has been prescribed by the Roman Pon-
tiffs, whether directly or through the Sacred Congregations, concerning the same matter, are to
be steadfastly observed." [45]

The Letter concluded with an earnest appeal
for the ending of the school controversy, and its
effect was decisive.

[45] Letter of Pope Leo XIII, dated May 31, 1893, to James
Cardinal Gibbons, in Amer. Cath. Quart. Rev., XVIII, p. 648.

CHAPTER X

STATE-SUPPORTED CATHOLIC SCHOOLS

EARLY CONDITIONS AND HOPES

FOR A considerable period after the Revolution, as has been seen, schools of the various denominations were, quite generally, given support out of the public funds.[1] It was natural for Catholics to expect the continuance of this support, even after the "non-sectarian" system of public schools arose. Catholic schools were on the ground. They antedated the public school system. They had been established in good faith, claiming the right of public support, along with other denominational schools; and they had actually received recognition of this right by the state in the grant of support. This recognition and support were accorded, to a greater or less extent, in almost every State. Sometimes, as in New York, it took the form of a general policy. Most often, however, it came about by arrangement with the local authorities. In some places it was very easy for the pastor to make such an arrangement; in many others it was difficult, if not practically impossible. In some places, again, nothing more than a mutual understanding between the pastor and the civil authorities or the

[1] Cf. The Cath. School System in the U. S., p. 360.

school board was required as a basis for public support; in others, formal written agreements were drawn up, with conditions on both sides.

Many examples of such agreements might be cited, and the arrangement is still made here and there. An instance that is specially instructive is offered in a certain city where several of the Catholic schools are under the agreement, which is still in force, after a trial of forty years. The conditions of the agreement in this case are as follows:

1. The Catholic schools shall be received under the control of the Board of Education.

2. Teachers in the Catholic schools shall be in all cases members of the Catholic Church, but to be subject to examination and appointment by the Board of Education.

3. The text-books used in these schools shall be the same as are used in the other public schools, except books on history, geography, and reading-books.

4. These schools shall be opened with reading the Scriptures and the Lord's Prayer. Such versions of Scripture may be used as the teacher may prefer.

5. The school buildings shall be under the control of the Board of Education.

6. The Trustees of the Catholic school buildings shall have power to withdraw them from the Board of Education at the end of any school year, whenever they are dissatisfied with the arrangement, provided that they shall give three months notice of such withdrawal.

7. In case of such withdrawal, the Board of Education may remove all apparatus, books,

movable fixtures, and furniture which they may have furnished for these schools.

8. The Board of Education shall have full control of the discipline, instruction, and general management of these schools, the same as of the other schools under their care, including also the length of sessions, the arrangement of school, courses of study, work, and duties, and all the interests of the schools.

9. The teachers of these schools will be expected to attend the meetings of the Normal class the same as teachers of other public schools. They will give respectful attention to the suggestions and instructions of the Superintendent, and are expected to exert themselves to carry out his views in the management and instruction of their schools.

10. The holidays shall be such as are usually given in Catholic schools.

The catechetical instruction in these schools is given from 8:30 to 9 A.M., before the beginning of the regular school hours. The buildings are owned by the parishes.[2]

DIFFICULTIES

State support of Catholic schools was much more frequent formerly than it is at the present day. The gradual exclusion of the Bible and religious teaching from the public schools brought with it a less tolerant attitude on the part of the public towards state support of denominational schools. On the other hand, the influx of

[2] From the original printed articles; cf. Rep. Comm. of Ed., 1894-5, p. 1659. The N. Y. Independent, Sept. 4, 1890, furnishes several other interesting examples.

religious orders during the Immigration Period made Catholics more eager to secure religious teachers for their schools, and to make these more thoroughly religious in spirit. The two tendencies operated towards the prevention of arrangements for the public support of Catholic schools.

The idea that state support should not be given to any school in which religious instruction was given, developed little by little into a fixed attitude of the non-Catholic mind, and it has been written into the constitutions of many of the States, particularly of those which are most progressive in matters educational. Legal and constitutional difficulties have thus been super-imposed upon popular sentiment, to form a barrier against state support of denominational schools. The Catholic attitude, however, did not change. Deeply convinced of the soundness of the principle of religious instruction in education, and with a strong sense of the righteousness of their cause, Catholics went on building schools and supporting them, trusting that their non-Catholic fellow-citizens would, sooner or later, come to see the justice of their claims. Even during the great wave of enthusiasm for the building of Catholic schools that came in the wake of the Immigration movement, the leaders of Catholic educational thought, while ever urging the erection of new schools, sought at the same time to move public sentiment towards effective recognition of the Catholic claim for state support.

Two distinct plans have been suggested with

the view of obviating the legal or constitutional
difficulties involved in such recognition, and to
avoid running counter to the prevailing feeling
against the expenditure of public funds for denominational teaching. In the one, this teaching
is excluded from the school curriculum proper,
and assigned to a time outside of the regular
school hours when the school building is no
longer under the state's control; in the other, it
is excluded from the *legal* curriculum, as a thing
not to be paid for by the state, but to be given
voluntarily by the teacher at the parents' request,
and during the regular school hours. The first
of these plans involves a change in the character
of the denominational school; the second leaves
the denominational school intact, while drawing a
legal and technical distinction between the secular and the religious content of the curriculum.
Both plans have had practical exemplification in
American Catholic school history. The first has
had trial in several instances which, from their
experimental nature, attracted general attention.
The second has also been acted on, and is still in
vogue in some places, but so far it has depended
for success chiefly upon a specially tolerant attitude of local public opinion.

BISHOP HUGHES' PLAN

The first of these two plans appears to have
been in the mind of Bishop Hughes when, at a
critical stage of the school controversy he became
engaged in, he submitted a series of "Propositions " to the Board of Aldermen of New York,

in 1840. It must be remembered that this great
champion of Catholic schools was, at the moment,
in severe straits. The tide was going against
him, and his supreme concern was, doubtless, to
save at all costs the principle of state support for
Catholic schools. The " Propositions " must
therefore be taken as representing, not what
he regarded as the full measure of Catholic rights, and still less an ideal condition,
but simply as the best practical compromise-
arrangement it seemed possible to bring about
under the circumstances. The teaching of religion in the schools had been proscribed by law, and
he was willing, he said, "to fulfill the conditions
of the law so far as religious teaching is proscribed during school hours." [3] He would accept
the same organization as other schools receiving
public aid—"the same hours, the same order, the
same exercises, even the same inspection." But
he reserved to the trustees of the Catholic schools
the right to appoint their teachers, and he reserved also the right to exclude text-books that
might be objectionable on the score of religion.[4]

THE POUGHKEEPSIE PLAN

Bishop Hughes' "Propositions" were rejected,
but in the year 1873 substantially the same plan
as he had proposed was accepted by the public
board of education for the city of Poughkeepsie,
N. Y. Some ten years before, the arrangement

[3] Works of Bishop Hughes, I, p. 106.
[4] For these propositions in full, and for an account of the
circumstances, cf. The Cath. School System in the U. S., p.
359 seq.

had been tried at St. Peter's Church, Hartford,
Conn., and had worked successfully for a time.[5]
The terms of the agreement at Poughkeepsie are
of special interest, not only because the arrangement went into effect, and was carried out to the
mutual satisfaction of the two parties concerned
for many years, but also because of the wide
publicity it achieved, and its historic influence
in both a theoretical and a practical way. The
plan adopted was, with the approval of Archbishop—afterwards Cardinal—McCloskey,[6] proposed to the board of education by the Rev. Patrick F. McSweeny, D. D., pastor of St. Peter's
Church, Poughkeepsie, who had under his charge
at the time two schools, one for boys and the
other for girls, with a total attendance of over
eight hundred pupils, the girls' school being
taught by the Sisters of Charity. The proposal
was referred to a special committee of the board,
whose report begins with the following statement of the situation and the arguments for the
proposition:

"The children who have attended this class of
schools are residents within the city and entitled
at any time to attend the public schools under the
charge of the board, and when they do come,
there can be no doubt of the duty of the board

[5] Cf. Centennial Celebration of First Mass in Conn. (pamphlet).
[6] The system of National Education in Ireland, although
much less favorable to Catholic interests than the Poughkeepsie plan, was tolerated by the Sacred Congregation of the
Propaganda, and this fact must have had influence with those
who, like Cardinal McCloskey, looked with favor upon the
Poughkeepsie plan.—For the system in Ireland, see Acta et
Decreta Sac. Conc. Recent., Collectio Lacencis, III, p. 795.

to provide for them. This duty becomes all the more apparent when we consider the fact that for years the parents, as tax-payers, have been and are contributing to the educational fund of the city, and in addition to this the children have been enumerated, and thus materially enlarged the amount allotted to the board by the State authorities. Thus both parents and children have been a continual source of revenue, which has been applied to the maintenance of the public schools, while these people have provided for the education of their children at their own expense.

"When the representatives of St. Peter's Church were before the board, the members of your committee understood it had been determined by those who heretofore had maintained their schools to discontinue them, as now constituted, with the present term, and that the gentlemen alluded to asserted the right of those they represented to have their children participate in the benefits and advantages of the common school system of the city; and also that they asked the board to make provision for them in common with the other children in the city and without distinction for or against them.

"Coupled with this was a proposition made by the pastor of St. Peter's Church to permit the board to use the school buildings and furniture owned by that church.

"Your committee proceeded to the consideration of the question involved, with the conclusion that a claim to a right having been made, the board was called upon to provide for a sudden and large increase of pupils, and that the measure of increase may be understood they remarked that by the records of the board it appears that the average attendance of pupils at the public schools during the last fiscal year was one thousand six hundred and seventy-one; at St. Peter's schools the average is reported at eight hundred and twenty."[7]

The committee recommended the acceptance of Dr. McSweeny's proposal upon the following terms and conditions:

"1. The board to pay the owner one dollar per year rent for each of said buildings and the school furniture therein, and in addition to keep the buildings in good repair and insured.

"2. The board to establish, according to its rules and regulations now or hereafter adopted, a public school in each of said buildings, and to have absolute and unrestricted control of the buildings and furniture during the school hours; at other times the owners to have control.

"3. The teachers for such schools to be selected, employed, paid and subject to dismissal by the board, in the same manner as the other teachers in its employ, and such teachers and the pupils attending such schools shall at all times during school hours be subject to the control and authority of the board and its rules and regulations, and such schools shall be open for the attendance of pupils and visitation by members of the board the same as other public schools.

"Either the board or the owners may terminate the lease at the end of any scholastic year by giving the other thirty days' previous notice of its intention to terminate."[8]

[7] Copied from the original report, and communicated to the author by the Rev. Joseph F. Sheahan, pastor of St. Peter's Church, Poughkeepsie, Apr. 12, 1910.
[8] Ib.

The report of the committee was adopted, and
the lease of the buildings made on August 21,
1873, to go into effect the first of the following
month.[9] The Catholic teachers in the two schools
were continued, and the order of daily exercises,
under the arrangement, was as follows:

8:45—Morning prayers.
9 to 12—Regular secular course, as in other
schools.
12—Short prayer; then recess.
1 P.M.—Religious instruction.
1:30—Regular secular course.
3—Closing religious exercises.[10]

The school hours were from 9 o'clock to 12,
and from 1:30 to 3. No child was compelled
to be at the religious exercises, unless by its own
parents' desire. Protestants were free to send
their children to the Catholic public schools,
should they so wish. It was tacitly understood
that Catholic teachers should be engaged for the
Catholic schools, so long as they were found to
be equally competent with the other teachers
under the control of the board.

The arrangement thus amicably arrived at
lasted for many years. After twelve years' trial,
Father McSweeny was able to state publicly that
it gave satisfaction both to the Catholics and
to the members of the board of education.[11]

[9] Original document of lease in possession of the pastor of
St. Peter's.
[10] Cath. World, XLIV, p. 796.
[11] Cath. World, XLIII, p. 510.

This was still the condition in 1891.[12] The difficulty created by the constitutional provision of the State against the appropriation of public funds for the support of denominational schools appeared to have been overcome by the peculiar conditions of the arrangement. The plan was not regarded by Catholics as ideal, but in the broad and tolerant spirit in which its provisions were interpreted by the school board, it was hailed by many as pointing the way to a satisfactory practical solution of the school question. Similar arrangements were made at Lima, Watervliet, Suspension Bridge, Ogdensburg, Corning, Rondout, and other places in the same State.[13]

THE FARIBAULT PLAN

It was to be expected that the solution of the school problem that had been effected at Poughkeepsie, and that had given satisfaction for so many years, would be applied elsewhere. The Poughkeepsie Plan came in time to be quite generally known throughout the country, and in many places hopes were entertained of its being successfully copied. In the Diocese of St. Paul, Minnesota, substantially the same agreement was entered into between the pastors and the

[12] Cath. World, LII, pp. 651, 652. See also N. Y. Independent, Sept. 4, 1890.
[13] Letter of Rt. Rev. Mgr. Burtsell to the author, May 7, 1910; Fr. Journal, Mar. 3, 1906. For a somewhat similar arrangement which was embodied in a bill presented to the legislature of New Jersey in 1893, and which had the approval of the Apostolic Delegate and the bishops of New Jersey, cf. Flynn, The Cath. Ch. in N. J., p. 498 seq.

school boards of Stillwater and Faribault. The arrangement effected in the case of these schools, which became known as the "Faribault Plan," attracted public attention, not only in the United States, but throughout the entire Catholic world. It entered largely into the theoretical educational discussions of the time, and it appears to have been, along with its Poughkeepsie prototype, their proximate occasion.[14]

The school question, it must be borne in mind, was the all-absorbing topic of the time. Especially since the Third Plenary Council, Catholics had been making themselves heard on the subject, and an impression had undoubtedly been made in the public mind. At the moment, they were probably nearer than they had ever been before, or have ever been since, to gaining the ear of the public for the full and unbiased hearing of their cause. Notwithstanding this, it was plain that no Catholic proposition could hope for general acceptance, in a practical way, which was not in the nature of a compromise. If the Poughkeepsie plan was the practical solution of the problem, the time seemed ripe for its presentation as such to the American people.[15]

[14] See preceding chapter, the Bouquillon Controversy.

[15] The propositions which Mgr. Satolli laid before the Archbishops at New York a little later afford evidence of the existence of a belief among Catholics that the time was favorable for reaching an agreement with the state authorities in respect to the public support of Catholic schools; and in the letter of the Holy Father to the Episcopate of the Province of New York, the previous year, the same opinion appears: "Hisce autem perspectis, passurum esse neminem istic putamus, ut catholici parentes cogantur ea condere tuerique gymnasia et scholas quibus uti nequeant ad filios suos instituendos."—Cf. Amer. Eccl. Rev., July, 1892, p. 66.

When the National Educational Association met at St. Paul in the summer of 1890, Archbishop Ireland, in an eloquent address, presented to the large and representative body of non-Catholic educators in attendance the claims of Catholics to state support for their schools. While firmly standing for the traditional Catholic doctrine that the education of the child belongs primarily to the parent, and not to the state, he frankly conceded to the state, as an agent, the right and duty of imparting instruction, as well as the power of compulsory education. Pointing out that the exclusion of religion from the school-room must lead to religious indifference as a creed in maturer years, and arguing that the interests of the Republic, no less than the preservation of Christianity, necessitated a return to the ideals of religious instruction that obtained in the earlier period of our national existence, he proposed as a solution of the problem the adoption of the denominational system of England and Prussia, or, in lieu of this, the compromise arrangement at Poughkeepsie.[16] It was evident from the general tenor of the address, that the latter plan was advanced merely as an alternative, not as embodying the full measure of justice due to the Catholic claims.

The address attracted attention throughout the country, and provoked discussion. In the Fall of the following year, the schools at Faribault and Stillwater, by an arrangement between the pastors and the school boards, were placed under the control of the latter during the regular

[16] Ann. Report of the N. E. A., 1890, p. 185.

school hours, and the Sisters listed on the pay-
roll as public school teachers. There was no
formal written agreement at either Faribault or
Stillwater, but simply a tacit understanding; and
the arrangement at both places was the same in
substance as that at Poughkeepsie. The following is an authoritative description of the practical
provisions of the plan:

"The schools are leased to the State authorities for one year, the contract being renewable at
the pleasure of the two parties. The same teachers (Religious of St. Dominic) are retained.
After hearing mass in the parish church, the
children are marched to school. At 3:30 P.M.,
at the close of the school hours, the pupils are
instructed in their catechism for an hour, and
then dismissed. No text-books to which the
Archbishop objects are retained. Instead of receiving a precarious and small compensation
from the parents, the teachers now receive a
salary of $50 a month each from the school
authorities. The teachers as well as the pupils
are subject to an examination by the school
board, and this arrangement has benefitted both
teachers and pupils. The schools are now more
numerously attended than before." [17]

In his address before the National Educational Association at St. Paul, Archbishop Ireland had, as has been pointed out, advocated the

[17] *Civilta Cattolica,* 1892, I, p. 756. This statement is taken
from a letter of Cardinal Gibbons to the Rt. Rev. D. J. O'Connell, Rector of the Amer. College, Rome, and represents the
description of the Faribault plan made by Archbishop Ireland
to the Archbishops at their meeting in St. Louis, the preceding
December.

arrangement simply as a tentative working agreement between the authorities of church and state. Unfortunately for the success of the plan, this aspect of it was soon lost sight of by both Catholics and non-Catholics. True, it would have been opposed by some, in any case, even as a tentative arrangement. From its very inception there were Catholics who strongly opposed it. Yet the arrangement at Poughkeepsie was practically the same. The latter was well known. It had stood for nearly twenty years, and had had the cordial approval of Cardinal McCloskey. Looked upon as a tentative plan to solve the "school question," it had aroused no general opposition. And practically the same arrangement existed at other places. The Faribault plan would probably have met with no great opposition, while exerting a far-reaching practical influence, had it not been drawn into the vortex of the exciting educational controversy that was going on at the time.

Friends of the Faribault and Poughkeepsie agreements became the defenders of Dr. Bouquillon's views, in whole or in part. The opposition, on the other hand, regarded his pamphlet as an attempt to justify, on the basis of Catholic educational principles, these complicated compromise arrangements, and to pave the way for their universal acceptance, with the replacement of the parochial school system altogether.[18] The " Faribault Plan," in fact, was made a party shibboleth. The matter was carried to Rome, and although

[18] See the literature of the Bouquillon Controversy, referred to in the preceding chapter, especially Father Conway's booklet, "The Parent First."

there was strong opposition, the arrangement was nevertheless approved as allowable under the particular circumstances, by the following decision of the Congregation of the Propaganda, April 21, 1892:

"The Decrees of the Baltimore Councils in respect to parochial schools remaining in full force, the agreement entered into by Archbishop Ireland relative to the schools of Faribault and Stillwater, in view of all the circumstances, may be tolerated." [19]

The decision, which came to be known, from its decisive terms, as the *Tolerari Potest,* was accompanied by a letter of Cardinal Ledochowski, Prefect of the Propaganda, which, recalling the decrees of the Third Plenary Council as to be firmly adhered to, made it plain that the favorable reply was given only for particular cases and in view of special circumstances.[20] This was likewise the tenor of a letter addressed soon afterwards, on May 3, to all the American bishops, by the same Congregation.[21] Nevertheless, the Faribault decision, instead of helping to allay the school controversy, proved to be only so much fresh material for it to feed upon. Each party sought to interpret it in a sense favorable

[19] The original text of this famous decision, the exact meaning of which became such a subject of dispute, was as follows: "Firmis in suo robore manentibus Decretis Conciliorum Baltimorensium supra scholas parochiales, compositio inita a R. P. D. Archiepiscopo Ireland relate ad scholas de Faribault et Stillwater, perpensis omnibus circumstantiis, tolerari potest." —Amer. Eccl. Rev., Supp., June 2, 1892.

[20] Ib., p. 12.

[21] Ib., p. 13 seq.

to its own views. Even members of the hierarchy feared that the Holy See, in formulating the decision, was not fully informed of all the circumstances, or of the effect it would have upon the parochial schools. In reply to a joint letter of the Archbishop and five of the bishops of the New York Province, in which this fear was voiced, the Holy Father, on May 23, explained the reasons upon which the decision was based, and, after showing that all the circumstances had been carefully considered, determined more clearly the legal force and meaning of the decision, with reference to the school legislation of the Baltimore Councils, in declaring that, "as in the case of all general laws, if any special or unexpected circumstances arise, equity suggests that an arrangement departing somewhat from the letter of the law may be tolerated"; and that it was felt that the case in question was to be decided "with moderation and prudence, rather than by the rigor of the law." [22]

The result of the Bouquillon controversy was, however, fatal to the practical success of the Faribault plan. Catholic sentiment was shown to be divided on the question. The attention of non-Catholics was directed to it, and an attitude of distrust and apprehension was engendered in the non-Catholic mind, which gradually changed into open hostility. After a couple of years, the arrangement was voluntarily discontinued in the schools of Faribault and Stillwater by the Catholic authorities. But practically the same arrangement was entered into by school boards

[22] *Amer. Eccl. Rev.,* July, 1892, p. 65.

the arrangement between the Poughkeepsie board and St. Peter's Church was, in accordance with the decision, terminated.

The continued friendly attitude of the local authorities at Poughkeepsie was shown by the fact that, when the boys' school in St. Peter's Parish was discontinued, in consequence of the decision, they rented the building for a public school, at a rental of $1,000 a year.[27] The burden that had been lifted so long from the parish by the arrangement was also evidenced by the expense-account of the girls' school the following year—$1800 being paid for Sisters' salaries, and upwards of the same sum for other school items.[28]

LIMA SCHOOL CASE

A similar decision was rendered by Superintendent Skinner in the Lima School Case, in 1902, the agreement at Lima having been substantially the same as that at Poughkeepsie and begun about the same time. The history of this case has a special interest, both from its peculiar circumstances and from the fact that it was

intendent held that the school law of the State forbade the *renting* of buildings for school purposes, except for temporary emergencies. For the decision of the Supreme Court of Illinois, in 1887, in the case of an arrangement similar to that at Poughkeepsie, cf. Amer. Cath. Quarterly Review, Vol. XXX, p. 527.

[27] Records of St. Peter's Parish.

[28] Ib. During the year 1909, the expenses of the two schools in the parish amounted to $5776.44, there being 642 pupils in the eight grades. The boys' school was reopened in 1904, and is now taught by the Marist Brothers. The Sisters of Charity have continued in charge of the girls' school.

brought before the highest court of the State. Although the majority of the voters of the school district were non-Catholics, they voted for the continuance of the Sisters, even after the Superintendent's decision.[29] It was the purpose of the pastor, the Rev. Simon. Fitzsimons, not so much to secure a continuance of the school arrangement as to obtain an authoritative judicial decision upon what he conceived to be the most vital point involved in the Superintendent's decision, viz., the right to wear the religious garb.[30] The Appellate Division Court rendered its decision in November, 1905, sustaining Superintendents Draper and Skinner in their condemnation of the garb. The decision was re-affirmed by the Court of Appeals, the highest tribunal in the State, April 17, 1906, the court holding that the commissioner of education had power, under the laws, to establish reasonable regulations for the management of the common schools, and that the regulation prohibiting teachers from wearing a distinctively religious garb while teaching was not unreasonable.[31] The decision, however, did

[29] Freeman's Journal, Mar. 3, 1906.

[30] Letter of Father Fitzsimons to author, May 12, 1910.

[31] For these decisions, see N. Y. Appellate Division Reports, 109, p. 361, O'Connor vs. Hendrick; and N. Y. Reports, 184, Court of Appeals, p. 421. See also letters of Fr. Fitzsimons to *Freeman's Journal,* Feb. 24, and Mar. 3, 1906; also, *Cath. World,* Vol. 92, p. 795.
The Supreme Court of Pennsylvania, in the Gallitzin School case, in 1894, decided that it was not unconstitutional to employ Sisters to teach in the public schools, while wearing their religious garb, the State not having as yet legislated against it. But the following year the legislature enacted a statute prohibiting the wearing of a distinctive religious garb by teachers in the public schools. In 1909, the Superior Court at Philadelphia sustained the constitutionality of this

not deal with the question of right in the abstract. It dealt with a concrete case. A superintendent of schools less unfavorably inclined towards Catholic schools might legally, perhaps, allow the wearing of the religious garb, even after the decision.

VOLUNTARY RELIGIOUS INSTRUCTION DURING SCHOOL HOURS

The second of the two general plans referred to for the securing of public support for Catholic schools, without a violation of the laws which prohibit appropriation of the public moneys to "sectarian" schools or for "sectarian" teaching, or a disturbance of that apparently fixed and permanent public sentiment lying back of the laws, is simply to exclude religious instruction from the curriculum of studies for which, and for which alone, the teacher is to be paid.[32] In the Pastoral Letter issued by the Third Provincial Council of Cincinnati, in 1861, the plan was outlined in brief as follows:

"In a country so divided in sentiment as ours is on the subject of religion, the only system which would be fair and equitable to all, would be that which would make education, like religion and like all other important pursuits, *entirely free;*

law in the case of a teacher who wore the Mennonite garb, reversing the judgment of the lower court. The decision of the Superior Court was confirmed by the Supreme Court of the State, in a decision handed down July 1, 1910.—*Phila. Ledger,* July 2, 1910. For the Gallitzin case, see 164 Penn. State Reports, p. 629 seq.

[32] Cf. p. 252.

and if taxes are collected from all for its encouragement and support, to apportion the amount of these taxes fairly among the scholars taught certain branches up to a certain standard, no matter under what religious or other auspices. This system would elicit educational industry and talent, by stimulating competition, and we have not a doubt that it would lessen the cost of education, greatly extend its blessings, and render it both sounder and more widely diffused. It would satisfy all classes, and it would render the schools really *public* and *common*—which they certainly are not at present except in name." [33]

This plan did not originate with the Third Provincial Council of Cincinnati. It had been proposed by Bishop Hughes in his great speech before the Board of Aldermen of New York City, in the year 1840.[34] Even before the days of Bishop Hughes, the idea had been put in practice through agreements entered into in many places between the representatives of the various religious denominations and the local representatives of the state. At Lowell, Mass., Catholic schools were, for many years, supported out of the public funds, under an agreement which was based upon this principle.[35] It was, in fact, for a considerable period, as has been noted, the basis of a commonly existing arrangement.

[33] Acta et Decreta Quatuor Conc. Provin. Cincinnat. 1855-1882, p. 148. The Pastoral Letter quoted from was written by Bishop Martin John Spalding, subsequently Archbishop of Baltimore. For his views on education, cf. Life of Archbishop Spalding. pp. 200-215.

[34] Works of Bishop Hughes, Vol. I, pp. 69, 87, 106. Cf. also, Cath. School System in U. S., pp. 366, 368.

[35] Cath. Sch. Sys. in U. S., p. 286.

Agreements based upon this same principle have continued to be made here and there down to our own days. In the State of New York, at the present time, Catholic secondary schools which are recognized by the Board of Regents, in common with other secondary schools, receive two and a half cents per day for actual attendance of each pupil holding an elementary certificate. The admission of pupils of the parish schools to the manual training classes of the public schools, as is done in a number of States at present, with the sanction of the courts, may also, perhaps, be regarded as a partial recognition of the same principle. This plan of Voluntary Religious Instruction has been frequently referred to, and often dealt with at length, in Catholic discussion of the school question in the United States.[36]

In his address before the National Educational Association at St. Paul, Archbishop Ireland pointed out that the plan involves no more than the adoption of the principle which is made the basis of the public support of the denominational school in England:

"I would permeate the regular state school with the religion of the majority of the children of the land, be it as Protestant as Protestantism can be, and I would, as they do in England, pay for the secular instruction given in denominational schools, according to results; that is, each pupil passing the examination before state officials, and in full accordance with the state program, would secure to his school the cost of

[36] Cf. references to the literature of the subject in preceding chapter.

the tuition of a pupil in the state school. This is not paying for the religious instruction given to the pupil, but for the secular instruction demanded by the state, and given to the pupil as thoroughly as he could have received it in the state school." [37]

This plan was endorsed by the American Federation of Catholic Societies, at its fifth national convention, held at Buffalo, in 1906. The text of the resolution adopted was as follows:

"Convinced that we are not called upon to suggest plans for the various non-Catholic denominations, we propose this solution of the school-fund problem as satisfactory to the Catholic body:

First, let no public moneys be paid out for religious instruction in any school; secondly, let the educational per capita tax be disbursed for results in purely secular studies only in our Catholic schools, our teachers receiving their salaries as other teachers receive theirs; thirdly, to obtain these results let our schools be submitted to state or city examinations. For in this way will the great principle of our government be preserved: 'No public moneys for sectarian purposes.' " [38]

Although this plan has been successfully tried, even in States that have constitutional or legal provisions against the appropriation of public moneys for so-called "sectarian instruction," its application, for many years past at least, has been

[37] Addresses and Proceedings of the N. E. A., 1890, p. 184.
[38] Cath. Standard and Times, Aug. 25, 1906. Cf. also, The Christian School—Pastoral Letter of Rt. Rev. Jas. A. McFaul, p. 29.

merely local, if the arrangement in the State of New York above alluded to be excepted; and its successful continuance has, with this exception, been entirely dependent upon local sentiment and conditions. Its constitutionality has never been brought to a satisfactory test. This would, of course, be done, if there was question of its application to the elementary schools on a larger scale. The constitutions of twenty-four States now contain provisions proscribing the payment of moneys for the support of "sectarian" schools.[39] But even if the plan were to be declared unconstitutional in some of the States, it would still remain the most equitable provision possible for Catholic school rights under our government. And the "school question," doubtless, would likewise still remain, for the power that makes laws and constitutions is also able to remake them.

[39] *Ed. Rev.,* v. 42, p. 131.

CHAPTER XI

THE ECONOMIC SIDE OF THE SCHOOL QUESTION

GENERAL METHODS OF SUPPORT

THE parish priest is one of the three controlling factors in the Catholic school system. By reason of his own position as well as the force of circumstances, he is charged with the responsibility of raising the money to build and to support the school. It is generally a heavy responsibility. The ordinary parish is not well-to-do. It is in debt and struggling. The only reliable source of revenue is that of the church contributions. To keep up the church and its equipment, and to pay off the debt, with the prospect, perhaps, of a necessary enlargement of the church in the future, or its replacement by a larger and finer structure,—this involves a problem which is difficult and persistent enough, in most cases, to tax the energies of the ablest and most zealous priest.

The support of the school would appear, at first sight, to involve a reduplication of the problem. Experience shows, however, that this is not the case. The pioneer bishops and priests, with a far-seeing wisdom, made church and school practically one, in a religious and also a financial way. No one could be a good Catholic who did not help to support both church and school; and, whatever the method adopted for the school's support, there was always the parish treasury to fall back on. The result has been that, generally speaking, wherever Catholics have been found sufficiently numerous to support a school, the pastor has been able to secure money enough to build and to maintain it.

But although the support of the school does not amount to a reduplication of the problem of the support of the church, it has, nevertheless, been always felt to be a real problem, and various methods have been tried in order to lessen its difficulties. It may be said, in general, that the money for the support of the school has been obtained in one of three ways,—tuition-fees, direct parish support, or endowment. The employment of these three methods dates back to the time of the foundation of the parish school system in this country. Sometimes all three have been employed in the case of the same school, part of the money being derived from endowments, part from tuition-fees, and the rest supplied from the general parish treasury.

The tuition-fee method has the apparent advantage of placing the expense of the school upon those who are directly benefitted by it, and who might therefore be supposed to be the most willing to bear the burden. This method has been largely used from the beginning. During the Immigration Period, and for long afterward, it was the most common way of providing for the support of the school. It is still widely in use, the parents paying the monthly tuition-fee,

usually from fifty cents to a dollar, to the
head of the school. Classes are generally large,
and a class of fifty pupils would thus, with
fifty cents from each, bring in just enough to pay
the Sister's salary of twenty-five dollars per
month. If less is brought in than what is needed
to pay the teachers' salaries, the balance is supplied from the parish treasury. The system is
simple enough, and financially efficient; yet it
has obvious disadvantages. One of these is that
it tends to throw the burden of the support of
the school upon the poor. It is the poor who
have the largest families. It is the well-to-do,
on the other hand, those who are best able to
contribute to the support of the school, who are
the most apt to send their children elsewhere,
and thus escape their share of the burden altogether. Another disadvantage comes from the
fact that there is, on the ground, a formidable
competitor for the patronage of the Catholic
parent, in the public free school. The necessity
of paying fifty cents a month for the education of
his child, comes home to many a hard-working
Catholic parent as a real and cogent argument
against the Catholic school.

For these reasons the Third Plenary Council
urged upon pastors the creation of free schools,
and expressed the hope that this might be
effected either directly through endowments from
the wealthy, or by means of associations of laymen, organized for the express purpose of raising
money for the support of the schools. In sug-
gesting such associations the Council adopted a
plan which had been devised by Bishop Neu-

mann, of Philadelphia, some thirty years before.
But Catholic free schools had existed even long
before the days of Bishop Neumann. There
were schools in Philadelphia before the close
of the eighteenth century which required no
tuition-fees, but which were supported directly
or indirectly by the parish. The term " free
school " has had various meanings throughout our educational history. Most often, perhaps, it has meant a school free from tuition-
charges, whether by reason of endowments or
parish support. Free schools, supported by the
parishes, have always existed, but within recent
times they have become very numerous. The
increasing tendency in the public-school system of
late years to eliminate every element of expense
to the parent, has greatly accelerated the movement toward Catholic free schools. The change
has been made quite generally in the larger cities,
as well as in many of the towns. In smaller
places and in country districts the tuition-fee
method still prevails. In many parishes text-
books are also furnished free. The change to
" free schools," or schools supported directly
from the parish funds, has been as rapid as it
has been noiseless, a fact which shows how firmly
the traditional view of the identity of the interests
of church and school is held by the Catholic mind.

Endowed schools have likewise existed all
along, but within the last decade or so there has
arisen a notable tendency toward more systematic efforts to secure endowment. In some
instances sufficient endowment-funds have been
donated by wealthy Catholics to provide for the

entire support of a school; more often, however, the endowment does not reach so far as this, and part of the school's expenses has to be met by one of the other methods outlined above. The most popular method employed for the securing of school endowments is that of scholarships or burses. At the St. Agnes' Parish School, New York, for instance, a gift of $500 will found a scholarship, and provide for the free schooling of a pupil, *in perpetuum*. Under the able administration of the Right Rev. Mgr. Henry A. Brann, a large number of scholarships have been secured for this school, in the form of personal memorial endowments. Other schools in New York and elsewhere have similar endowments. The amount of the scholarship may vary, being generally less in smaller places, where the cost of living and schooling is correspondingly lower. A plan involving a larger endowment-unit is followed by the Right Rev. Mgr. James P. Sinnott, Pastor of St. Charles' Church, Philadelphia. The unit here is a fund the interest from which is sufficient to provide for the salary of a teacher, and the name of the donor of such a fund is placed on a brass tablet, which is attached to the door of a class-room. While many schools may in time become completely endowed in these ways, and part of the burden of school support may be lifted from many others, it is hardly to be expected that the greater number of Catholic parish schools can ever be made altogether free. The past history of the schools, at any rate, offers no warrant for any such expectation. It is far more likely that the schools will have to continue to rely upon the parishes for their support.

With this survey of the methods most commonly employed for the support of the schools, the way is now clear for the consideration of those larger elements in the problem of school support which have special historical as well as practical importance. These may be classed under the titles of teachers' salaries, the financial value of the parish schools to the state, and their actual cost.

TEACHERS' SALARIES

The number of lay teachers engaged in parish schools is relatively small. In some of the larger dioceses they constitute only about one-thirtieth of the whole number of teachers. In the Archdiocese of New York, on the other hand, they number nearly one-half as many as the religious teachers.[1] The religious teacher is generally preferred, but when a sufficient number of religious can not be had, lay teachers become a necessity. The large parish schools of New York, Chicago, and other great cities have grown so fast that the religious orders have been unable to supply them with teachers enough, and as a result lay teachers are sometimes found outnumbering the religious in a school. But throughout the country as a whole, lay teachers probably form only from one-tenth to one-fifteenth of the entire number of parish-school

[1] Sixth Annual Rep. of the Supts. of Cath. Schools for the Archd. of N. Y.

teachers. Their salaries are usually not much above those of religious employed in the same grade and kind of teaching.

During the Immigration Period the salaries of Sisters and Brothers were much lower than they are at present. It was not uncommon, as late as even a couple of decades ago, to find Sisters teaching at a salary of one hundred dollars a year. There has been an upward movement in the salaries of religious teachers which has, to some extent, accompanied the rise in public-school salaries. The salary most commonly received by Sisters engaged in parish-school work is $20 per month, or $200 per year, where the parish furnishes their dwelling-house and pays for light, heat, etc. Where the Sisters provide their own dwelling-house, and meet these latter expenses themselves, the salary is increased by $5 per month, or $50 per year. Within the past few years, owing to the increased cost in living expenses, the upward movement in salaries has been given a new impetus. In 1909 in the Archdiocese of New York the salary of the Sisters of Charity—the diocesan sisterhood—was raised from $300 to $400. The Archbishop of Chicago, during the same year, fixed the salary of Sisters teaching in the Archdiocese at a minimum of $250 per year—an advance of $50. Several other dioceses have done the same. In many parishes in the larger cities the Sisters receive $300 per year. Nevertheless, there are not a few parishes, especially in towns and country places, where they receive considerably less than $200,

It is difficult to see how, with such comparatively small remuneration, and with the cost of living so high universally, the individual establishments or schools in charge of religious teachers can save anything to send to the religious mother-house. Yet, something has to be saved and sent. This is of imperative necessity. The mother-house is the centre of energy, and the hope for the future. From it the young teachers come, and there they are trained. To the mother-house the old teachers look, as to their home, where they will be tenderly cared for when they are no longer able to teach. The novitiate and normal school, the infirmary and home for the aged, must be supported, and to this end each establishment or school must contribute its quota. The amount each is able to save for this purpose varies, naturally, with the place. Some are able to save very little; others can send annually a considerable sum. It may safely be said that the amount that each school sends annually to the mother-house rarely falls below ten per cent of the total of salary receipts, whilst it is usually at least twice as much as this.

It often happens, undoubtedly, that the amount which the Sisters receive by way of salary is added to incidentally by gifts of varying amount and kind, through the kindness and generosity of lay friends in the parish. But this is more usual in country parishes and small places, where the salary is notably below the common figure. The fact should not, therefore, be taken as indicating that the common salary of $250 is ordinarily increased in this way to any notable extent.

It is true, however, that the remuneration received for the teaching of special branches, such as music and drawing, does increase the salary-average somewhat, at least in many schools. Such special branches, if studied beyond the elementary grades, are charged for as extras, and, where the school is large, one teacher—sometimes more than one—is retained for the special purpose of teaching the " extras." In this case the teacher receives no salary from the parish. The amount derived from the teaching of the " extras " in parish schools is difficult to estimate; it is usually more than the common salary, though it is of course far less than these " extras " bring in the academies, where they constitute one of the most important sources of revenue. A conservative estimate would probably be that, in a large school, a teacher of the special branches is able to earn at least one-half as much again as the common salary. But this particular element of school revenue does not enter into the question of the cost of the school to the parish, since the "extras" are always paid for by the parents of the children who take them.

Brothers who teach in the parish schools generally receive from $300 to $400 per year. Notwithstanding this, the per capita saving in their schools is not much, if any, above that in the schools of the Sisters. The living expenses of women are not so high as those of men. Nor do men understand as women do the art of economizing.

Thus, Catholic teachers do not receive more

than one-half as much salary as public-school
teachers engaged in the same district and in the
same class of work. In many cases they do not
receive one-third as much. In the State of New
York, for instance, the average annual salary of
teachers in the public elementary schools, in the
year 1909, was $769.23[2]; the average for the
teachers in the parish schools was probably
between $250 and $300. Yet parish-school
teachers have to live, and they have also, as has
been said, to contribute their share to the support of the mother-establishment. The self-
sacrifice of Catholics in building up and supporting a separate system of schools has been frequently pointed out in discussions of the school
question. But the self-sacrifice of the people in
the matter is slight indeed when compared with
that of the teaching Sisters and Brothers. The
brunt of the heavy burden really falls upon them.
The pinch of real poverty and privation, in so far
as anything of the kind really results from the
up-keep of the parish-school system, is felt only
by them. The parish priest and his people of
to-day little feel the burden of the schools, as did
the immigrant priests and settlers of half a century ago. Economically, as well as socially,
there have been vast changes in the Catholic
body. The economic condition of the teachers,
nevertheless, has remained relatively almost un-
affected. With the Sisters and Brothers who are
engaged in teaching in the schools, it is still a
struggle for existence—a struggle " to make ends
meet," and to save something to help support

[2] Sixth Annual Rep. Ed. Dept., State of N. Y., p. 49.

the home of their religious youth and their declining years. There is always present, too, the shadow of the even greater problem of the securing of new vocations or subjects in number sufficient to prevent the religious organizations from dwindling away. The parish-school system of to-day has been rendered possible only because its cost has been far less than that of the public-school system. The economic basis upon which the parish school rests is therefore revealed by the simple statement that Catholic teachers work for from one-third to one-half the salary of teachers in the public schools; for, in the maintenance of the school, it is the salary that is the chief item of expense.

THE SAVING TO THE STATE.

An interesting question is that of the direct financial value of the Catholic school system to the state, or, in other words, of the amount of money it would cost the state to replace the parish-school system, if all Catholics, in the exercise of their constitutional rights, were to send their children to the public schools. This question has often been dealt with by eminent Catholic educators and apologists. The answer has been sought by assuming, as a basis, that the present per capita cost of public-school education, in any given place, represents what would also be the per capita cost of educating in the public schools the pupils who are now in the parish schools of that place. If, for example, the per capita cost in the

Catholic schools of a certain town is $7, and the corresponding cost in the public schools of the same town is found to be $21, it is taken for granted that it would cost just $21 for the education in the public schools of each pupil now in the parish schools, or just three times as much. But can this be safely assumed? The question is important, not only for ascertaining the amount which the parish-school system saves annually to the state, but also for the study of the more difficult matter of the possible economic value to Catholics of the change to state support.

If the parish-school system were to be taken over by the state intact, and no distinction of cost made between denominational schools and public schools, the assumption would certainly be valid. On the other hand, if Catholics, in the exercise of their constitutional rights, were simply to close their own schools and send their children to the public schools, its validity might, to some extent, be called in question. There are seats to spare in many public-school class-rooms. Thousands of parish-school pupils could, undoubtedly, find place in the public schools, without any addition to the element of cost, save in the matter of such incidentals as books and stationery; while such increase in numbers, without additional expense, would at the same time lower the per capita cost.

Although the validity of this assumption may, therefore, be questioned, in the hypothesis of Catholic schools being closed and their pupils sent to the public schools, the possible error from this source would not be likely to amount to very much. It must be remembered that the empty seats in the public schools are chiefly in the upper grades. The lower grades are nearly always overcrowded, especially in the larger cities. Now, the vast majority of parish-school pupils are in the lower grades, and provision would have to be made at once for these by the erection of new buildings and the employment of more teachers. As a matter of fact, does not a phenomenon similar to that which is involved in the hypothesis that is being considered, actually take place in the larger cities whenever there is a heavy and unexpected increase in the school enrollment? The addition to the public-school enrollment in New York has sometimes been so large as to approximate the entire parish-school enrollment there.[3] Yet no permanent lowering of the per capita cost of public-school education has resulted. The reason of this lies in the fact that, in the case of any large city school-system taken as a whole, the present attendance, at least in the lower grades, is really commensurate with the size of the school-system itself. In other words, although some of the class-rooms may have spare seats, others have already more pupils than they can conveniently hold; and when the pressure of the new and larger enrollment comes each fall, the saving that is represented by the existing empty seats of certain class-rooms is about balanced by the extra expense caused by the overflow of already full or crowded rooms. Practically the same phenomenon would appear,

[3] Cf. Twelfth Annual Rep. of the Supt. of Schools, N. Y. City, p. 29.

so far at least as the lower grades are concerned, if all parish-school pupils were to be sent to the public schools.

With the reservation, then, that there would be apt to be some lowering of the per capita cost, at least for several years, due to the filling of the empty seats in the upper grades, it may be accepted that the present per capita cost of educating pupils in the public schools would continue to be, approximately, the per capita cost of public-school education, if all the Catholic children were to be sent to the public schools.

What would be, therefore, the probable cost of educating all the parish-school pupils in the public schools? The method most commonly employed for ascertaining this has been to take the cost of education per pupil for the whole United States, as given in the Report of the Bureau of Education, and multiply this by the total number of pupils in the parish schools. This method is, however, open to two objections. The average cost per pupil, as given by the Commissioner of Education, includes expenditure for high schools as well as elementary schools; while the diocesan systems include, as yet, comparatively few high schools. Another objection is that the Commissioner's average includes the cost of public-school education in the southern states, as well as in the northern and western. Catholic schools are mostly in the northern and western states, and it is there accordingly that they would have to be replaced. The cost of public education is very low in most of the southern states; in two of them it averages less than

$7 annually per pupil.[4]   Hence, the general average that is obtained in this way cannot be safely made use of in computing the probable cost to the state of educating the children in the parish schools.

A more accurate method was followed by the Catholic Superintendent of Schools of Philadelphia.[5]   This consisted in ascertaining the average cost per pupil in the public schools in each town of the Archdiocese, and multiplying by the number of Catholic pupils in each place respectively. The same method was employed by the Catholic Superintendent of Schools of Boston.[6]   While the results obtained are, undoubtedly, reliable, so far as they go, the inquiry has not been extended beyond a comparatively limited field.

Until fuller data appear, the most trustworthy method of arriving at the amount of the direct financial value of the Catholic schools to the state will probably be to base the estimate for the entire United States upon the ascertained cost of the public *elementary* schools in some one State which may be regarded as fairly representative in this way.   The State of New York, if New York City be excluded, might perhaps be chosen. It contains some large cities, and many thriving manufacturing towns, and it is in such places that Catholic schools are found most numerously. New York, furthermore, furnishes more complete statistics about the cost of education than

[4] Rep. Comm. of Ed., 1909, p. 1331.
[5] The Right Rev. Mgr. P. R. McDevitt, in Report for 1900-1901.
[6] The Rev. Louis S. Walsh; in 1908, consecrated Bishop of Portland, Me.; cf. *Sacred Heart Review*, Jan. 3, 1903.

other States. The inquiry, then, being restricted
to the elementary schools, and the figures being
based upon registration,[7] it is found that, in New
York State, exclusive of the metropolis, the average annual cost of education per pupil in 1909
was $22.50. This includes teachers' salaries, the
cost of apparatus, books for school libraries, and
all other incidental expenses. If expenditures for
sites, furniture, repairs, and other permanent
improvements be included, the average cost per
pupil becomes $24.66.[8] If this latter figure be
now multiplied by 1,237,251, the total number of
pupils enrolled in the Catholic parish schools of
the United States during the year 1909-10,[9] the
result is $30,511,010—approximately the sum it
would cost the state annually at present to educate
the pupils who are in the parish schools.

But this is, of course, only the cost of maintenance. Room would have to be made for these
pupils, and equipment provided. The inquiry
being pushed a step further along the same lines,
it is found that, in New York State, excluding
the metropolis, the average value of elementary
schoolhouses and sites, together with apparatus,
library, and all other property, is $71.99 per pupil
registered. This, in other words, represents the
amount of ground, building, and equipment
required for each pupil at the time of registration.
For the whole number of pupils in the parish

[7] For the sake of comparison, the number of pupils *registered* is taken here, because the number of pupils in the parish
schools, as given in the *Catholic Directory,* represents registration rather than average daily attendance.

[8] Sixth Annual Rep. of the Ed. Dept., State of N. Y., from
the statistics on pp. 49, 94, 122, 124, 149.

[9] Cath. Directory, 1910.

schools, therefore, the amount that would have to be expended for this purpose would be $89,069,699. The interest on this sum at 4 per cent would be $3,562,788. If this be added to the above calculated expense of state maintenance of Catholic schools, the total of $34,073,798 is obtained, which will thus represent the probable sum saved annually to the state by the parish-school system.

ACTUAL COST

No attempt has yet been made to compute accurately the actual cost of the parish schools throughout the whole country. Diocesan school reports, with the exception of that from the Archdiocese of New York, have not, as yet, supplied the necessary data for such an undertaking. Hence it will not be possible to do more here than to offer a rough estimate of the actual cost.

It has been stated that the salaries of public-school teachers are from two to three times as much as those of Catholic teachers. This would lead to the expectation that the annual cost of parish-school education ought not to prove to be more than from one-third to one-half that of elementary education in the public schools, for the chief item in the annual cost is that of teachers' salaries.[10] Furthermore, the expense for heat, light, and janitor-service is less in parish schools than in public schools, for the general reason that such things cost less to private enterprise than to

[10] For a discussion of the possible economic benefit to Catholics of a change to state support, cf. Amer. Eccl. Rev., XLIV, p. 531.

the state. Moreover, heat and light are often
supplied from the adjoining church plant, just as,
in parishes of moderate size, one janitor does service for both church and school. An examination of such scattered data as have been furnished
from the dioceses confirms the expectation of a
proportionate lowering of the cost of parish-
school education, resulting from these conditions.

In St. Louis, for instance, the entire per capita
cost of education for the large schools of SS.
Peter and Paul's Parish, containing 1203 pupils,
with two Brothers of Mary at a salary of $375
each, and twenty-three Sisters of Notre Dame at
a salary of $300 each, was, in 1908, $8.64.[11]
For all the public elementary schools of St. Louis,
the same year, the per capita cost, based upon
registration, was $22.76—over two and a half
times as much.[12]

In the Archdiocese of New York, in 1909, the
per capita cost of maintenance, based upon enrollment, and including salaries, supplies and apparatus, heat and light, repairs, interest and insur-
ance, for all the schools of the Archdiocese, was
$11.13.[13] For all the public elementary schools
of the State of New York, the same year, the
corresponding per capita cost, based upon registration, was $28.66,[14] which is, again, over two

[11] *America*, May 29, 1909.
[12] Report of Board of Ed. of St. Louis, 1908-9, pp. 244, 301.
[13] Sixth Ann. Rep. of the Rev. Superintendents of Cath.
Schools, 1909.
[14] Sixth Ann. Rep. of the Ed. Dept. of the State of N. Y.,
p. 49. The average cost per pupil given in the report is $36.70.
But this includes the cost of new buildings and sites, which are
not included in the archdiocesan average. The public-school
average was therefore reduced correspondingly. There is still
some discrepancy, however, inasmuch as "repairs and furni-

and a half times as much as the cost of the Catholic schools. If New York City proper, or the Boroughs of Manhattan, Bronx, and Richmond, be excluded, the average cost in the Archdiocese per pupil is but slightly reduced, becoming $10.56, instead of $11.13. The average value of school property per pupil is, of course, considerably greater in the metropolis than throughout the rest of the Archdiocese, being $156.39 in the case of the former, and $129.96 in that of the latter. It would evidently be unsafe, however, to make the property-value per pupil in the Archdiocese of New York a basis for the calculation of the property-values of parish schools throughout the country. The property-value per pupil for all the dioceses of the State of New York might, perhaps, be reasonably assumed as a basis for such a calculation, but this is not yet available.

What is, now, the *average* actual cost of Catholic parish-school maintenance per pupil throughout the country? The amount cannot be stated with any degree of accuracy. At best, no more than a probable estimate can be made at present. The cost appears to vary within almost as wide limits as the cost of public-school education. There are numerous schools in which the total annual per capita cost of maintenance is not more than $5, while in the Archdiocese of New York, as has been seen, it is slightly over $11. In

ture" are, in the state report, classed with "sites and buildings"; and expenditures for repairs and furniture are therefore excluded from the above estimate of cost for the public schools, while they are included in the estimate of cost for the parish schools. The estimate taken for the public schools is thus slightly lower than it should be.

particular schools in the large cities the cost runs up to even a much higher figure than this; and in some schools, too, the cost is considerably under $5. But only conditions that are more or less general need be considered, and the above figures may be taken as representing the ordinary extremes. It may therefore be said that the average cost of maintenance per pupil, based upon enrollment, ranges from $5 to $11. The mean of the range is $8, and this may accordingly be taken as the most probable common average of the annual cost of education per capita in the parish schools the country over.[15] For the 1,237,-251 pupils in the parish schools during the year 1909–10, this would represent an actual annual outlay of $9,898,008. Under the public-school system at present the corresponding cost of the education of all the children in the parish schools would, according to a foregoing estimate, amount to $30,511,010.

[15] This conclusion, which is based upon observation and statistics, appears to be confirmed by the following calculation: The most common salary is $250, and the average class probably numbers about 40. This would give an average per capita expense for salaries of $6.25. Now, all other school expenses combined probably make about 30 per cent. of the salary-expense—in this case, $1.87. The addition of these two gives $8.12 as the average cost of parish-school maintenance per pupil.

CHAPTER XII

SCHOOLS OF FOREIGN NATIONALITIES

A GENERAL VIEW

WHEN Governor Seward, in the year 1840, declared himself as in favor, not only of the support of denominational schools by the state but also of the policy of providing children of foreign nationalities with teachers who were of the same language and religious beliefs as their own, he expressed, at the same time, his conviction that this policy was best adapted to prepare them for their life and responsibilities as American citizens.[1] It was a view diametrically opposed to that prevailing generally among American-born citizens of the country. The arrival of foreign immigrants in such vast numbers, especially during the period beginning with the later '30's, aroused fears for the preservation of the English language, as well as American political institutions. Hence, the Native American and Know-Nothing movements, with their savage hostility towards everything Catholic, and particularly the Catholic school.

Time has, however, completely vindicated the soundness and the far-sightedness of Governor

[1] Cf. Cath. Sch. Sys. in U. S. p. 362.

Seward's view. The state did not, it is true, adopt his plan; but its main provisions had been adopted, even before his time, by the American Catholic hierarchy, and they have been firmly adhered to. The Church has seen to it that children of Catholic immigrants, speaking a foreign language, have been provided with teachers who were of the same faith and could speak the same tongue. And the result has been, unquestionably, such as the great statesman anticipated. The process of assimilation has gone on quietly, smoothly, rapidly. There has been no friction, no reaction. The movement has proceeded along the lines of natural growth. Schools which began with practically all the teaching in a foreign language have become, after one generation or two at most, schools in which practically all the teaching is done in English. The process of assimilation will be dealt with more in detail in considering the schools of certain nationalities. But there could be no clearer evidence of the thoroughness of the work of assimilation effected in the Catholic school than the fact that the German or Polish young man, removed by but two generations—and sometimes by only one—from his immigrant ancestry, has become the strongest advocate of the use of English in his children's school.

The chief factor in the sum of the influences making for this assimilation, has been, of course, the language, character, habits, institutions and conditions of the American people—in a word, the new atmosphere of the American life. The young man of foreign-born parentage who is ambitious to make his way in life, soon comes to see that it is essential for him to be able to hold his own in every respect against competition, within the field of his chosen occupation. Reverence for the parental language and nationality will not, therefore, generally speaking, prevent his striving after the most rapid Americanization that is possible for him.

A second factor in the process of assimilation, one which had influence during the Immigration Period at least, was the attitude of the Irish immigrants towards the English language. The Irish came to this country speaking, as a rule, only the English language. Thrown into a congregation together with German immigrants, they awoke for the first time to a full realization of their attachment to the English tongue under the use of German alternately with English in the church, in accordance with the custom obtaining in such "mixed" parishes. In the school, however, a "mixed" arrangement of this kind was manifestly impossible. There had to be two schools. Thus, however small the number of the Irish in a place, a Catholic English-speaking school usually came to be established. And the Catholic English-speaking school stood out clearly to all Catholics as the representative of the ideal, for the advantage of its training in English became in time quite evident. There are hundreds of places in this country, most of them, perhaps, in the middle western States, where such "mixed" congregations formerly existed, and where, consequently, the attitude of the Irish towards the use of the English tongue in both

church and school has been an important factor
in the process of assimilation.

Legislation has been a third factor. With the
growth of compulsory school legislation and child
labor laws, one State after another has added to
the requirements for obtaining an employment-
certificate the provision of being able to read and
write the English language. Forty-nine States
in 1909 had child-labor and compulsory school
laws. Of these, the following require, among
other things, the ability to read and write English
before the child is free to engage in gainful
employment: Arizona, Arkansas, California,
Indiana, Kansas, Maine, Maryland, Massachusetts, Michigan, Minnesota, Montana, New
Hampshire, New York, Ohio, Oregon, Pennsylvania, Rhode Island, Texas, and Vermont[2].
The prevailing tendency, too, is towards the
increase of the requirement in English, as well
as towards its extension throughout the States.
The legislature of Ohio, in the year 1910,
substituted for the simple requirement of
being able to read and write English the
condition of passing satisfactorily a fifth-
grade test in reading, writing, spelling, English,
grammar, geography and arithmetic.[3] Legislation has helped on the movement making for the
use of English by the foreign nationalities, but
it would be difficult to estimate its influence. It
may even be questioned if it has had so very
much influence at all. The rapid assimilation, by

[2] Report Comm. of Ed. for 1909, p. 228; cf. also Report for
1906; Carrigan, The Law and the Amer. Child, p. 141.
[3] Rep. Comm. of Ed. for 1910, p. 206.

the children of the older immigrants, of the life
and spirit and language of the country, before
the era of compulsory education, seems to show
that the assimilative process could hardly be less
rapid in these latter times, even if there were no
legislative efforts to quicken it.

A fourth important factor is the Catholic for-
eign-language school itself, paradoxical as this
may seem. Yet it is a fact that the process
of assimilation has gone on all the more surely
and thoroughly by reason of its being rendered
a *gradual* process through the Catholic foreign-
language school. Efforts to hasten the process
artificially could only result in a reaction in the
contrary direction. The Catholic foreign-lan-
guage school, in teaching the child his parental
mother-tongue as well as English, and at the same
time equipping him with the knowledge requisite
for the duties and opportunities of American
citizenship, has formed the most natural and easy
agency of transition. As has been well said by
Cardinal Gibbons:

" Our Catholic schools afford a much easier
pathway for the foreigner to enter the American
life than is the case in the public school. There
the child must enter at once upon the use of the
English language—perhaps under the guidance
of one who does not know the habits and customs of the immigrant child, and hence cannot
enter into complete sympathy with his work. . . .
In the Catholic school they come under the instruction of those who know the respective languages and can understand their peculiar idioms
of thought and speech. With the English lan-

guage as a constantly enlarging part of their course, they are gradually, almost unconsciously, brought into complete sympathy with American ideals, and readily adapt themselves to American manners and customs. This assimilation is constantly going on in our Catholic schools, and is quite an important factor in our national development." [4]

GERMAN SCHOOLS

This process of assimilation has had its most complete exemplification in the German immigrant and his descendants. German immigrants outnumber those of any other nationality, and they have been coming to this country longer than most of the others. The total membership of Catholic parishes in which German was used exclusively or in connection with English, in the conduct of church services, was, according to the Religious Census of 1906, 1,519,978.[5] Since the German immigrant, on his arrival, could speak only his native tongue, schools had to be established for his children in which German should be, at least for a time, either the only or, at any rate, the chief medium of instruction. The German immigrant, moreover, was strongly attached to his mother-tongue, and where, as often happened, German settlements were formed, or even entire districts peopled mainly by Germans, it was natural that their mother-tongue

[4] Quoted in *Cath. Standard and Times,* Dec. 21, 1907.
[5] Census of 1906, I, p. 118. This does not include children under nine years of age. This reservation is always to be understood in the case of the figures for Catholic "membership" from the Religious Census of 1906.

should be made the language of the school as
it was of the home and church, and that if
English were to be taught at all, it should be
taught much as French and German are taught
to-day in the high school, and for much the same
reason. This was a condition that obtained in
Bucks County and other districts in Pennsylvania
before the Revolutionary War. It obtained also
in several parts of Ohio and Wisconsin, and
in other middle western States, during the Immigration Period. The condition gave rise to
alarm, and sometimes in minds that were altogether untinged by religious or nationalistic bias.
For, if the language of the school as well as the
church and the home were German, would not
the condition of segregation necessarily continue? Might it not become permanent, and so
constitute a menace to the development of the
national life?

The condition, however, has not continued;
and it passed away all the more quickly and completely, it must be evident now, by reason of the
German immigrants being left strictly to themselves,—free to preserve as long as they chose
the cherished language, habits and institutions of
the Fatherland, and subject only to the play of the
racial, social and civic forces naturally at work
around them. It was due to these forces that
English came to have a larger and larger place in
the curriculum, even in the schools established
during the Immigration Period. The father and
mother naturally made the mother-tongue the
language of the home, and, in union with their
pastor, they held firmly to the principle that it

must also be the language in their church. But
with their children it was different. The learning
of English thoroughly was seen to be necessary
for advancement along any but the lowest
levels of social and economic life; and immigrant
parents, accordingly, were not only anxious for
their children to learn English thoroughly, but
also favored the steady enlargement of English
in the curriculum. Thus, as the years went by,
one branch after another came to be taught at
least partly in English. The movement was
accelerated when, in the early '80's, the second
generation of descendants of the early immigrants began to reach the schoolroom. These
children came from homes where English was
spoken. They could not, in many cases, speak
German at all. Yet it was these who formed
the bulk of the attendance at German Catholic
schools in the closing years of the nineteenth century. Under such conditions, the teaching of all
the common branches in English became a practical necessity, for English had become the only
available medium of instruction. It is interesting
to note—although it is somewhat beside the question—that, in connection with this movement in
the German school, German began, a little later,
to be replaced also in the churches. The causal
connection between the two movements is
obvious.

The result of this process of assimilation has
been, that the schools in German parishes and settlements have quite ceased to be " German," in
the sense that formerly attached to the term
when used in this connection. It is true that, in

some German parishes, the catechism is taught in German; but even in these the catechism is also taught in English. It is likewise true that, in almost all schools in German parishes, German reading is taught; but even many non-German parish schools—and public schools as well—have introduced German reading into the work of the upper grades. There are, of course, exceptional conditions here and there, and there are still some schools in which German is the chief medium of instruction. But the condition which generally obtains to-day, in schools in German parishes throughout the country, may be gauged from the fact that in the Archdiocese of Philadelphia, which includes the ancient German strongholds of Berks and Bucks Counties, there are no schools which do not follow the regular diocesan school program, in English; and that, in the Archdiocese of Cincinnati, which has been one of the strongest German centers, there are no longer any real " German " schools, English being everywhere the common medium of instruction.

FRENCH SCHOOLS

HISTORICAL

French Canadians constitute the bulk of the French-speaking population in the United States. Like the Poles, Germans and Irish, the French Canadians have proceeded on the principle that the Catholic school constitutes the most effective practical test of loyalty to the Church as well as the surest guarantee of the Church's future; and, in proportion to their number and means, they have proved their devotion to this principle by results that will compare favorably with those achieved by any other nationality. The stream of French-Canadian immigration began at a very early period in our history. The development of manufacturing industries, especially in New England, drew immigrants in increasing numbers southward across the Canadian border. Thirty years ago, it was estimated that the number of French Canadians in the States amounted to half a million, and of these one hundred and fifty thousand were in New England.[6] Since then, this number has been swelled by many thousands every year. The census of 1906 gives the total membership of Catholic parishes using French only or French together with English, as 1,031,530.[7] Eighty-five per cent of the French Canadian school attendance to-day is in New England.

The concentration of the French-Canadian population in New England has, to a certain extent, rendered the problem of the parish school less difficult than in the case of the other foreign nationalities. It led to the building up of strong, populous parishes, which could easily provide for the erection and support of parish schools; in fact, in many towns through these States, the French Canadians make up more than one-half of the population. It also made more easy of

[6] John Gilmary Shea, The Canadian Element in the U. S., in Amer. Cath. Q. Rev., IV, p. 581 seq.

[7] Census of 1906, p. 118.

solution the problem of the teacher. Quebec abounded in religious communities; and it was much less difficult, and much less expensive to bring teachers from Canada to thriving New England, than to induce them to cross the Atlantic and take up their work in the pioneer towns and settlements of the West, as in the case of the Irish and German immigrations of an earlier date.

TEACHING COMMUNITIES

This comparatively greater facility of obtaining teachers is doubtless the chief reason why the average number of pupils to a teacher is so much less in the schools of this nationality than in the case of certain others. For 161 French Canadian schools, for instance, the average number of pupils to a teacher is 43; while for 293 Polish schools, the average number is 55. Forty-one communities are engaged in teaching in French-Canadian schools in the United States. Many of these are American communities, in charge of a single school or two of this class. Most of the work, however, is done by teaching orders from Canada and France, several of which have established provincial houses in this country. Among these may be mentioned, in the order of the numerical strength of the teaching membership and the school attendance: the Presentation Nuns, Sisters of St. Ann, Sisters of the Holy Cross and Seven Dolors, Sisters of Jesus and Mary, Sisters of St. Joseph (several branches), Sisters of the Holy Ghost, Sisters of the Assumption, Sisters of the Congregation of Notre Dame,

Sisters-Servants of the Immaculate Heart, Sisters of St. Chretienne, and the Little Franciscan Sisters of Mary,—all of these, except some of the Sisterhoods of St. Joseph, being from the Province of Quebec. Several schools are taught by the Little Brothers of Mary or the Marist Brothers, and the Brothers of St. Gabriel. Lay teachers form only about three per cent of the whole number of teachers engaged in the schools.

THE CURRICULUM

The amount of time devoted to the study of French or to teaching in French, in this class of schools, varies considerably with locality. In New England and New York, it may be said that five or six hours a week represents the amount of time that is most commonly given to French. In certain localities, one-half of the day is given to French, and the other half to English; but this condition is exceptional. As a rule, French-Canadian parents are anxious for the advancement of their children in English, and are quite satisfied with the teaching of their mother-tongue for no more than an hour a day. French-Canadian schools, therefore, usually follow the ordinary diocesan school program. Half an hour a day is devoted to teaching the catechism in French, and another half-hour to French reading, which, in the upper grades, is replaced by French Grammar.

The following table shows the number and distribution of the French and French-Canadian schools, teachers and pupils. The figures are

NUMBER AND DISTRIBUTION OF FRENCH SCHOOLS.

Diocese.	Parishes without Schools.	Schools.	Religious Teachers.	Lay Teachers.	Pupils.
Boston, Mass.....	4	17	165	14	8,637
Chicago, Ill.......	......	6	70	1	2,202
New Orleans, La ..	......	1	5	......	160
New York, N. Y...	......	3	36	......	1,518
St. Paul, Minn....	4	2	9	......	627
San Francisco, Cal.	......	......	......	......	......
Albany, N. Y.....	4	5	16	2	1,311
Brooklyn, N. Y. ..	......	1	......	2	36
Buffalo, N. Y.....	......	1	3	......	86
Burlington, Vt....	2	7	62	3	1,769
Cleveland, O......	......	1	2	......	50
Duluth, Minn.....	......	2	10	......	380
Fall River, Mass ..	1	14	113	9	6,786
Gr'ndRapids,Mich.	......	7	32	4	1,410
Hartford, Conn ...	......	6	46	......	1,910
Lincoln, Neb......	1	......	......	......	......
Manchester, N. H .	......	16	165	2	7,420
Marquette, Mich..	3	4	30	1	943
Ogdensburg, N. Y .	......	6	62	......	1,520
Portland, Me.....	......	17	159	......	6,508
Providence, R. I...	1	12	141	4	6,366
Rockford, Ill......	......	1	5	......	90
St. Cloud, Minn. ..	......	1	6	......	200
Sioux City, Ia.....	1	......	......	......	......
Springfield, Mass..	5	29	294	......	12,829
Superior, Wis.....	......	1	2	......	90
Syracuse, N. Y. ...	1	1	5	......	200
Total.........	27	161	1438	42	63,048

Total membership of French and French-English parishes 1,031,530.

derived from the official diocesan reports to the *Catholic Directory*, for the year 1909-10.[8]

[8] From the method employed at this date and previously in gathering the school statistics published in the *Catholic Directory*, it is evident that the figures given for school enrollment for the year 1909-10 represent, in part, the enrollment during the previous scholastic year. According to the system adopted by the publishers in 1911, the school statistics will be gathered in October, and the enrollment given will therefore be for the scholastic year during which the *Directory* is published. It is

Here, as well as in the tables relating to other nationalities, the number of pupils represents enrollment at the beginning of the school year; mission stations are excluded; as are also parishes and schools of mixed nationalities, whenever this condition is made known in the *Directory*.[9]

From statistics furnished by the Immigration Commission, it would appear that the French Canadian pupils in the public schools are about equal in number to those in the parish schools.[10] However, the Commission's figures for the parish schools are in some cases too low. Thus, for the parish schools in Manchester, N. H., the number of pupils given is 923, while, according to the *Catholic Directory*, the number is over 3,500.

ITALIAN SCHOOLS

According to the census of 1906, there were 826,023 members of Catholic parishes in which the Italian language was used, either exclusively or in connection with English.[11] In other words,

published soon after January 1st. The population-figures are sent to the *Directory* between November 15th and January 1st. —Letter of Editor of *Directory, 1911*.

[9] The information furnished by the *Catholic Directory* in regard to French schools is evidently not complete for certain dioceses. Thus, for the Archdiocese of New Orleans only one school is given as French. While the statistics furnished by the *Directory* for the general Catholic population are far from being reliable, there is good reason for regarding the figures given for school attendance in the individual schools as fairly accurate in the aggregate. The tables given in this and the following chapter have been compiled from the reports sent in from individual schools.

[10] Abstract of the Report, 1911, on The Children of Immigrants in Schools, pp. 66, 73.

[11] Census of 1906, p. 119.

this represents the number of persons who belong to Italian parishes. In strength of church membership, therefore, the Italians rank third among the nationalities using a foreign tongue in the Catholic Church in the United States, being preceded only by the Germans and the French Canadians. Yet comparatively few Italian parishes have parish schools. The chief reason for this appears to be an almost entire lack of appreciation of the importance of the Catholic school. Italian children generally attend the public schools.

In response to the efforts of the bishops, promising Italian schools have been organized in a number of places within recent years. Archbishop Farley, of New York, has taken the lead in this work, and the future appears to hold out better hopes for the education of Italian children under Catholic auspices. One of the difficulties has been to secure proper teachers. This difficulty has now been largely overcome. Several Italian teaching communities have established themselves in the United States, and are doing efficient work in the schools for Italian children. Chief among these is the community known as the Missionary Sisters of the Sacred Heart, which has erected a novitiate in New York City. Among other Italian sisterhoods are the Missionary Franciscan Sisters of the Immaculate Conception, the Sisters of the Third Order of St. Francis, Allegany, N. Y., and the Baptistine Sisters.

Italian immigrants are but little concerned, as a rule, about the retention of the mother-tongue by their children. Frequently, catechism and reading, with some grammar, are taught in Italian; but frequently, too, all the teaching in the Italian parish schools is in English. This is the case, for example, in all the schools for Italian children in New York City. The second generation of Italian children know so little Italian that they have to be taught even the catechism in English.[12]

NUMBER AND DISTRIBUTION OF ITALIAN SCHOOLS.[13]

Diocese.	Parishes without Schools.	Schools.	Religious Teachers.	Lay Teachers.	Pupils.
Boston, Mass.....	6	1	9	1	471
Chicago, Ill.......	9	1	10	......	702
Cincinnati, O.....	1	......	......	......	......
Milwaukee, Wis...	2	......	......	......	......
New Orleans, La ..	1	......	......	......	......
New York, N. Y...	15	7	47	29	3,700
Oregon City, Ore..	......	1	2	......	82
Philadelphia, Pa...	14	3	25	......	1,633
St. Louis, Mo.....	2	1	......	3	171
St. Paul, Minn....	1	......	......	......	......
San Francisco, Cal.	1	......	......	......	......
Albany, N. Y.	3	1	2	2	100
Altoona, Pa.......	1	2	......	2	109
Brooklyn, N. Y.. .	8	3	14	6	952
Buffalo, N. Y.....	9	5	19	1	989
Cleveland, O......	9	1	5(?)	......	202
Columbus, O......	1	......	......	......	......
Davenport, Ia.....	1	......	......	......	......
Denver, Colo.....	1	2	16	......	720
Detroit, Mich.....	1	1	3	......	120
Duluth, Minn.....	2	......	......	......	......
Erie, Pa..........	1	......	......	......	......
Fall River, Mass ..	1	......	......	......	......
Galveston, Tex....	1	......	......	......	......
Gr'ndRapids,Mich.	1	......	......	......	......
Harrisburg, Pa....	2	......	......	......	......
Hartford, Conn ...	6	2	5	......	225
Indianapolis, Ind..	1	......	......	......	......
Little Rock, Ark..	2	......	......	......	......

[12] Cf. Lord, The Italian in America, p. 242 seq.
[13] From parish reports in Cath. Dir. for 1909-10.

NUMBER AND DISTRIBUTION OF ITALIAN SCHOOLS—*Continued*

Diocese.	Parishes without Schools.	Schools.	Religious Teachers.	Lay Teachers.	Pupils.
Marquette, Mich..	2	......	......	......	......
Mobile, Ala.......	1	1	......	1	45
Monterey and Los Angeles, Cal....	2	......	......	......	......
Newark, N. J.....	13	8	26	5	1,638
Peoria Ill.........	2	......	......	......	......
Pittsburgh, Pa.....	9	3	11	1	514
Providence, R. I...	3	......	......	......	......
Richmond, Va....	1	......	......	......	......
Rochester, N. Y. ..	1	1	10	......	575
Rockford, Ill......	1	......	......	......	......
Sacramento, Cal...	1	......	......	......	......
Scranton, Pa......	13	1	6	......	211
Springfield, Mass..	6	......	......	......	......
Superior, Wis.....	1	......	......	......	......
Syracuse, N. Y....	1	......	......	......	......
Trenton, N. J.....	13	2	6	......	600
Wheeling, W. Va..	2	......	......	......	......
Winona, Minn....	......	1	4	......	79
Total.........	175	48	220	51	13,838

Total membership of Italian and Italian-English parishes 826,023.

CHAPTER XIII

SCHOOLS OF FOREIGN NATIONALITIES.—*Continued*

POLISH SCHOOLS

BEGINNINGS

THE stream of Polish immigration reached the United States in the year 1855, when the Polish settlement of Panna Marya was formed in Texas. The following years witnessed the arrival of other Polish colonies in Texas, as well as in Michigan and Wisconsin. In the year 1870, with the inauguration by Prussia of a fresh policy of persecution and proscription against the Poles, a great tide of immigration set in towards the United States. Between the years 1855 and 1880, eighty-five Polish churches were built. Wherever a Polish parish was established, a parish school, as a rule, also arose; and the erection of the school was usually coincident with the erection of the first church. Each year after the last mentioned date witnessed a fresh influx of Polish immigrants, and the building of a corresponding number of churches and schools.[1] According to

[1] Kruszka, Historya Polska w Ameryce, VI, p. 8 seq., I, p. 71 seq.; *America*, III, p. 411; Fronczack, art. on The Poles in America, quoted in *New Century* (Wash.), Oct. 6, 1906; Van

the Religious census of 1906, the membership
of Catholic parishes using Polish alone or Polish
and English amounted to 736,150.[2]

Problems of the most difficult character confronted the early Polish parish priests in their
efforts to establish Polish schools. It was a
situation like that which confronted the pastors
in the Irish and German settlements during the
period 1840-1860. The Poles were even poorer,
perhaps, than the immigrants of that period,
and, like the Germans, they were, on their arrival,
unable to speak a word of English. Although
poor, however, the Poles were generous even to
a fault where their religious interests were concerned; and the churches and schools, even
though heavily debt-burdened, which sprang up
everywhere in the midst of their new settlements,
testified eloquently to their piety and to their
lively interest in the education of their children.
A more difficult problem was that of providing
teachers for the schools. The schools were
built, as a matter of fact, without any one stopping to consider the problem of the teacher. The
first teachers were the best that could be procured on the spot or in the vicinity, the better
educated among the immigrants being pressed
into service for the purpose. Men were usually
employed for the larger boys, and women for the
girls and smaller boys.

In Chicago the first Polish parish, that of St.
Stanislaus, was organized in 1869. By the year

Norman, Poland, The Knight among Nations, p. 326 seq.;
The Confessions of a Polish Priest, in *Cath. Standard and
Times,* Mar. 12, 1910.
  [2] Census of 1906, p. 119.

1874, when the Rev. Vincent Barzynski, of the
Order of the Resurrection, who had come from
Poland some years before, took charge, it had
about four hundred and fifty families. Father
Barzynski was a remarkable man, and his life
and labors have left deep and lasting traces in
the history of his countrymen in America. We
are concerned here with his work as a church-
man only in so far as it bears upon education;
and it will suffice to say of his church work that,
during his twenty-five years' pastorate, St. Stanislaus Parish grew to be one of the largest Catholic parishes in the world, and became the chief
focal point of influence for the entire Polish
body in the United States. He established the
first Catholic Polish paper, and the first Catholic Polish daily. An ardent believer in Polish
Catholic schools, his power as an organizer was
shown, not only in his development of the St.
Stanislaus Parish School until it came to be nu-
merically probably the largest single elementary
school in the world—counting to-day 3,820
pupils, with 65 teachers,—but also in his efforts
to make the work of the school the most highly
efficient possible. Under his direction, the earliest Polish text-books were issued. He lent a
helping hand in the formation of the first teaching corps of Polish Sisters, brought from Europe
one of the two largest Polish teaching communities in this country, and founded a third community. He developed secondary schools for
boys and girls in the parish, and the St. Stanislaus
College for boys.[3]

[3] Confessions of a Polish Priest, in *Cath. Stand. and Times,*
Mar. 12, 1910; Kruszka, op. cit., I, p. 76 seq., III, p. 14 seq.

Another priest who had a great influence in the educational development of the Poles in America was the Rev. Joseph Dombrowski. He brought the Felician Sisters to America while pastor at Polonia, Wis., and helped to establish them in Detroit after he took charge of a parish in that city. His most notable educational work was probably the founding in that city, in 1884, of the Polish College and Seminary of SS. Cyril and Methodius, an institution which has given to hundreds of priests, along with a theological training, the knowledge of the Polish language, literature and history requisite for an effective ministry in Polish parishes.[4]

TEACHING BODIES

The first attempt to found a Polish teaching order in the United States was made by the Rev. Felix Zwiardowski, a Resurrectionist, pastor at Panna Marya, Texas, about 1873. But the community did not long survive.[5]

A colony of the Felician Sisters was brought from Cracow, Poland, to Polonia, Wis., by Father Dombrowski, in 1874. Fire destroyed their house, and they moved to Detroit in 1882, having in the meantime opened a school at Bay City, Mich. With the aid of Father Dombrowski, now also at Detroit, the Sisters established their mother-house in that city, and, with the growth of the community's membership, they were sent to Polish schools in various parts of the

[4] Kruszka, Historya, II, p. 112 seq.
[5] Ib., II, p. 101.

country. In 1900, they took charge of a school
at Buffalo, N. Y., which has become the provincial-house of their schools in the East. The
Felician Sisters are the largest of the purely
Polish teaching orders, numbering to-day about
800 Sisters.[6]

The Sisters of the Holy family of Nazareth
were brought to this country by Father Barzynski, in 1885. They opened an academy on West
Division St., Chicago, two years later, and took
charge subsequently of Polish schools in that city,
and in many dioceses throughout the country.
The central establishment is at Desplaines, Ill.
They constitute the second largest of the purely
Polish communities. The Sisters number 440.[7]

There are several other Polish teaching orders.
The Polish Franciscan School Sisters were
founded by Father Barzynski, in 1893. Their
mother-house is at St. Louis, and they have
charge of seven schools.[8] The Sisters of the
Resurrection came to America in the year 1900.
The central establishment is in Chicago. The
Sisters number 63.[9] The Polish Sisters of St.
Joseph were founded in 1901, with the mother-
house at Stephen's Point, Wis. Under Mother
Felicia, forty-two members of the Sisters of St.
Francis, of Milwaukee, were, in that year, canonically authorized to separate from the Order
to form the new body, which has to-day 218
members.[10] The Bernardine Sisters of St. Fran-

[6] Kruszka, Historya, II, p. 112 seq.; Cath. Dir. for 1910.
[7] Kruszka, op. cit., II, p. 119 seq.; Cath. Dir.
[8] Kruszka, op. cit., II, p. 110.
[9] Ib., p. 123.
[10] Ib., p. 129.

cis have their principal establishment at Reading, Pa. The Sisters of St. Francis, under the patronage of St. Cunegunda, have their mother-house in Chicago. The community known as the Filiae Mariae have a school at Manayunk, Pa.[11]

Among the non-Polish communities which have charge of Polish schools, the School Sisters of Notre Dame, of Milwaukee, occupy the first place. Some of their Polish schools have grown to be very large, notably St. Stanislaus' and St. John Cantius', Chicago, with 65 and 27 teachers respectively, and St. Josaphat's, Milwaukee, with 25 teachers. The community began this work as early as 1873.[12]

A number of other non-Polish communities have charge of Polish schools, among which may be mentioned the Sisters of the Incarnate Word and the Sisters of Divine Providence, Texas; the School Sisters of St. Francis, Milwaukee, who conduct nine schools; the Sisters of St. Francis, St. Francis, Wis.; the Sisters of St. Francis, Lafayette, Ind.; the Sisters of the Holy Cross, Notre Dame, Ind.; the Benedictine and Dominican Sisterhoods; the Sisters of Mercy, and of St. Joseph; and various other branches of the Franciscan Sisters.[13]

There is no Polish teaching community of Brothers. The Brothers of the Congregation of the Holy Cross have charge of the large and flourishing school of Holy Trinity Parish, Chicago, where, in 1909, they also established a Polish high school.

[11] Cath. Dir.; Rep. Supt. of Schools, Phila., 1910.
[12] Kruszka, p. 106; Cath. Dir.
[13] Kruszka, op. cit., II, passim; Cath. Dir.

Fully fifty per cent of the Sisters in Polish schools speak English and Polish with equal fluency, and about eighty per cent or so were born in America or have spent all but the years of their earliest infancy here.[14]

The following table shows how the work of the Polish schools is divided among the Polish teaching orders, and also the large share of it that is being done by the School Sisters of Notre Dame—the only non-Polish community in the list:

Teaching Body.	Schools.	Teachers.		Pupils.	Av. No. Pupils to Teacher.
		Sisters.	Lay.		
Felician Sisters........	98	656	4	36,285	55
Sisters of the Holy Family of Nazareth......	25	244	5	15,907	64
Polish Sisters of St. Joseph.............	22	151	1	8,503	56
Bernardine Sisters of St. Francis............	6	18	1	1,333	70
Sisters of the Resurrection..............	3	21	.....	1,229	58
Sisters of III Order of St. Francis (Chicago)	5	22	.....	695	31
Polish Franciscan School Sisters.............	7	?	.....	506	......
Filiae Mariae.........	1	3	1	192	48
School Sisters of Notre Dame.............	18	251	6	15,587	61
Lay teachers.........	64	116	.....	6,728	58

The number and distribution of the Polish parishes, schools, teachers and pupils may be seen in the following table:

[14] Confessions of a Polish Priest, *Cath. Stand. and Times,* Feb. 12, 1910.

NUMBER AND DISTRIBUTION OF POLISH SCHOOLS.[15]

Diocese.	Parishes without Schools.	Schools.	Religious Teachers.	Lay Teachers.	Pupils.
Baltimore, Md....	......	3	25	......	1,616
Boston, Mass.....	5	3	7	2	414
Chicago, Ill.......	3	26	334	6	21,641
Cincinnati, O.....	......	2	......	2	92
Milwaukee, Wis...	2	16	139	7	8,031
New York, N. Y...	3	6	9	6	901
Oregon City, Ore..	1	......	......	......	......
Philadelphia, Pa...	7	14	52	6	3,470
St. Louis, Mo.....	......	4	17	......	812
St. Paul, Minn....	4	4	20	2	1,225
Albany, N. Y.....	4	5	15	13	1,541
Altoona, Pa.......	4	3	......	5	336
Belleville, Ill......	......	1	3	......	117
Brooklyn, N. Y....	5	5	22	2	1,035
Buffalo, N. Y......	......	20	152	1	8,248
Burlington, Vt....	1	1	......	2	64
Cleveland, O......	8	12	72	10	4,991
Columbus, O.....	......	1	......	1	50
Denver, Colo.....	1	......	......	......	......
Detroit, Mich.....	1	16	134	......	7,804
Duluth, Minn.....	2	1	3	......	150
Erie, Pa..........	......	1	13	1	830
Fall River, Mass...	2	2	7	1	372
Fargo, N. Dak....	1	......	......	......	......
Fort Wayne, Ind..	......	12	60	6	3,005
Galveston, Tex....	......	1	2	......	40
Gr'ndRapids,Mich.	......	12	72	2	3,860
Green Bay, Wis...	1	19	45	4	2,701
Harrisburg, Pa....	......	4	21	......	1,754
Hartford, Conn. ..	1	11	14	21	1,845
Helena, Mont.....	......	1	3	......	100
Kansas City, Mo..	......	1	1	......	40
La Crosse, Wis...	1	6	15	3	677
Leavenworth, Kan.	......	2	6	......	211
Lincoln, Neb......	......	1	4	......	94
Manchester, N. H.	......	1	5	......	184
Marquette, Mich..	1	1	......	1	93
Mobile, Ala.......	3	......	......	......	......
Monterey and Los Angeles, Cal....	1	......	......	......	......
Newark, N. J.....	3	7	39	1	2,970
Ogdensburg, N. Y.	1	......	......	......	......
Omaha, Neb......	3	8	31	3	1,188

[15] Summary of parish reports in Cath. Directory for 1909-10.

NUMBER AND DISTRIBUTION OF POLISH SCHOOLS—*Continued*

Diocese	Parishes without Schools.	Schools.	Religious Teachers.	Lay Teachers.	Pupils.
Peoria, Ill........	1	5	26	2	1,429
Pittsburgh, Pa....	3	21	74	16	4,799
Providence, R. I...	4	......	......	......	......
Rochester, N. Y...	......	3	11	......	496
St. Cloud, Minn. ..	2	1	4	......	70
St. Joseph, Mo....	......	1	4	......	190
San Antonio, Tex .	......	......	10	33	884
Scranton, Pa......	20	10	20	12	2,179
Sioux City, Ia.....	1	......	......	......	......
Sioux Falls, S. Dak.	1	1	8	......	175
Springfield, Mass..	4	4	25	......	1,437
Superior, Wis.....	2	2	10	......	417
Syracuse, N. Y....	2	2	6	1	436
Trenton, N. J.....	1	7	25	4	1,687
Wheeling, W. Va..	2	......	......	......	......
Wilmington, Del ..	......	1	8	......	500
Winona, Minn....	3	2	18	......	925
Total.........	115	293	1591	176	98,126

Total membership of Polish and Polish-English parishes 736,150.[16]

The above statistics, as well as those relating to the other foreign nationalities, are a summary of the Polish school reports in the *Catholic Directory* for the Census-Year 1909-10. Where Polish parishes are without schools, it may be taken for granted that they are either newly founded or small. It may also be remarked that where Polish schools have lay teachers exclusively, it is due to one or both of these same conditions, as is evident from the small number of teachers in the individual schools.

What proportion, it may be asked, does the total enrollment in Polish schools bear to the total

[16] Census of 1906, p. 119.

number of Polish children of school age, and to the total Polish population? These questions cannot be answered directly, for neither the Polish population nor the number of Polish children of school age is accurately known. The Polish population of the United States has been variously estimated at from two to four millions.[17]

In the years 1908-10, inquiry was made by the Immigration Commission in the public schools of thirty-seven leading cities, and in the parish schools of twenty-four of these same cities, concerning the nationality of the pupils.[18] It was intended that the investigation should include all the children attending the public and the parish schools in the cities selected. If the Commission's figures for public-school attendance be accepted, and allowance be made for the discrepancies in its parish school enrollment,[19] it would appear from the report that there are about as many Polish children attending the public schools as attend the parish schools. This would indicate a total Polish enrollment, in parish and public schools of the United States, of about 200,000, which would correspond to a population of about 1,000,000.[20] It must be noted, however, that the Commission's figures for Polish attendance at the public schools do not include the chil-

[17] Cf. Kruszka, op. cit.
[18] Cf. Abstract of the Report on the Children of Immigrants in Schools: Washington, 1911.
[19] The parish school enrollment, as given in the report, is undoubtedly too low in some cases. The Polish parish schools in Milwaukee are credited with an attendance of 1979, and those in Cleveland with an attendance of 705. Cf. p. 66. The actual attendance, in each city, is probably three times as great. Cf. p. 307 supra.
[20] Cf. Rep. Bureau of Ed. for 1909, II, p. 606.

dren of Polish fathers who were born in this country; and also, that the Polish parish school enrollment of 98,126, as given in the above table, does not include Polish pupils attending non-Polish parish schools. The number of these latter is very large; but there is no means at present of ascertaining just how large the number is. The total Polish school enrollment would be at least doubled, in all probability, by the inclusion of both these elements; and this would mean a corresponding Polish population in the United States of at least two millions.

GROWTH IN EFFICIENCY—THE CURRICULUM

A glance at the above tables shows one of the great evils that Polish educators have to contend against—overcrowding. The evil is not, it is true, confined to Polish schools. It exists in most Catholic city schools. It exists also in the public school systems of many of the large cities, where thousands of children are kept out of school for one-half of each school day. Overcrowding is one of the most acute problems with which Polish educators have to deal. The school buildings are too small, the teachers are too few, and there is no playground or even breathing-place for the pupils, in many cases, except the street. It must be said that the evil, in the two first of these respects, at least, is far less than it was. New and larger school buildings are appearing in the city parishes, and the growth of the Polish teaching orders, as well as of Polish membership in the non-Polish orders, has been very marked. But Polish immigrants are still pouring into the country, and the average Polish family is very large. The growth of the parishes is consequently so rapid that the Polish city pastor finds it quite impossible to provide all the teachers and all the class-room space requisite for a well conducted school, just as various city boards of education find it impossible to provide sufficient seating capacity for the annual increase of pupils in the public schools.

To the rapid increase of the Polish population is also due, to some extent, the unprepared state of many of the teachers. Most of the Polish teaching orders are passing through the stage of growth which marked the early history of the other teaching orders in this country. The supply of vocations is not equal to the demand for teachers, resulting from the overwhelming increase of pupils in the schools. Competent lay teachers who are willing to work for a teacher's wages, are few and hard to find. It is, then, either the religious teacher, or none. This is the dilemma in which the pastor is placed, whether he is opening a new school, or making an imperatively needed enlargement. The problem of the maintenance of the school presents itself to him as a matter of life and death for the Faith. And it is this view that very often prevails with the mother-superior of the teaching order. A not unfriendly critic has thus described the result:

" A girl enters the convent; she is perhaps possessed of an elementary education, and perhaps she is not. If she has advanced to the threshold of the high school she has done well.

Now she is coached as strenuously as possible, and the " degree work " is given as quickly as possible. Three years later, perhaps but two years later, little Wladislawa, whom you prepared for First Holy Communion four or five years ago, is hurried out to your neighbor's parish, where . . . she is doing a work that will soon wear the life out of her, for it is beyond her power. There has been no time for training her along educational lines, certainly not along pedagogical lines." [21]

This condition still exists to a large extent among Polish teaching orders, but it is far from being universal. It is found chiefly in the newer communities, in those organized within the past dozen years. The older Polish communities and English-speaking communities doing Polish work, have profited by experience. In some of these, the pedagogical training of the Sisters is still far from perfect; in others, like the School Sisters of Notre Dame, it has reached a very high standard. It is in recently founded parishes, as a rule, that the crudest teaching is found.[22]

Another obstacle to efficiency which the Polish educator has had to contend with, especially in the teaching of English, has been the duality of the medium of instruction. Polish as well as English had to be taught as a living language, and not only as a living language but as a language no less important for the pupil than English. This condition necessarily increased the number

[21] Confessions of a Polish Priest, in *Cath. Stand. and Times,* Jan. 29, 1910.
[22] Ib.

of school-room subjects, and the time devoted to
English had to be cut down. Certain of the
" non-essential " subjects were also omitted, and
in these ways the curriculum of the Polish schools
has been generally constructed so as to provide
time sufficient for a full elementary study of
Polish, without an undue lengthening of the
school hours. Religion is usually taught only in
Polish. The following curriculum [23] may be

A TYPICAL POLISH SCHOOL CURRICULUM.

	1st Grade	2d Grade	3d Grade	4th Grade	5th Grade	6th Grade	7th Grade	8th Grade
Catechism(Polish)	135	135	135	135	135	135	90	90
Bible History (Polish).......	90	90	90	90	90	90	...	...
Church History (Polish).......	...	...	...	...	...	...	60	60
Reading (Polish) .	315	285	210	150	150	150	135	135
Grammar & Composition (Polish)	...	...	60	90	90	90	90	90
History of Poland (Polish).........	...	30	30	60	60	60	...	...
Literature(Polish)	...	...	...	...	...	...	90	90
Arithmetic (Eng.)	300	300	300	300	300	300	300	300
Reading & Spelling (English)....	360	300	210	150	150	150	150	150
Grammar & Composition (Eng.)..	...	...	60	90	90	90	90	90
History of United States (Eng.) ...	...	...	60	90	90	90	90	90
Geography (Eng.)	...	60	60	60	60	60	60	60
Penmanship.	90	90	90	90	90	90	90	90
Drawing........	60	60	60	60	60	60	60	60
Vocal Music (Eng. and Polish).....	105	105	90	90	90	90	90	90
Recess..........	150	150	150	150	150	150	150	150
Total no. minutes per week..	1605	1605	1605	1605	1605	1605	1605	1605

[23] Curriculum of the Holy Trinity School, Chicago, communicated by Bro. Peter, C.S.C., Principal. The school is taught by both Brothers and Sisters. For a fuller enumera-

cernible in them? and how do these effects compare with those which have been noted in the case of the Germans? The inquiry is the more interesting, and the less easy at the same time to answer off-hand, because of the tendency of the Poles to form compact, self-sufficient settlements, whether in town or country.

No one can walk through a group of Polish children at play in a school-yard or in the street without being struck by the fact that these children already form an English-speaking generation. Children of the Polish immigrants, even though living in closely crowded and self-sufficient communities, appear to take to English as readily as did the children of the German immigrants. And this, too, even though only Polish is heard in the home and in the church. Says the keenly observant author of the *Confessions of a Polish Priest* which has more than once been referred to:

" Not two boys out of twenty employ Polish in their conversation with one another; and in all probability the two boys, could they be found, would be newly arrived immigrants, or perhaps but one of them would be such. The girls are slower in abandoning Polish as a medium of conversation. The boys' games, whether foot-ball, baseball, marbles, kite-flying, tag, black-man, run-sheep-run, make the boys think in English and think quickly. I have still to discover what games they play in Poland. The average Polish boy in the vicinity of Irondale [representing a typical Polish settlement] speaks English with scarcely a perceptible Polish accent.

" When our boys and girls leave school, at the age of fourteen or fifteen, they have a command of purer Polish than that spoken by their elders, for they speak it with less dialectic accent and have learned at least the elements of Polish Grammar. But the same boys and girls five years later speak Polish with less ease. The young man and the young woman of twenty-two or three years do not devote an hour a week to the reading of Polish books or papers, while of writing in Polish there is practically none. It is a growing difficulty to find a young man or young woman equipped with a sufficient knowledge of Polish to assume the duties of recording secretary in our parish and national societies." [25]

It seems not unlikely, then, that the second generation of the Polish immigrants would be quite as completely Americanized as was the second generation of the German immigrants, were it not for the steady stream of fresh arrivals from Poland. Nevertheless, the facts that have been cited show that the Americanization of the Polish population is proceeding rapidly and irresistibly. The Polish school has served the same purpose here as did the German school, in the corresponding movement affecting the German population. It has, apparently, delayed the movement, but, in reality, it has forestalled the danger of a reaction, by restraining the movement within the lines of natural laws, and has thus made the results all the more sure and thorough. But this is only one aspect of the work of the Polish parish school. Its chief work,

[25] *Cath. Standard and Times,* Feb. 12, 1910.

the work for which it was founded and for which
it still stands, has been to teach the Polish people
in America to be true to themselves, — to the
faith, the patriotic and social traditions, and, so
far as may be also, the language of the Fatherland. This ideal, far from being inconsistent
with American citizenship, is, as the parallel history of other foreign nationalities shows, the very
condition for its most effective realization under
the circumstances. Such has been the conviction,
from the first, of leading Polish priests and laymen. For this ideal the Polish parish school will
doubtless continue to stand, long after the differences between its curriculum and that of the
other schools of the diocese shall have disap-
peared.

Spanish Schools

The census of 1906 gives 356,329 as the total
membership of the 514 Spanish and Spanish-
English parishes in the United States.[26] Almost
all of these parishes are in New Mexico, Arizona, Texas and California. There are but few
distinctively Catholic schools; the *Catholic
Directory* gives only six. But in many districts
throughout the southwest in which the population
is entirely or almost entirely Catholic, the public schools naturally reflect the attitude of the people towards religion and assume more or less of
a Catholic tone.

[26] Census of 1906, p. 119.

Bohemian Schools

About one-third of the children who are of
school age, in Catholic Bohemian parishes, attend
Bohemian parish schools. Considering the
difficulty of securing teachers for these schools,
this result bespeaks a sturdy devotion on the part
of Bohemian Catholics to the principle of the
Catholic school.

Chief among the teaching orders engaged in
the work of the Bohemian parish schools are the
School Sisters of Notre Dame. This powerful
organization has charge of seven schools, with
forty-eight teachers, and its work here as elsewhere reaches a very high degree of pedagogical efficiency. The Sisters of the Third Order of
St. Francis, of Joliet, Ill., are also doing highly
successful work, and have charge of a number of
Bohemian schools. The same may be said of the
Bohemian Benedictine Sisters, whose mother-
house is at St. Procopius School, Chicago, which
has eighteen teachers and over eight hundred
pupils; of the School Sisters of St. Francis, Milwaukee; and of the Sisters of Notre Dame, of
Cleveland.

In regard to the curriculum, the time-schedule,
and the assimilative forces at work within and
without the school, it may be said that the same
conditions which have been described in connection with the Polish schools exist in the case of the
Bohemian schools, and of those of other Slavic
nationalities.

NUMBER AND DISTRIBUTION OF BOHEMIAN SCHOOLS.[27]

Diocese.	Parishes without Schools.	Schools.	Religious Teachers.	Lay Teachers.	Pupils.
Baltimore, Md.... ..	......	1	9	......	565
Chicago, Ill.......	......	9	72	......	3,198
Dubuque, Ia......	1	1	7	......	150
Milwaukee, Wis...	......	3	10	......	362
New York, N. Y...	1	1	15	......	754
Philadelphia, Pa...	1	......	......	......	......
St. Louis, Mo.....	......	2	11	......	579
St. Paul, Minn.....	2	2	7	1	310
Cleveland, O.... ..	......	6	43	......	2,507
Dallas, Tex.......	1	......	......	......	......
Davenport, Ia...	1	......	......	......	......
Detroit, Mich.....	1	......	......	......	......
Fargo, N. Dak....	1	......	......	......	......
Green Bay, Wis...	1	......	......	......	......
La Crosse, Wis....	......	2	6	......	264
Lincoln, Neb......	5	......	......	......	......
Little Rock, Ark...	1	......	......	......	......
Omaha, Neb......	2	......	......	......	......
Pittsburgh, Pa....	......	1	2	......	96
Richmond, Va	1	......	......	......	......
Sioux City, Ia.....	1	......	......	......	......
Wichita, Kan.....	......	1	2	......	40
Winona, Minn....	3	2	10	......	153
Total.........	23	31	194	1	8,978

Total membership of Catholic Bohemian and Bohemian-English parishes 154,073.[28]

LITHUANIAN SCHOOLS

The organization of parishes and schools for the Lithuanians has been rendered difficult by the lack of both priests and religious teachers. The *Catholic Directory* gives reports from thirty-nine parishes, sixteen of which have schools. The Archdiocese of Chicago has five of these schools, three of them being in charge of the Sisters of the Holy Family of Nazareth.

[27] Summary of parish reports in Cath. Dir., 1909-10.
[28] Census of 1906, I, p. 118.

Recently, a Lithuanian teaching order of Sisters, known as the Congregation of St. Casimir, was founded by the Rt. Rev. John W. Shanahan, Bishop of Harrisburg.[29] The development of this new community promises to stimulate greatly Catholic educational work among the Lithuanians, whose number in the United States is being largely added to each year by immigration. The following table shows the number and distribution of the existing schools, teachers and pupils:

NUMBER AND DISTRIBUTION OF LITHUANIAN SCHOOLS.[30]

Diocese.	Parishes without Schools.	Schools.	Religious Teachers.	Lay Teachers.	Pupils.
Baltimore, Md....	1	......	......	......	......
Boston, Mass.....	4	......	......	......	.....
Chicago, Ill.......	2	5	11	3	664
Milwaukee, Wis...	2	......	......	......	......
New York, N. Y...	1	......	......	......	......
Philadelphia, Pa...	5	2	4	......	165
Albany, N. Y.....	......	1	......	2	88
Alton, Ill.........	1	......	......	......	......
Belleville, Ill......	1	......	......	......	......
Brooklyn, N.Y....	2	......	......	......	......
Cleveland, O......	......	1	2	......	120
Detroit, Mich.....	1	......	......	......	......
Gr'ndRapids,Mich.	......	1	2	......	138
Harrisburg, Pa....	1	1	3	......	147
Hartford, Conn ...	2	1	5	......	309
Newark, N. J.....	3	......	......	......	......
Omaha, Neb......	1	......	......	......	......
Peoria, Ill........	2	1	2	......	112
Pittsburgh, Pa....	2	2	5	1	276
Rochester, N. Y...	1	......	......	......	......
Scranton, Pa......	7	1	1	......	85
Total.........	39	16	35	6	2,104

Total membership in Lithuanian and Lithuanian-English parishes 82,530.[31]

[29] *Cath. Standard and Times,* Aug. 13, 1910.
[30] Summary of parish reports in Cath. Directory for 1909-10.
[31] Census of 1906.

Slovak Schools

The Slovaks, who come from the northern part of Hungary, are usually Catholics. In the United States, they are found most numerously in the coal and iron regions of Pennsylvania and in Cleveland, O.[32] They belong, some to the Latin, and some to the Greek Rite.[33] Probably one-half of the children attending school in Catholic Slovak centers are registered in the parish schools. This high proportion appears to be due to two facts, the strong attachment of the people to the Catholic faith, as the result of their long struggle against heresy, and the generous devotedness of certain of the teaching orders to the work of educating Slovak children. Among these may be mentioned the Sisters of Notre Dame, of Cleveland, Ohio; the Bohemian Sisters of St. Benedict, Chicago; the Sisters-Servants of the Immaculate Heart, Scranton; the Sisters of the Third Order of St. Francis, Joliet; and the Sisters of the Incarnate Word, of Texas.

An event of very great import for the future of Slovak education was the founding recently, by Bishop Michael J. Hoban, of Scranton, of a distinctively Slovak teaching community, known as the Sisters of Sts. Cyril and Methodius.[34] The new organization has already given promise of a rapid growth, and with the large accession of Slovak immigrants every year, the present num-

[32] Cf. Capek, The Slovaks of Hungary.
[33] Cf. Shipman, Greek-Catholics in the U. S., in Cath. Encyclopedia, VI.
[34] *Cath. Stand. and Times,* Aug. 13, 1910.

ber of Slovak parish schools will, doubtless, continue to increase. Another distinctively Slovak community, the Slovak Sisters of Charity, has charge of a school at Braddock, Pa.

NUMBER AND DISTRIBUTION OF SLOVAK SCHOOLS.[35]

Diocese.	Parishes without Schools.	Schools.	Religious Teachers.	Lay Teachers.	Pupils.
Chicago, Ill......	3	3	11	......	625
Milwaukee, Wis...	......	1	1	......	79
New York, N. Y...	1	......	......	......	......
Philadelphia, Pa...	5	8	16	2	961
St. Louis, Mo.....	......	1	......	1	50
St. Paul, Minn....	1	......	......	......	......
Altoona, Pa.......	1	2	11	1	537
Brooklyn, N. Y. ..	1	......	......	......	......
Buffalo, N. Y.....	1	......	......	......	......
Cleveland, O......	2	8	29	1	1,896
Columbus, O......	1	......	......	......	......
Harrisburg, Pa....	2	1	......	2	68
Hartford, Conn. ..	......	1	4	......	170
Leavenworth, Kan.	1	......	......	......	......
Marquette, Mich..	1	......	......	......	......
Newark, N. J.....	1	1	6	1	301
Peoria, Ill........	1	1	5	......	277
Pittsburgh, Pa....	9	5	18	1	1,192
Scranton, Pa......	14	5	10	......	913
Syracuse, N. Y....	1	1	5	......	350
Wheeling, W. Va..	1	......	......	......	......
Total.........	47	38	116	9	7,419

Total membership of Catholic Slovak and Slovak-English parishes 78,353.[36]

GREEK SCHOOLS

Catholics who follow the Greek Rite in the United States belong to a number of distinct nationalities—the Ruthenians proper, the Slo-

[35] Summary of parish reports in Cath. Directory for 1909-10.
[36] Census of 1906, I, p. 119.

vaks, and Rumanians, from the North and East
of Austria, and the Croatians, Slovanians, Dal-
matians, and Slovenes from the South and
West.[37] Besides these, there are also the Syrians,
and those Italians who adhere to the Greek Rite.
The greater number of the Greek-Catholics come
from Austria, and belong to the Slavic race. The
first Greek-Catholic priest to labor in the United
States was the Rev. Ivan Volanski, who organized a parish at Shenandoah, Pa., in 1885, erecting a church and also the first parish school.
With increasing immigration, other priests came,
and in 1907 the Rt. Rev. Stephen Soter Ortynski, a Basilian monk, was consecrated as the first
bishop of the Greek Catholics in the United
States. By 1909, there were about 140 so-called
Ruthenian Greek-Catholic churches, comprising
those of the Ruthenians proper and the Slovaks
who follow the Greek Rite. There is also, all
told, a considerable though lesser number of
churches belonging to the other nationalities
mentioned above.[38]

Bishop Ortynski, whose residence is in Philadelphia, has done much to further the establishment and progress of Catholic schools. Altogether, there are about fifty parish schools of
the Ruthenians. Besides the teaching of catechism and Ruthenian, the curriculum embraces
the study of English and the other common branches in American schools. Lay teachers are generally employed.[39] In 1911 a colony of Basilian

[37] Capek, The Slovaks of Hungary, p. 2.
[38] Shipman, The Greek-Catholics in the U. S., in Cath. Encyclopedia, VI.
[39] Shipman, loc. cit.

Sisters, from Galicia, came to Philadelphia for the purpose of devoting themselves to the work of the Ruthenian schools.[40]

There are also a few Catholic schools of the other nationalities mentioned above, and here and there Sisters are found in charge of a school. Among these may be mentioned the Sisters of St. Francis, the Dominican Sisters, and the Sisters of Notre Dame, of Cleveland.

PORTUGUESE SCHOOLS

According to the Religious census of 1906, there were forty Portuguese Catholic parishes in the United States, with a membership of 48,227, but there is no mention of a Catholic school in connection with any of these parishes in the diocesan reports furnished to the *Catholic Directory*.

HUNGARIAN (MAGYAR) SCHOOLS

The census of 1906 gives 26,472 as the membership of the twenty Catholic Hungarian parishes in the country.[41] There are nearly half a million Catholic Hungarians in the United States, but they are widely scattered, and not numerous enough in most places to form distinct parishes.[42] In the year 1909-10, there were thirty-one parishes and ten parish schools, with twenty-six religious and eight lay teachers, and an attendance

[40] *Cath. Standard and Times,* Dec. 9, 1911.
[41] Not counting mixed parishes, other than Hungarian-English.
[42] Shipman, Hungarian Catholics in America, in Cath. Encyclopedia, VII.

of 1,880. The three largest schools are those conducted by the Ursuline Sisters at Cleveland, the Sisters of Notre Dame of Cleveland, at Toledo, and the Sisters of the Holy Ghost, at Bridgeport, Conn.[43]

BELGIAN SCHOOLS

The diocesan reports in the *Catholic Directory* for the year 1909-10 show the existence of six Belgian parishes, with four schools, twenty-three religious teachers, and 955 pupils.

SUMMARY.[44]

Nationality.	Parish Member-ship.[45]	Parishes without Schools.	Schools.	Relig-ious Teachers	Lay Teach-ers	Pupils.
French........	1,031,530	27	161	1,438	42	63,048
Italian........	826,023	175	48	220	51	13,838
Polish........	736,150	115	293	1,591	176	98,126
Bohemian....	154,073	23	31	194	1	8,978
Lithuanian...	82,530	39	16	35	6	2,104
Slovak........	78,353	47	38	116	9	7,419

[43] Cath. Dir., 1910.

[44] In addition to the works referred to, cf. the respective articles on the various foreign nationalities in the Cath. Encyclopedia and the International Encyclopedia; Lord, The Italian in America; the Italians in America, in *Forum* for Jan., 1911; Balch, Our Slavic Fellow-Citizens; More, Bohemia and the Czechs.

[45] Census of 1906. Including only parishes where language of specified nationality is used either exclusively or together with English, and not including children under nine years of age.

CHAPTER XIV

SCHOOLS FOR THE INDIANS, NEGROES, ETC.

Indian Schools

ALONG with the efforts of the Church to Christianize the Indians, there went hand in hand, from the very beginning, the work of educating them by means of schools, and this work has been continued down to the present time.[1] In most places, the same general plan was followed, the idea of Catholics being that industrial training should be given a prominent place in the education of Indian children, whether boys or girls. Outside of the old mission-systems of the Franciscans and Jesuits, there was little attempt, until a comparatively recent period, to systematize the work or to centralize its directing agencies. This result has been brought about gradually, under the pressure of hostile instrumentalities bent apparently upon the extinction of the Catholic Indian school.

President Grant's so-called " Indian Peace Policy," proclaimed in the year 1870, inaugurated an era of governmental hostility to Catholic Indian schools, as the policy was carried out

[1] Cf. Cath. School System in U. S. Cf. also Chapter VI supra, The Far Western States.

practically, and eighty thousand Catholic Indians were thrown under Protestant control. Four years later, Archbishop Bayley, of Baltimore, appointed General Charles Ewing as Commissioner of Catholic Indian interests, with whom the Rev. J. B. A. Brouillet, Vicar-General of the Diocese of Nesqually, was associated, their headquarters being established at Washington, D. C. Vigorous efforts were made from this newly constituted center of the work to combat hostile legislation and unfair administrative discrimination, as well as to raise money by voluntary contributions for the support of the Indian missions and schools. The Third Plenary Council, in 1884, completed the organization of this central agency at the National Capital by formally constituting it as the Bureau of Catholic Indian Missions, under the authority of the Church, a committee of prelates being appointed as supervisors. In 1894, the Bureau was chartered by the State of Maryland, the Archbishops of Baltimore, New York and Philadelphia being the incorporators. The Rev. J. A. Stephan became Director of the Bureau in 1884, occupying the position until his death in 1901. He was succeeded by the present Director, Rev. William H. Ketcham.

The work of the Bureau has shown that its establishment and organization was the result of wisdom no less than necessity, and its effectiveness has constantly increased. With only a few Indian schools remaining under Catholic control, the Bureau, in 1877, induced the United States Government to inaugurate the " Contract School System," under which forty-three boarding and seventeen day schools were established for Catholic Indians by the year 1890, with Government allowances amounting to over three hundred thousand dollars. This success aroused a storm of bigoted hostility, under the influence of which Congress repudiated the Contract System in 1896, announcing its settled policy to be, "to make no appropriation whatever for education in any sectarian school," In the year 1900, appropriations were accordingly declared at an end. Catholic Indian schools were thus again suddenly thrown upon the charity of the Catholic public. The Bureau struggled hard to meet the situation, which seemed almost hopeless. The raising of several hundred thousand dollars a year was a gigantic task, and its accomplishment would have been impossible except for the providential generosity of Mother M. Katherine Drexel, a daughter of Francis A. Drexel, of Philadelphia, who has contributed over one-half of the amount disbursed by the Bureau in recent years. Recognition of certain fundamental rights of Indian parents was also, in time, secured from the Federal Administration. Chief among these rights was that embodied in the ruling by President Roosevelt, in 1904, that Indian Tribal Funds could be drawn on by Catholic Indians for the education of their children in the mission schools, a ruling that was sustained by the Supreme Court of the United States. The following table shows the amount of money expended by the Bureau during the year 1907, and also the sources from which the funds were derived. The table is illustrative of the means through which the support of the

Indian schools and missions has been secured within recent years:

Preservation Society, Marquette League, bequests and donations..	$11,850.90
The annual Lenten Collection.....	63,749.50
Indian Tribal Funds.............	28,073.51
Mother M. Katherine Drexel.....	127,843.40
	$231,517.31

In addition, the aid to the schools, during the same year, resulting from the issuance of rations for the pupils, may be computed at $20,000.

Besides its work of providing means for the support of the schools, the Bureau has, through the exercise of its powers of supervision and inspection, brought them closer together and induced a greater uniformity in studies and methods, thus raising the standard of many of the schools. Father Stephan, during the seventeen years he was connected with the Bureau, devoted much of his time to this work of inspection and supervision, and his efforts in this way have been ably continued by his successor.

For the census-year 1910, the report of the Bureau shows the existence of 55 Catholic boarding schools and 8 day schools, with an enrollment of 4,924 pupils. The school workers numbered 606, and included 57 priests, 72 Brothers, 373 Sisters, and 104 lay teachers and employes. The Catholic Indian population was 61,456, out of a total Indian population of about 300,000. Catholic Indians in Government schools numbered 6,010.

Catholic Indian schools have thus, in spite of apparently insurmountable obstacles, continued to exist, and have even increased in number and efficiency. Much of the credit for this must also be given to the religious teachers, who have devoted themselves unselfishly to the work, in spite of the hardships it necessarily entails. Jesuit priests and brothers have been foremost here, among the teaching orders of men. Of the communities of women engaged in the work, the Sisters of the Blessed Sacrament were organized by Mother M. Katherine Drexel, in 1889, for the express object of educating the Indians and colored people. The novitiate and mother-house is at Cornwells, Pa., and the Sisters now number 143. The Ursulines of Montana have likewise been prominent in Indian school work, as also the Sisters of Divine Providence of Texas, and several branches of the Franciscan Sisters.[2]

SCHOOLS FOR COLORED CATHOLICS

The history of organized educational work among negro Catholics began with the founding of the first community of colored Sisters in Baltimore, in 1825.[3] The new religious body was

[2] Reports of the Director of the Bureau of Cath. Indian Missions; Our Cath. Indian Missions—a paper by Rev. Wm. H. Ketcham, Director of the Bureau, at the Cath. Missionary Congress, Chicago, 1908; Our Indian Schools—a paper by Rev. C. W. Currier, at Fourth Ann. Meeting of Cath. Ed. Assn., Milwaukee, 1907; Cath. Encyclopedia, VII, art. on Indian Missions, Bureau of; Ann. Reports of the Mission Work among the Negroes and Indians, by the Members of the Commission. See also Chapters II and III supra on Religious Communities, and Chapter VI on The Far Western States.

[3] Cf. Cath. Sch. Sys. in U. S., p. 254.

approved by the Holy See in 1831 under the title of the Oblate Sisters of Providence. The growth of the community has been slow, but it has furnished a very considerable supply of efficient teachers for the colored schools. In 1910, the Sisters numbered 139, and had charge of two schools and two academies in the Archdiocese of Baltimore, two schools in the Archdiocese of St. Louis, a school in Leavenworth, Kansas, and several schools in Cuba.

Another community of colored Sisters, known as the Congregation of the Sisters of the Holy Family, was founded in New Orleans in 1842, and its development has had an important influence upon educational work among colored Catholics. The number of Sisters, in 1910, was 105, who were in charge of an academy and thirteen schools in the Archdiocese of New Orleans, two schools in Galveston, Texas, and one in Houston.

The Sisters of Mt. Carmel, of New Orleans, opened a colored school there as early as 1838. They took charge subsequently of several other schools for colored children in the Archdiocese.

Franciscan Sisters from England who established themselves in Baltimore, in the year 1881, and later on at Richmond and Norfolk, aim chiefly at work among the colored people, and have several schools for colored Catholics. In 1910, there were 58 of the Sisters in this country.

The Sisters of the Holy Ghost, whose motherhouse is at San Antonio, Texas, are also specially devoted to educational work among the colored people, and have a number of colored schools.

The Sisters of the Blessed Sacrament were

established for the education of both Indians and colored people. They have a flourishing academy and an industrial school for colored girls in Nashville, Tennessee.

Several other religious communities have engaged in the work of the colored schools. One of the great drawbacks is the poverty of the colored people. The support of the school thus becomes a burden that must be borne by others than the parents of the pupils, or the parishes to which the parents and children belong. A collection is taken up annually in all the Catholic churches of the United States for the benefit of the Indian and Colored Missions, and the total usually amounts to about $100,000. A considerable share of this goes to the support of schools for colored children.

There are about 150,000 colored Catholics in the United States, with 119 Catholic schools, and an attendance of about 8,000. In the Archdiocese of New Orleans, there were, in 1907, 80,000 colored Catholics and 52 schools, with an attendance of 2312.[4]

INDUSTRIAL SCHOOLS

In the year 1910, there were 117 Catholic industrial schools in the United States, with about 15,000 pupils. Various teaching orders have charge of these schools, and many of them will compare favorably with the best non-Catholic institutions of the kind. In some instances, they

[4] Annual Reports of the Mission Work among the Negroes and Indians; Cath. Directory; Cath. World, articles on Negro.

have a reformatory purpose in view. Many girls' schools, also, have manual training classes, especially in the upper grades.[5]

ORPHANAGES

In 1910 there were 258 Catholic orphan asylums in the United States, in which 45,343 children were being educated. Religious communities are usually in charge. These institutions are found in all the dioceses, and also in all the larger cities. A number are endowed in whole or in part, but most of them depend upon the continual charity of the faithful.[6]

SCHOOLS FOR THE DEAF AND DUMB

Catholic schools for the deaf and dumb in the United States number 13, with an enrollment of 1,002 pupils. Four of these are in the State of New York. Most of these schools are in charge of religious communities of women, and the greater number of the pupils are girls, as there is no community of men devoted to the work of the education of the boys. These are generally obliged, in consequence, in order to obtain an education, to attend institutions that are non-Catholic. There are upwards of 15,000 Catholic deaf in the country. The number of non-Catholic schools for the deaf is 126.[7]

[5] Cath. Dir., 1910; Hist. Cath. Ch. in the U. S., Vol. II.
[6] Cath. Dir., 1910.
[7] Rep. of Fourth Ann. Meeting of Cath. Ed. Assn., paper of Rev. F. A. Moeller, S.J., on Ed. Status of the Cath. Deaf in U. S., p. 37; Cath. Encyclopedia, V, art. on Ed. of Deaf and Dumb.

CHAPTER XV

CURRENT MOVEMENTS AND PROBLEMS

The Curriculum

THE GENERAL SITUATION

A STUDY of the curriculum of the Catholic school will show the concurrent influence, in many instances, of the three essential factors in its organization and administration that have been considered,—the parish, the diocese, and the religious community.[1] The influence of all three is often discernible in the framing of the curriculum. Certain subjects like catechism, bible-history, and singing may be prescribed by the diocese, with a given time-minimum for each; the pastor, in view of local needs or conditions, may insist on certain studies; while the regulation of many of the subjects is generally left to the religious superiors. Most often, the determination of the curriculum is left to the religious superiors and the pastor, the diocesan authority not interfering, except in the matter of religious instruction. The condition is not unlike that which obtains in the public school system, where the framing of the curriculum by the educational

[1] See Chapter VIII, Organization and Administration.

officers of the state or county is frequently subject to revision at the hands of the city or district school board. The pastor, in the Catholic system, has much the same control as the city or district board in the public school system. But very often he maintains a passive attitude with regard to the curriculum, and permits his religious teachers to carry out their own plans.

Each of the larger religious communities has its own school curriculum, to which it is bound more or less by rule, tradition, or custom derived from a long experience. Each community has its own traditions, also, about methods of teaching. Fundamentally, there is, fortunately, no very great difference between either the respective methods or the curricula. This is especially true of the larger and more progressive communities. Subjected to common conditions, and face to face with common educational needs or demands, the traditional curriculum of each community has undergone a development which has resulted in making them all alike, except in certain matters of detail.

The differences, however, while not so important in themselves, have, nevertheless, been a constant source of inconvenience to pastors and parents, as well as to the diocesan educational authorities. In the matter of text-books, for instance, there has been much confusion. In cities, the changing of schools by pupils is frequent, and, inasmuch as each community may have its own series of chosen text-books, it has often happened that pupils, on entering another school, would find themselves under the necessity of purchasing an entirely different set of text-books. " There is not an instance in the Diocese, as far as we can now see," said the Fort Wayne School Board, in 1879, " where a pupil can take a full set of text-books from one congregation and use them all in another.[2]   This condition has caused an altogether unjustifiable expense to Catholic parents.   Furthermore, the examination and inspection of schools was seen to have little value for purposes of comparison, unless the time-allotment of the various subjects were the same in each school.   Hence, it has happened that the establishment of the diocesan board of education, and the regular visitation and examination of schools, which necessarily involved an official comparison of teachers, methods, and schools, has tended inevitably towards the adoption by each diocese of a common curriculum, with well defined subject-matter and fixed time-allotments, and with a single series of text-books for all the parish schools.

Many of the dioceses have, within recent years, adopted such standards of uniformity.   Philadelphia took the lead in the matter, for the Philadelphia system of inspection and supervision makes strongly for diocesan uniformity in everything pertaining to the schools.   In the prescribed courses of studies adopted there about fifteen years ago, the subject-matter of the work of each grade is defined in detail, and there are suggestions as to the best methods to employ in each branch and grade; but no text-books are prescribed, and no time-limits imposed, it being left to the principals to arrange programs of rec-

[2] Report for 1878-9, p. 5.

itations for the several classes in the schools over which they preside. Some dioceses, on the other hand, prescribe the series of text-books to be used in the schools; and some have gone further still, and fixed the recitation-periods for each subject through all the grades of the course.

PRESENT AND FUTURE PROBLEMS

It is evident that the movement towards uniformity is still only in process of development. All Catholic educators agree as to the need of greater diocesan uniformity. There is lack of agreement, however, as to just how far such uniformity should go, and as to just what means should be made use of in order best to bring about as much uniformity as is needful. One extreme view is that nothing more is desirable than a brief prescribed course of study, containing the matter that a school should cover each year, together with a thorough visitation of all the schools once a year, everything beyond this being left to the regulation of the pastors and religious superiors. Another view is, that the curriculum, with all that it involves,—subjects of study, methods of teaching, time-schedules, and text-books,—ought to be completely regulated by the diocesan educational authority. Between these two extremes, Catholic educators entertain varying shades of opinion. There can be no doubt, however, that the advocates of greater diocesan uniformity have been gaining ground. As in the case of the public school system, the tide is running strongly towards

increased centralization. Difference of conditions between district and district, and between
city, town, and country, argues forcibly in favor
of a diversified or at least a flexible curriculum.
The tendency is, nevertheless, the other way.
The final result will probably be reached sooner
in the Catholic system than in the public school
system, because the diocese can, whenever it
wishes, impose its will in this respect upon the
teachers and the local authorities, whereas the
state educational authorities most often can not
do this.

Generally speaking, the curriculum of the
Catholic school, outside of the matter of religious
instruction, does not differ very greatly from that
of the corresponding public schools in the same
place. There are two reasons for this. One is,
the desire of the pastor and Catholic teachers to
have the parish school recognized as fully abreast
of the public schools, so that parents may not
have cause to complain. Another reason is
found in the fact that the same general causes
that have operated to bring about changes in the
public school curriculum, have had influence also
upon the course of studies of the Catholic school
—an influence not so great, perhaps, but still
direct and constant. For purposes of comparison, time-schedules of the curricula of some representative parish schools are here given, and,
below these, the time-schedule of a series of typical public schools. The first school considered
is at Michigan City, Ind., in the Diocese of Fort
Wayne, and is conducted by the School Sisters of
Notre Dame, the largest and most wide-spread

of the teaching orders of women. The curriculum is typical of the work of this Order, which counts about four thousand Sisters. This is followed by a time-schedule adopted several years ago for parish schools in the Diocese of Pittsburgh. The third is a schedule prescribed for all the public grammar schools in the District of Columbia.

TIME-SCHEDULE OF A TYPICAL PARISH SCHOOL.[3]

	1st Grade	2d Grade	3d Grade	4th Grade	5th Grade	6th Grade	7th Grade	8th Grade
Religion	210	210	150	150	150	150	150	150
Writing	150	150	150	150	120	120	120	120
Music	150	150	120	90	90	60	60	60
Drawing	60	60	60	60	60	60	60	60
Physiology	...	...	...	...	...	60	60	90
Needlework	...	...	...	60	60	60	60	60
Geography	...	...	150	150	150	120	90	90
Mathematics:								
Arithmetic	270	270	240	210	240	240	240	120
Algebra	...	...	...	...	...	...	...	120
History and Civics	...	...	...	...	60	120	150	150
Language & Composition	150	150	150	210	...	...	...	...
Grammar & Composition	...	...	...	...	210	60	210	240
Reading & Literature	240	240	210	150	150	150	150	150
Spelling	150	150	150	90	90	60	60	60
German	...	...	...	...	...	150	150	150
Supplementary	150	150	150	90	...	...	...	...
Total minutes per week	1530	1530	1530	1410	1380	1410	1560	1620

[3] Michigan City, Ind., 1910. This school is in a "mixed" English-speaking and German parish and has an attendance of 360.
[4] The Diocesan Plan calls for 14 weeks of algebra. This is taken during the latter part of the term.

TIME-SCHEDULE OF PARISH SCHOOLS IN DIOCESE OF PITTSBURGH.[5]

	1st Grade	2d Grade	3d Grade	4th Grade	5th Grade	6th Grade	7th Grade	8th Grade
Religion.........	250	250	250	250	200	200	150	150
Spoken & Written English.......	230	230	230	230	250	250	270	270
Reading & Literature..........	420	420	345	235	205	200	200	200
Arithmetic......	200	200	200	275	250	200	200	200
Algebra.........	...	...	...	...	...	...	60	60
Geography......	...	...	75	100	125	150	150	100
History.........	...	...	...	30	90	120	150	150
Drawing........	100	100	100	90	90	90	90	90
Physiology & Hygiene.........	50	50	50	40	40	40	40	40
El'm'nt'ry Science	50	50	50	30	30	30	30	40
Civics..........	...	...	...	20	20	20	20	40
Vocal Music.....	100	100	100	100	100	100	100	100
Recess..........	100	100	100	100	100	100	100	100
Total minutes per week....	1500	1500	1500	1500	1500	1500	1560	1500

[5] Adopted provisionally Nov. 25, 1907.

ATTENDANCE

GROWTH OF PARISH SCHOOL ATTENDANCE

The enrollment in the parish schools during the year 1909-10 was, according to the *Catholic Directory*, 1,237,251; and the Catholic population of the United States the same year was 14,347,027.[6] The *Directory* has shown a steady increase in the school attendance from year to year. It would be interesting to ascertain the exact ratio of this increase to that of the Catholic population. An examination of the data fur-

[6] For the time and method of gathering the statistics published in the *Directory*, see p. 306, note.

TIME-SCHEDULE OF PUBLIC SCHOOLS IN DISTRICT OF COLUMBIA.[7]

	1st Grade	2d Grade	3d Grade	4th Grade	5th Grade	6th Grade	7th Grade	8th Grade
Writing.........	60	75	90	75	50	50	15	15
Music..........	60	60	60	60	60	60	60	60
Physical Culture .	50	50	75	75	75	75	75	75
Drawing, Art, & Construct.....	90	90	90	90	90	90	90	90
Physiology......	15	15	15	15	15	15	15	15
M. T. & Household Arts......	...	...	60	60	60	90	90	90
Geography......	...	...	90	150	150	150	150	150
Nature Study....	75	75	75	75	75	...	...	...
Science.........	...	...	...	...	...	60	60	60
Mathematics: Arithmetic.....	90	100	150	150	200	200	200	150
Algebra.......	...	...	...	...	...	...	...	90
History and Civics	75	75	75	75	90	120	150	120
Language & Composition.......	50	100	120	120	120	150	...	...
Grammar & Composition.......	...	...	...	...	...	...	200	240
Reading & Literature..........	300	320	240	200	200	120	120	90
Spelling & Word Analysis.......	...	...	60	60	60	60	60	80
Unassigned Time.	85	90	140	135	95	100	55	45
Total minutes per week....	950	1050	1340	1340	1340	1340	1340	1370

[7] In 1910.

nished by the *Directory* shows that, on the basis of these data, the ratio of Catholic school attendance to the total Catholic population is about the same now as it was ten years ago, and also that it was substantially the same as now sixteen years ago. This argues a very rapid Catholic school growth. To hold firmly the actual attendance, while providing ample facilities for the enrollment of new pupils corresponding to the rapid growth of the Catholic population—the means for all this being, at the same time, provided by voluntary contributions—has been a gigantic task, and the most generous loyalty of American Catholics to the principles of Catholic education might well have proved to be no more than equal to it. It is not, unfortunately, possible to carry the examination back farther than about sixteen years, for the data furnished by the older *Directory* are too incomplete, the reports from some of the dioceses being lacking.

NUMBER OF CATHOLIC PUPILS IN PUBLIC SCHOOLS

A question of no less interest is that of the number of Catholic pupils attending public schools. The answer to this question can at present be approached only in an indirect way, and the easiest way is by ascertaining the ratio of the total Catholic school attendance to the Catholic population, and then comparing this with the ratio of the total school attendance in the country to the total population. The difference might be assumed to represent, roughly, the number of Catholic children attending non-Catholic or public schools. Some reservations must be made, however, in instituting this comparison. It is assumed that the difference between the ratios would represent the number of Catholic pupils attending the public schools, or, in other words, that *all* Catholic pupils not attending the parish schools are pupils of the public schools. But this is not necessarily the case. It might well be that Catholic children, in certain places, would be put to work sooner than non-Catholic children generally in the same places. This condition would have the effect of diminishing the Catholic school attendance, without such diminution really indicating any corresponding increase of Catholic pupils in the public schools. There is good reason to believe that this very condition does obtain in many places, and this fact must be borne in mind in comparing parish and public school attendance.

Again, a source of inaccuracy occurs in the getting of the figures for the Catholic population. It may be assumed that the figures for school enrollment furnished annually by the *Catholic Directory* are substantially accurate. But its figures for the Catholic population have been gravely called in question. Nor do the compilers claim that these figures are more than an approximation to the truth, although they are supplied by the diocesan chanceries. They are justly regarded as too low. Still, for the purpose in view here, they may be regarded as accurate enough. They probably represent, within fair limits of accuracy, the number of regular church-going Catholics, who alone can be depended on to send their children to the parish schools, or indeed can be expected to do so. Catholics who are such merely by reason of baptism should not be numbered among those whose children may be practically expected to attend Catholic schools.

It is convenient, in considering the question of school attendance, to take the scholastic year 1908-9, since the latest report of the Commissioner of Education goes no farther than that year. It is found, then, that the number of children enrolled in Catholic parish schools during the year 1908-9 was 8.42 per cent of the Catholic population.[8] The number of pupils receiving elementary instruction, in primary and grammar grades, in all schools throughout the country, both public and private, the same year, was 19.92 per cent of the population of the United States.[9] This second ratio is two and one-third times as great as the former; or, in other words, the number of children attending the parish schools is only three-sevenths of what it ought to be, judged by the norm of school attendance generally throughout the country; and, instead of an attendance of 1,197,193 in 1908-9, the parish schools ought to have had an attendance of 2,835,701. Does this mean that 1,638,508 Catholic children—represented by the difference between these numbers—were attending the public schools? No; for it is certain that children of the poorer Catholics, especially the immigrants, in many places quit school sooner than the children of non-Catholics in the same places. Yet, the figures undoubtedly do mean that a very large proportion of Catholic children, probably more than a million, attend the public schools.

[8] Cath. Dir. for 1909.
[9] Rep. Comm. of Ed., 1910, Vol. II, p. xviii Introduction, and pp. 669, 670.

WHY CATHOLIC CHILDREN ATTEND THE PUBLIC SCHOOLS

In attempting to account for this large enrollment of Catholic children in the public schools, the lack of Catholic schools in country districts very generally must be given foremost consideration. No reliable estimate of the number of Catholics living in country districts can at present be made, but the number must be, in the aggregate, very large. About one-half the public school enrollment is in country or district schools, and sixty-seven per cent of the public school enrollment during the year 1907-8 was in schools outside of cities containing four thousand population and over.[10] The Catholic population, on the other hand, is concentrated in the cities and larger towns. In villages and country districts, where the Catholic population is small or scattered, parish schools are in most cases scarcely possible. Probably from one-fourth to one-third of the whole number of Catholic children live outside of cities containing four thousand population and over.[11]

If a fair allowance is made for the number of Catholic children attending public schools on account of the condition just mentioned, it will appear that the number of those who are drawn to the public schools by reason of other causes cannot be so very large, and that it is probably well under half a million. The Superintendent of

[10] Rep. Comm. of Ed., 1909, p. 599.
[11] Cf. Rep. of Fifth Ann. Meeting of Cath. Ed. Assn., p. 46.

Catholic Schools of the Archdiocese of Philadelphia has summed up the causes which bring Catholic children to the public schools as follows:

"1. In sparsely settled districts a Catholic school is impossible.

"2. In certain small towns Catholics are so few that their resources are inadequate to build and support a school.

"3. Even in those places where Catholics are numerous the debt on the Church property is so great that common prudence dictates that a pastor should not increase his burden, already too heavy, by the erection of a parish school.

"4. In large cities where ground is valuable a newly-organized parish can do little more, at first, than provide for the erection of a church.

"5. Sometimes the parish school is too small for all the children of the parish and many must of necessity go elsewhere.

"6. Again, the school may be large enough to house all the children of the parish, but the parish revenue is inadequate to educate all, and the pastor limits the number in attendance so as to keep within his resources.

"7. In certain instances the Catholic population of a place is in the majority, the environment is Catholic, and hence neither priest nor people feel that a separate school is a necessity.

"8. A certain proportion of Catholic children attend non-Catholic schools in order to prepare more directly to teach in the public schools.

"9. Catholics often attend non-Catholic secondary schools because of the inability of the Church at present to provide everywhere Catholic high schools.

"10. Some attend secular high schools, colleges, and universities because Catholic schools of the same grade are not near at hand.

"11. Sometimes a pastor is indifferent to Catholic education, and his people, reflecting his attitude, send their children to the public schools.

"12. Some people are imbued with the idea that the secular school is superior to the Catholic school.

"13. Some again in their reaching for social prestige and advancement think these reputed advantages can be best secured in secular institutions."

And he concludes very justly:

" When these reasons are given due consideration it will be quite well understood why thousands of Catholic children attend non-Catholic schools. Many are there with sufficient reason, and comparatively few are there in open defiance of the legislation of the Church. Keeping in view the above explanation for the non-attendance at Catholic schools of so many of our children, we may look forward hopefully and confidently to the time as not far distant when every Catholic child in the United States may enjoy his true inheritance—a Catholic education."[12]

[12] Rt. Rev. Mgr. Philip R. McDevitt, Report for 1910, p. 17.

Catholic High School Movement

HISTORICAL

Catholic schools of secondary grade have existed in the United States almost from the beginning of our Catholic educational history. Forming distinct departments in Catholic colleges for boys and academies for girls, these schools have continued in the same connection down to the present day. With the rise of the private · secondary school known as the " academy," after the Revolution, many Catholic institutions of this class were established, both for boys and for girls. Some of these were founded and conducted by lay teachers, and others by the religious orders. These also have continued to exist, and have been constantly growing in number. When the public high school movement began, and public high schools in organic relationship with the public elementary school system came gradually to replace the independent " academies," Catholics were not in a position, even had they so desired, to parallel the new educational creation by the organization of secondary schools in close connection with the existing system of parish schools. They had not the means to do so, and the parish school system was not sufficiently developed at the time for the attempt. At Lowell, Mass., where the parish schools received public support, there was a Catholic public high school in 1843, according to the *United States Catholic Magazine* for that year.

The feeling of Catholics in Lowell at the time was thus expressed: " Our schools may now compete with any in the Commonwealth. The schoolhouses are handsome and commodious buildings; the *high school* house is beautiful." [13] But educational conditions in Lowell were, at the time, rather exceptional, and it was not until nearly half a century later, as will be shown, that the movement for Catholic high schools in organic connection with the parish schools really began.

COLLEGE HIGH SCHOOLS

That Catholics, however, were keenly alive to the necessity of providing facilities for secondary education under Catholic auspices, is shown by the fact that secondary schools or departments were established at all the Catholic colleges, and that these have been continued, except in one or two instances, down to the present time; as also by the fact of the continued growth of the number of independent secondary schools. A report made to the Catholic Educational Association in the year 1908 showed that, in 101 Catholic colleges for boys in the United States there were 10,798 students of secondary grade in the high school departments of these colleges. The number of collegiate students was 4,232. The colleges for girls have likewise always maintained secondary departments, with the exception of Trinity College, Washington, which does not admit pupils below the Freshman grade.

[13] Vol. 2, . 5 (1843), art. Statistics of Lowell, Mass.; cf. Cath. Sch. Sys. in U. S., p. 287.

INDEPENDENT SECONDARY SCHOOLS

The secondary schools of this class are independent of parish control, and are generally supported by tuition-fees. Most of them are conducted by the religious orders, whether of men or women. Many of these schools are of long standing. In the case of boys' schools, the curriculum usually extends only to the Freshman year exclusively, but it includes the studies of the grammar school. In 1901, there were 90 schools of this class for boys, with an attendance of over 5,000 pupils of secondary grade, and about 9,000 belonging to the grammar department.[14]

There are 709 Catholic academies for girls in the United States, according to the *Catholic Directory* for 1910, with an attendance of between 80,000 and 90,000 pupils. Approximately 25,000 of the pupils attending these institutions are of secondary grade, about 50,000 are in the elementary grades, and the remainder are in the collegiate departments.[15] The total number of girls in Catholic secondary schools appears to be considerably greater than that of boys. Many of these academies have developed strong collegiate departments, and a number have been chartered by the state as colleges. The larger institutions will compare favorably with the best equipped male colleges, and the number of Catholic girls' colleges is growing rapidly. But the greater number of the academies for girls have

[14] Cath. Secondary Schools, in Amer. Cath. Q. Rev., July, 1901.
[15] Ibid., compared with Cath. Dir. for 1910.

no collegiate departments strictly so called, and must be classed as secondary schools, although many of them have a year or two of collegiate work.

In Catholic academies for girls there are usually three main departments, from the standpoint of the curriculum: the academic course or department, comprising the studies of the high school, which may also, as said, include considerable collegiate work; the preparatory department; and the primary department,—the last two divisions covering jointly the eight grades of the ordinary elementary school. There are also departments of art and music. These latter features are characteristic of the Catholic academy for girls. They impart to it a certain cultural tone, and distinguish it academically from the public high school. They also attract to it popular favor and support.

PARISH AND DIOCESAN HIGH SCHOOLS

The movement for the establishment of high schools in connection with the parish schools has been spontaneous, and first showed itself in the efforts of individual pastors, in widely separated parts of the country, to add high school courses, if not a complete high school, to the parish school. A great impetus, as well as a clear and high ideal, was given to the movement when the Catholic High School of Philadelphia was founded, through the generous gift of Mr. Thomas E. Cahill, of that city. Mr. Cahill's will was dated August 23, 1873, and provided for the purchase of property and the erection and equipment of a large and suitable building, at a cost of $280,000, besides a perpetual endowment fund, the annual interest from which amounts to over $30,000. The building was dedicated in 1890. The parish schools of the city were brought into affiliation with the new institution, and their graduates who went on for secondary studies passed up to it after examination. It was thus placed in the position of a central superior school, while remaining an integral part of the parish school system, under the control of the head of the diocese. The school is for boys only. The attendance at present is over four hundred, and the faculty comprises a rector, a vice-rector, and eighteen lay instructors.[16]

Several other Catholic high schools have since been erected and endowed by generous benefactions, but most of the new parish high schools have had to depend upon the parishes for their support. Since the opening of the Catholic High School in Philadelphia, these schools have multiplied rapidly. In 1901, the Commissioner of Education reported 53 such schools, the attendance comprising both boys and girls, and three years later the number had risen to 70. These were, too, only the more important schools of this class. There existed several times as many parish schools in which one or more grades of high school work was taught; for in all the large parish schools the tendency was to keep

[16] Henry, The Roman Cath. High School, Phila., in First Ann. Report of Cath. Ed. Assn., p. 61.

the pupils as long as possible, and thus as much high school work was taken up by the school as it could provide for.[17] With the view of ascertaining more fully the actual number of Catholic high schools of this class and collecting other useful data for a careful study of the problems presented by the high school, a committee was appointed by the Catholic Educational Association in 1908, which made its report at the Chicago meeting of the Association, in July, 1911. The investigation of the committee was directed to all the larger parish schools, and the work of 893 such schools was studied. The list of high schools published by the committee included Catholic high schools for boys and also those for both boys and girls, exclusive of the preparatory departments of colleges. The list contains 310 schools. About three-fourths of these are under parish or diocesan control, and the remainder are under the control of religious orders.[18] The former are often free schools, while the latter are usually supported by tuition-fees.[19] Not all of the independent secondary schools, or schools under the control of religious orders, are included in the list. Furthermore, reports were not received from many of the larger parish schools that do high school work, and it was estimated that in all there are to-day between four and five hundred Catholic high schools for boys or for

[17] Cath. Secondary Schools, in Amer. Cath. Q. Rev., July, 1901; Report of the Joint Committee on High Schools, in First Ann. Rep. of the Cath. Ed. Assn., p. 39.

[18] The list of these schools was published in the February *Bulletin* of the Cath. Ed. Assn., 1911.

[19] See above, "Independent Secondary Schools," p. 362.

both boys and girls, exclusive of the preparatory departments of colleges.[20]

The total number of pupils doing work above the elementary grades in these 310 high schools amounted to 14,824. The boys numbered 8,212, and the girls, 6,612. One-half of the high schools have four full grades. Of the remainder, 66 have three grades; 60 have two grades; and 29 have only one grade. It is interesting to observe that this condition of incompleteness obtains also to a considerable extent in the case of public high schools. Over one-third of the 10,213 public high schools given in the Report of the Commissioner of Education for the year 1909-10 had a curriculum lasting only from one to three years.

Nearly all these high schools are conducted by religious. Brothers teach in 69 schools, and Sisters in 234. Brothers are generally preferred for high school work, in the case of boys; but there is not a sufficient number of teaching Brothers to meet the demand. It may be noted that the majority of teachers in the public high schools, if the teachers be considered in the aggregate, are women.[21] Two hundred and twenty-two of these schools have courses in Latin, and more than two dozen teach Greek also. Fully one hundred of them offer a curriculum that is practically equivalent to the entrance requirements for the Freshman year in Catholic and non-Catholic colleges of excellent standing. Yet only 23 of these schools are affiliated to, or have any

[20] Bull of the Cath. Ed. Assn., Feb., 1912, p. 9; also, Rep. of Eighth Ann. Meeting of the Cath. Ed. Assn., p. 47 seq.

[21] Rep. of Comm. of Ed., 1910, p. 1131.

direct connection with, Catholic colleges. About the same number are affiliated to non-Catholic colleges or normal schools.

The relation of these high schools to the parish schools exhibits an even greater lack of practical co-ordination. Only 19 occupy the position of "central" high schools, while 263 are directly connected with but a single parish school. A high school that is attached to a parish school is usually regarded as a strictly parish affair, and hence fails to obtain patronage or support outside of its own parish. As a result, the attendance is apt to be small, and the teaching staff incomplete. The establishment of "central" high schools, or the conversion into such of certain of the existing high schools that are now attached to elementary schools, is evidently indispensable for the further progress of this high school movement. Evidently, too, such "central" high schools, if the elementary schools are to be effectively connected with them, must be under the same control as the elementary schools. This can be brought about only by the direct intervention of the supreme diocesan authority, or by the formal and hearty co-operation of the pastors of a town or city, with the bishop's approval.[22] It has been calculated that the total annual cost of a complete Catholic high school, with seven teachers, is from $3,000 to $4,000. Most of the existing parish high schools cost far less than this. Catholic high schools fully equal to the

[22] For a further discussion of this problem, cf. Report of Joint Committee on High Schools, in First Ann. Rep. of the Cath. Ed. Assn., 1904, p. 48.

public high schools in point of efficiency, can be conducted and maintained at about one-third of the cost of the latter.[23]

An important feature of this new high school movement is the growing demand for Catholic high schools for girls. Philadelphia has, here again, taken the lead. The practical work of organizing a Catholic high school for girls began there in 1900, and soon four high school "centers" in as many parts of the city, were established, each with a two years' course. Each of these "centers" was in charge of a teaching community of Sisters. The attendance increased so rapidly that the "centers" were, in a few years, unable to accommodate all the pupils that applied. Through the untiring efforts of the Superintendent of Schools, the Rt. Rev. Mgr. Philip R. McDevitt, a practical movement was inaugurated to build a central high school for girls, to match the splendid Boys' High School; and with the gift of $100,000 for the purpose from a devout Catholic lady, and the generous co-operation of the Catholics of the city, means were provided for the erection and equipment of a modern high school building capable of accommodating a thousand pupils or more. The building was begun on April 27, 1911. About 450 pupils were in attendance at the high school "centers" in the year 1911.[24] An interesting feature of the new Girls' High School in Philadelphia is that several religious communities are to co-operate in supplying the teaching staff.

[23] Cf. Eighth Ann. Rep. of the Cath. Ed. Assn., p. 59.
[24] Cf. Ann. Reports of the Supt. of Cath. Schools, Phila., especially for 1908 and 1911.

Catholic high schools for girls have also been established in a number of other places, and it is likely that this feature of the Catholic high school movement will continue to develop. There is a growing demand for free high schools for girls, in which the course of instruction shall be the continuation and complement of the course of instruction in the elementary schools. The existing academies for girls do not appear to satisfy this demand, valuable and indispensable as is the work that they are doing, partly because they are not free schools, and partly because the academies are, by tradition, inclined to emphasize the cultural element in education rather than the useful. The new girls' high schools have, as one of their foremost aims, the training of girls along lines that are closely connected with commercial and industrial pursuits.

It is evident that the continued progress of the Catholic high school movement will have far-reaching effects. It is promoting higher standards of efficiency in parish elementary schools, by reason of the competitive rating of their graduates in passing up to the high school, as has notably been found to be the case in Philadelphia. It is beginning to exert a quickening influence upon the academies for girls and the high schools for boys under the control of the religious orders. It has helped to swell the Freshman classes in Catholic colleges, and to stop the present drift of Catholic boys and girls to the non-Catholic colleges and universities. There is a growing feeling among Catholic college men that the preparatory department ought to be separated altogether or at least more widely from the college proper, and this can be effected safely only through the systematic multiplication of strong Catholic high schools. These schools are, moreover, increasing the attendance at the seminaries, both secular and religious, by fostering and developing vocations. The movement is thus rich in possibilities of good, and it seems destined to round out and complete the organization of Catholic education in the United States, by furnishing an effective bond of union between the parish school and the college, which have hitherto stood practically apart.

THE CATHOLIC EDUCATIONAL ASSOCIATION

The growth of the Catholic high school movement, as well as the general effort that is being made to perfect the curriculum, the teaching, the organization and administration of the parish schools, as has been described under these topics, shows that the Catholic school system in the United States has been, within recent years, undergoing a rapid development. The keynote of all these progressive movements appears to lie in the general recognition of the need of a greater unification of all Catholic educational forces. The present study of the growth and development of the schools would therefore not be complete, within its professed scope, unless some account were given of the Catholic Educational Association, which, although not organically connected with the parish school system, has unquestionably done much to foster the movement for unification. Indeed, the Association is probably the chief factor in the present healthful stir which is apparent throughout the entire field of Catholic education.

THE COLLEGES

The Catholic Educational Association grew out of the Association of Catholic Colleges, which was organized in St. James' Hall, Chicago, April 12 and 13, 1899. The initiative in the matter was taken by the Rt. Rev. Thomas J. Conaty, at that time Rector of the Catholic University. Bishop Conaty had previously proposed the matter to the Archbishops, at their annual meeting, and received their most hearty encouragement. Fifty-one delegates, representing fifty-three colleges, were in attendance. Seven papers had been prepared, and, along with the discussion of these, there was a general exchange of ideas all along the line of Catholic college work. A plan for permanent organization was framed, and a committee appointed to draft a constitution, which was adopted the following year. The constitution provided for a board of directors, consisting of a president and a standing committee of five members, all to be elected annually. The board prepared the programs for the annual meetings, and had charge of the business affairs of the Association, subject to the approval of that body. Bishop Conaty to whom is due the chief credit for the founding of the Association of Catholic Colleges and its happy guidance through the early trial-years of its existence, continued to occupy the position of president until he was named Bishop of Monterey and Los Angeles, in 1903.

The number of colleges in the Association has increased from year to year, and also the attendance at the annual meetings. Rev. John A. Conway, S. J., of Georgetown, who was elected to the presidency in 1904, continued the conservative and prudent policy of his predecessor. He was succeeded, in 1908, by the Rev. Charles B. Moulinier, S. J., of Milwaukee, who gave way, after two years, to the Very Rev. M. A. Hehir, C. S. Sp., of Pittsburgh.

The Association of Catholic Colleges, during the thirteen years of its existence, has had much to do with the shaping of recent Catholic college growth. It has, for instance, labored from the very beginning to raise the entrance requirements of the smaller or weaker colleges up to the level of those of the larger institutions. Scarcely a year has failed to witness the discussion of this matter, in some form, before the convention. These discussions have borne fruit. Many of the colleges have raised their entrance requirements, and at the last annual meeting the report of the committee that had this matter in charge showed that the Association is preparing, as a result of these years of discussion and work, to adopt a definite standard of entrance requirements, to be demanded of all colleges joining the organization. Another instance of the good effected by the Association is seen in the development of the Catholic high school movement. Discussions, following the reading of carefully prepared

papers dealing with the subject, were frequently
had, and the importance and need of high schools
were thus urged upon both clergy, teachers, and
laity. A prominent place was naturally given, in
the annual meetings, to papers and discussions
dealing with college discipline as well as methods
of teaching the ordinary college branches.[25]

THE SEMINARIES

Even before the organization of the Association of Catholic Colleges, a movement looking
towards the unification of Catholic educational
efforts was inaugurated by the establishment,
through the efforts of the Rt. Rev. Mgr. Conaty,
of the Conference of Catholic Seminaries. A
meeting of representatives of various seminaries
was held at St. Joseph's Seminary, Dunwoodie,
N. Y., on May 25, 1898, and an organization
effected. A second meeting was held in Philadelphia, the next year, the Very Rev. A. L. Mag-
nien, S. S., of St. Mary's Seminary, Baltimore,
being elected president. Further meetings were
not held, however, until 1904, when the Conference assembled at St. Louis, at the same time and
place as the College Conference. Among those
who have been prominent in the work of the Seminary Conference may be mentioned: Very Rev.
Patrick McHale, C. M., of St. John's Seminary,
Brooklyn; Very Rev. James F. Driscoll, St.
Joseph's Seminary, Dunwoodie; Very Rev. M.

[25] Cf. Ann. Reports of the College Conference, 1899-1903;
for an historical sketch of the College Conference and a list
of all the papers read, up to 1904 inclusive, see Rep. of First
Ann. Meeting of Cath. Ed. Assn., p. 12 seq.

S. Ryan, C. M., Kenrick Seminary, St. Louis;
Very Rev. E. R. Dyer, S. S., St. Mary's Semi-
nary, Baltimore; Very Rev. Francis P. Havey, S.
S., St. John's Seminary, Boston; Very Rev. E. J.
Walsh, C. M., Niagara University; and the Very
Rev. Walter Stehle, O. S. B., St. Vincent's Semi-
nary, Beatty, Pa.[26]

THE SCHOOLS

The formation of an organization to be composed of representatives of the parish schools,
and to be in affiliation with the College organization, was first broached at the Chicago meeting
of the Association of Catholic Colleges, in 1900.
The proposal met with some opposition, as there
was doubt in the minds of certain of the college
men as to the relations which ought to subsist
between the two bodies. Through the efforts of
Monsignor Thomas J. Conaty, acting in conjunction with the bishops, school superintendents and
delegates from eight dioceses met with the Association of Colleges at the Palmer House, Chicago, in 1902, and on July 9 effected an organization as the Parish School Conference, with
Monsignor Conaty as president. The next year,
when the two bodies met at the High School in
Philadelphia, the Parish School Conference,
representing twenty-five dioceses, elected an
executive committee and adopted a permanent
constitution. When Bishop Conaty was succeeded in the rectorship of the Catholic Univer-

[26] Cf. History of the Educational Conference of Seminary
Faculties, in First Ann. Rep. of Cath. Ed. Assn., p. 25.

sity by the Rt. Rev. Mgr. D. J. O'Connell, the
same year, the latter was elected to the presidency
of the Parish School Conference, as also of the
Association of Catholic Colleges.

The membership of the Parish School Conference increased rapidly, many pastors and
teachers joining the organization. The attendance at the annual meetings soon mounted into
the hundreds, and at the last annual gathering
there were over a thousand in attendance, the
greater number of these being teachers in the
parish schools. The papers read and discussed
in these meetings have generally had relation to
the curriculum and the methods of teaching its
component subjects, the teaching of Christian
Doctrine being given special prominence. These
discussions reached many thousands of teachers
annually, for frequently a small group of teachers
attending the convention represented an entire
community, and were expected, on their return, to
make a report of the proceedings. The discussions
were widely circulated also through their publication in the annual reports. The influence of
the Parish School Conference upon the teaching
in the parish schools has thus been very great
and very helpful. Special teachers' meetings, for
the benefit of the local teachers, are held in connection with the annual Conference.

Rev. Louis S. Walsh, Superintendent of
Schools of Boston,[27] was elected president of the
Conference in 1904. Rt. Rev. Mgr. Philip R.
McDevitt, Superintendent, of Philadelphia, occu-
pied the position from 1906 to 1910. He was

[27] Later Bishop of Portland, Me.

succeeded by the Superintendent of the Archdiocese of New York, the Rev. Joseph F. Smith.
All three were specially active and prominent in
the work of organizing the Parish School Conference and shaping its growth and policy.[28]

CATHOLIC EDUCATIONAL ASSOCIATION

The idea of a general union of Catholic educational societies was in the mind of Bishop
Conaty and other members of the College Association when it was first suggested in the Chicago
Meeting, in 1900, that representatives of the
diocesan school systems be invited to form an
affiliated organization. The actual accomplishment of the projected union was due chiefly to
the Rt. Rev. Mgr. Dennis J. O'Connell, who
made it one of his principal concerns, on his
assuming the rectorship of the Catholic University, in 1903. Monsignor O'Connell was ably
assisted in this work by influential members of
the three independent associations whose foundation has been described. Conspicuous among
these were the Rev. Francis W. Howard, of
Columbus, Ohio, secretary of the Parish School
Conference; the Rev. M. P. Dowling, S. J., of
Creighton University, who was chairman of the
joint committee to which the matter was referred
for settlement at the St. Louis Meeting of the
three bodies; and the Rev. John P. Carroll, who
subsequently became Bishop of Helena.

The adjustment of the relations between the

[28] For an hist. sketch of Par. School Conf., cf. First Ann.
Rep. of Cath. Ed. Assn., p. 18 seq.

three organizations involved delicate and difficult questions, and called for the exercise of tact and a broad-minded and far-seeing zeal. At the Philadelphia Meeting, in 1903, the Parish School Conference took the initiative, by appointing a committee to confer with the Association of Colleges about a plan of union. In response to this, the College Association empowered its executive committee to act in the matter and report, and during the winter and spring of 1903-4 the two committees were busy with the discussion of the problems and questions involved. When the two societies met at St. Louis, in the summer of 1904, in conjunction with representatives from the seminaries, the way had thus been cleared for a complete agreement, and a carefully framed plan of union had been prepared. This plan was accepted substantially without change.[29]

The constitution adopted for the general association which was now formed, and which was to be known as the Catholic Educational Association, left complete autonomy to each of the three component bodies, in all that regarded their respective independent interests. The control of the finances, however, was lodged in the general association, it having been determined that each seminary was to contribute twenty dollars annually, each college ten dollars, and each individual member or school in the School Conference two dollars. The several bodies composing the Association were to be designated as depart-

[29] Cf. Proceedings of Joint Committee on Organization, in First Ann. Rep. of Cath. Ed. Assn., p. 30 seq.

ments. The admission of new departments was
also provided for. The officers of the Association were to be, a president-general, who was to
preside at all meetings of the Association; several vice-presidents general, to correspond in
number with the number of the departments; a
secretary-general; a treasurer-general, and an
executive board. This last was to consist of the
above general officers, the presidents of the
departments, and two other members elected
from each department of the Association. All
officers were to be elected annually.[30]

Monsignor O'Connell, who had worked so
hard for the accomplishment of this result, was
elected president-general. Upon his becoming
Auxiliary-Bishop of San Francisco, in 1909, Rt.
Rev. Thomas J. Shahan, the newly chosen Rector of the Catholic University, was elected president-general of the Association. Rev. Francis
W. Howard has been the secretary-general of
the Association since its formation.

The constitution of the Catholic Educational
Association appears to have been wisely framed,
for the departments have so far worked together
in harmony and with an ever growing success.
The membership of each department has
increased, and also the attendance at the departmental meetings. The treasurer's report for the
year 1910-11 showed a paying membership for
that year of 12 seminaries, in the Seminary
Department, 76 colleges in the College Department, and 1,106 members in the Parish School
Department, the latter comprising individual

[30] Constitution of Cath. Ed. Assn., in Ann. Reports.

persons, schools, academies, and religious houses. The total cash receipts for the same year were $4,253.38. The bulk of the money received goes to the dissemination of the educational literature published by the Association, which includes chiefly the official *Bulletin* of the Association, published quarterly, and the *Annual Reports*.

The growth of the Association and its influence are also indicated by the expansion of the departmental work. The College Department has organized three sections for the more effective prosecution of its work in the special fields of languages and literature, mathematics and science, and philosophy and history; while in the Parish School Department there is a section whose membership is made up of the diocesan superintendents of schools, and another which is devoted to the study and discussion of educational work among Catholic deaf-mutes.[31]

[31] Eighth Ann. Rep. of the Cath. Ed. Association.

APPENDIX A

STATISTICAL SUMMARY.

Catholic population of the United
States[1] 14,347,027
Enrollment in parish schools....... 1,237,251
Enrollment in Catholic educational
institutions of all kinds........ 1,450,488
Parish schools 4,845
Parishes without schools[2]......... 4,004
Teachers in parish schools[3]....... 31,000
Teaching communities of women[4].. 264
Teaching brotherhoods 11
High schools[5] 310
Enrollment in these high schools
     Boys 8,212
     Girls 6,612

[1] Cath. Directory for 1910.
[2] Not including missions with churches.
[3] Approximate.
[4] Including, as a rule, single independent establishments.
[5] Exclusive of preparatory departments of colleges. The above number includes only those high schools reporting to the committee of the Cath. Ed. Association in 1910; over 100 high schools did not report. See p. 365.

APPENDIX B

BIBLIOGRAPHY

Documentary Sources

Original records of many of the teaching communities, at the respective mother-houses.

Letters and documents relating to various events in American Catholic educational history. Reference to these has sometimes been given in the foot-notes.

Books, Pamphlets, etc.

General histories are not, as a rule, included in this list, nor are works of which only a very limited use is made. Reference to the latter has been given in the footnotes.

ABBELEN, RT. REV. MGR. P. M. Mother Caroline Friess, First Commissary-General of the School Sisters of Notre Dame in America. A sketch of her life and Character. With an Introduction by Rt. Rev. J. L. Spalding, D.D. St. Louis: B. Herder, 1893, pp. 287.

ALERDING, RT. REV. H. A History of the Catholic Church in the Diocese of Vincennes. 1883, pp. 636.

AMERICAN CATHOLIC HISTORICAL RESEARCHES. Philadelphia: Founded in 1884.

ANNUAL REPORT OF THE SUPERINTENDENTS OF
PARISH SCHOOLS of the Archdiocese of New
York. 1904-1910.

ANNUAL REPORT OF THE SUPERINTENDENT OF
PARISH SCHOOLS of the Archdiocese of Philadelphia. 1895-1911.

ANNUAL REPORTS OF THE SUPERINTENDENTS
OF CATHOLIC SCHOOLS of the Dioceses of
Pittsburgh, Cincinnati, St. Louis, Newark.

ASSOCIATION OF CATHOLIC COLLEGES, ANNUAL
REPORTS OF THE. 1899-1903.

From the year 1904, the papers and proceedings of the
Association of Catholic Colleges are included in the Reports
of the Catholic Educational Association.

BALCH, EMILY GREENE. Our Slavic Fellow-
Citizens. New York: Charities Pub. Com.,
1910, pp. 536.

BOUQUILLON, REV. THOMAS, D.D. Education:
To Whom does it Belong? Second Edition,
with a Rejoinder to Critics. Baltimore:
John Murphy & Co., 1892, pp. 31+42.

BROSNAHAN, REV. TIMOTHY, S.J. Dr. Harris
and the Agnostic School House. 1903, pp.
31.

BROWNSON, ORESTES A. Literary, Scientific and
Political Views. Selected from his Works,
by Henry F. Brownson. New York: Benziger Bros., 1893, pp. 418.

BRUNOWE, MARION J. A Famous Convent
School (Mt. St. Vincent's-on-the-Hudson).
New York: The Meany Co., 1897, pp. 153.

BURNS, JAMES A. The Catholic School System in the United States: Its Principles, Origin, and Establishment. New York: Benziger Bros., 1908, pp. 415.

CAMPBELL, REV. THOMAS J., S.J. The Only True American School System. An Address. New York: The Messenger Office, 1902, pp. 24.

CAPEK, THOMAS. The Slovaks of Hungary. New York: The Knickerbocker Press, 1906, pp. 214.

CATHOLIC CHURCH, THE, IN THE UNITED STATES OF AMERICA. To Celebrate the Golden Jubilee of His Holiness, Pope Pius X. Vol. 1: The Religious Communities. New York: The Catholic Editing Co., 1908, pp. 458.

CATHOLIC DIRECTORY. Annual. New York: P. J. Kenedy & Sons.

CATHOLIC EDUCATIONAL ASSOCIATION, Annual Reports of. 1904-1911.

CATHOLIC EDUCATIONAL ASSOCIATION, Bulletin of. Issued Quarterly.

COMMISSIONER OF EDUCATION, ANNUAL REPORT, for 1897-8. Chapter XVII, Notes on the History of American Text-books on Arithmetic, pp. 788-868.

COMMISSIONER OF EDUCATION, ANNUAL REPORTS, especially Report for 1894-5, which contains a lengthy study of the Parochial Schools (pp. 1617-1671).

COMPULSORY EDUCATION. The State of Ohio
vs. the Rev. Patrick Francis Quigley, D.D.
New York: Robert Drummond, 1894, pp.
598.

The three arguments of Judge Dunne, before the Court of
Common Pleas, the Circuit Court, and the Supreme Court of
Ohio, contain a strong and clear exposition of the traditional
Catholic view of the respective rights of the parent, the state,
and the Church in education. Pp. 354-403 are devoted to a
criticism of Dr. Bouquillon's pamphlet, "Education, to Whom
does it Belong?"

CONCILII PLENARII BALTIMORENSIS TERTII,
ACTA ET DECRETA. Baltimore: John
Murphy & Co., 1886, pp. cix+321.

CONCILIORUM PROVINCIALIUM ET PLENARII
BALTIMORENSIUM, DECRETA. Baltimore:
1853.

Contains the Decrees of the first Seven Provincial Councils
and the First Plenary Council of Baltimore.

CONCILIORUM PROVINCIALIUM CINCINNATEN-
SIUM, ACTA ET DECRETA, 1855-1882. Cincinnati: Benziger Bros., 1886.

CONWAY, REV. JAMES, S.J. The Respective
Rights and Duties of Family, State, and
Church in regard to Education. New York:
Fr. Pustet & Co., 1890, pp. 60.

CONWAY, REV. JAMES, S.J. The State Last: A
Study of Dr. Bouquillon's Pamphlet,
"Education: to Whom does it Belong?"
With a Supplement reviewing Dr. Bouquillon's "Rejoinder to Critics." Third Edition. New York: Fr. Pustet & Co., 1892,
pp. 116.

DUNNE, HON. EDMUND F. Our Public Schools:
Are they Free for All, or are they not? A
Lecture. Second Edition, 1875, pp. 40.

EDUCATIONAL BRIEFS. Issued Quarterly by the
Philadelphia Diocesan School Board.

The *Briefs* are usually reprints of educational studies of
notable importance.

FLYNN, REV. JOSEPH M. The Catholic Church
in New Jersey. 1904, pp. 695.

Contains a Sketch of the Sisters of Charity, of Convent
Station.

GLEANINGS OF FIFTY YEARS: The Sisters of
the Holy Names of Jesus and Mary in the
Northwest. 1859-1909, pp. 230.

GOLDEN BELLS IN CONVENT TOWERS. The
Story of Father Samuel (Mazzuchelli) and
Saint Clara. Chicago: Lakeside Press,
1904, pp. 126.

GUÉRIN, MOTHER THEODORE, LIFE AND LIFE-
WORK OF. Foundress of the Sisters of Prov-
idence at St. Mary-of-the-Woods, Vigo Co.,
Ind. By a member of the Congregation.
New York: Benziger Bros., 1904, pp. 499.

HARTMANN, REV. B. Religion or No Religion
in Education. Alton: Melling & Gaskins,
1894, pp. 54.

HISTORICAL SKETCHES OF THE CATHOLIC
CHURCHES AND INSTITUTIONS OF PHILA-
DELPHIA. A Parish Register and Book of
Reference. Philadelphia. Daniel H.
Maloney.

HOLAIND, REV. RENE I., S.J. The Parent First: An Answer to Dr. Bouqillon's Query, "Education: to Whom Does it Belong?" New York: Benziger Bros., 1891, pp. 34.

HOWLETT, REV. W. J. Life of the Rt. Rev. Joseph P. Machebeuf, D.D., First Bishop of Denver. 1908, pp. 419.

HUGHES, RT. REV. JOHN, WORKS OF. In two volumes, 1864.

JOHNSON, CLIFTON. Old Time Schools and School Books. New York: The Macmillan Co., 1904, pp. 381.

VON KETTELER, RT. REV. W. E., BISHOP OF MENTZ. Public Schools or Denominational Schools? Pastoral Letter, 1873. New York: Benziger Bros. 1892, pp. 30.

KRUSZKA, WENCESLAUS. Historya Polska w Ameryce. 6 small vols., Milwaukee, 1905.

MCAULEY, CATHERINE, LIFE OF. Foundress of the Institute of the Sisters of Mercy. By a Member of the Order. New York: D. & J. Sadlier, 1871, pp. 508.

MCFAUL, RT. REV. JAMES A., D.D. The Christian School. Pastoral Letter. New York: Benziger Bros., 1907, pp. 32.

MCQUAID, RT. REV. BERNARD J., D.D. A Lecture on School Education and School Systems, 1874, pp. 16.

MCQUAID, RT. REV. BERNARD J., D.D. Christian Free Schools. Two Lectures. 1872, pp. 30.

McQuaid, Rt. Rev. Bernard J., D.D. The Public School Question. A Lecture. 1876, pp. 44.

Manning, Henry Edward, Cardinal. National Education. London: Burns & Oates, 1890, pp. 47.

A collection of articles, expressive of the traditional Catholic view of the parent, the Church, and the state in education.

Mannix, Mary E. Memoirs of Sister Louise, Superior of the Sisters of Notre Dame. With Reminiscences of the Early Days of the Order in the United States. Boston: The Angel Guardian Press, 1907, pp. 338.

Montgomery, Hon. Z. The School Question from a Parental and non-Sectarian Standpoint. Fourth Edition. Washington, 1889, pp. 138.

National Educational Association, Annual Report, for 1889. Discussion on Denominational Schools, by Cardinal Gibbons, Bishop Keane, Edwin D. Mead, Ph.D., and Hon. John Jay. Pamphlet, pp. 71.

O'Hara, Rev. Edwin V. Pioneer Catholic History of Oregon. Portland: Glass & Prudhomme Co., 1911, pp. 236.

Palladino, Rev. L. B., S.J. Indian and White in the Northwest, or A History of Catholicity in Montana. Baltimore: John Murphy Co., 1894, pp. 409.

Chapters XIII-XVI contain a discussion of methods of educating the Indian, with an exposition of the method followed in Catholic Indian schools, and of the principles upon which this method is based.

RECORDS OF THE AMERICAN CATHOLIC HISTOR-
ICAL SOCIETY OF PHILADELPHIA. Begun in
1884.

REEDER, RUDOLPH R., Ph.D. The Historical
Development of School Readers, and of
Method in Teaching Reading. Columbia
Univ. Contributions to Philosophy, Psy-
chology and Education. Vol. 8, No. 2.
New York: The Macmillan Co., 1900, pp.
92.

RIVAUX, ABBÉ. Life of Mother St. John Fontbonne, Foundress of the Sisters of St. Joseph
in Lyons. New York: Benziger Bros.,
1887, pp. 295.

Contains an account of the first mission of the Congregation in the United States, with some valuable statistics.

SADLIER, AGNES. Elizabeth Seton, Foundress of
the American Sisters of Charity: Her Life
and Work. New York: D. & J. Sadlier,
1905, pp. 289.

SETON, MOTHER, Foundress of the Sisters of
Charity. Sisters of Charity, Mt.-St.-Joseph-
on-the-Ohio. 1909, pp. 74.

SHEA, JOHN GILMARY. History of the Catholic
Church in the United States. Four Volumes.

SHEEDY, REV. MORGAN M. The Catholic Parochial Schools of the United States. In Report of the Commissioner of Education for
1903, Chapter XXI, pp. 1079-1101.

SMYTHE, HON. CHARLES R. Letters on Public
Schools, with Special Reference to the Sys-

tem as Conducted in St. Louis. 1870, pp. 51.

SOUVENIR OF THE GOLDEN JUBILEE OF THE THIRD ORDER OF ST. FRANCIS. Glen Riddle, Pa., 1905.

STANG, RT. REV. WILLIAM, D.D. Pastoral Letter on Christian Education. 1907, pp. 21.

STORY OF FIFTY YEARS, A. From the Annals of the Congregation of the Sisters of the Holy Cross. 1855-1905. Notre Dame, Ind., *Ave Maria* Press, 1905, pp. 214.

TAXATION AS RELATED TO PUBLIC EDUCATION. Report of the Committee of the National Educational Association. Pamphlet. July, 1905, pp. 87.

TRAHEY, REV. JAMES J. The Brothers of Holy Cross. Notre Dame, Ind., 1907, pp. 168.

UNITED STATES CATHOLIC MAGAZINE. Founded in Baltimore in 1842, and Conducted for a year under the Title of *The Religious Cabinet*. Vols. I-VIII.
Contains important educational data.

WALSH, RT. REV. LOUIS S. Origin of the Catholic Church in Salem. Boston, 1890, pp. 151.

WARDE, REV. MOTHER M. XAVIER, Foundress of the Order of Mercy in the United States. The Story of Her Life, with Brief Sketches of Her Foundations. By the Sisters of Mercy, Manchester, N. H. Boston: Marlier & Co., 1902, pp. 287.

PRINTED BY BENZIGER BROTHERS, NEW YORK.

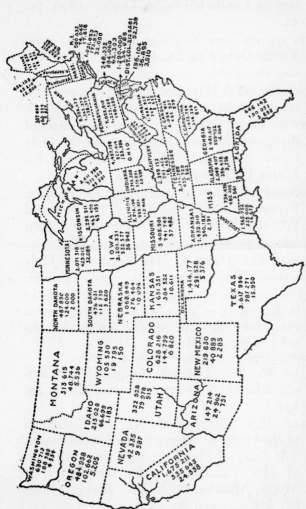

The first line of figures shows the population of the State, the second line shows the public school attendance, the third line, the parochial school attendance.

(From the report of the Commissioner of Education for the year ending June 30, 1908, and the Catholic Directory for 1909.)

INDEX

Jersey City, N. J., estab. of
Sisters of Mercy, 52; of
Srs. of Charity, 69; of
Dominican Srs., 79.

Jesuits, Indian missions and
schools in Montana, 154;
open college in Denver,
157; and Pious Fund of
Cal., 172; foremost in
Indian school w o r k
among orders of men,
342.

Johnstown, Pa., 90.

Joliet, Ill., 85.

KANSAS CITY, MO., 109.

Kansas, schools of Sisters of
St. Joseph, 33; of San-
guinist Srs., 59; of Do-
minican Srs., 79; of
Benedictine Srs., 89;
earliest schools, 151-153,
156; compulsory school
legislation, 297.

Keane, Most Rev. John J.,
229.

Kenrick, Most Rev. Francis
Patrick, archb. of Phila.,
difficulty in securing
teachers, 19; and Sisters
of St. Joseph, 32.

Kenrick, Most Rev. Peter R.,
archb. of St. Louis, plans
to unite branches of Sis-
ters of St. Joseph, 30;
secures Christian Bros.,
108.

Kentucky, estab. of Ursuline
Sisters, 56.

Kerney, Martin J., author of
Cath. text-books, 139-141.

Ketcham, Rev. William H.,
339 seq.

Key West, Fla., 94.

Kieran, Mother John, of Sisters of St. Joseph, 32.

Kim, Bro. J. B., of Bros. of
Mary, 119.

Know-Nothing Movement,
influence on Catholic ed-
ucation, 18, 26, 200; attitude of Mother Warde,
52; Xaverian Bros., 120;
school Sisters, 131, 222.

Kulturkampf, causes Ursu-
lines to come to U. S., 57;
Sanguinist Srs., 59;
Franciscan Srs., 85;
causes Polish immigra-
tion to U. S., 311.

Kundeck, Rev. Joseph, 36.

LA CROSSE, diocese of, schools
of Benedictine Srs., 89.

La Crosse, Wis., 85.

Lafayette, Ind., 154.

La Grange, Ill., Sisters of St.
Joseph, 34.

Laity, attitude towards parish
schools, 16 seq.

Lake City, Minn., 56.

Lamy, Rt. Rev. John B., ed.
work in N. Mexico, 68;
176-178.

Lannen, Mother Clement, of
Sisters of St. Joseph, 32.

Laporte, Ind., 47.

Laramie, Wyo., 158.

Laredo, Tex., 54.

La Salle College, Phila., 107.

Las Cruces, Ariz., 177, 178.

STANDARD CATHOLIC BOOKS

PUBLISHED BY

BENZIGER BROTHERS,

CINCINNATI: NEW YORK: CHICAGO:
343 MAIN ST.   36–38 BARCLAY ST.   211–213 MADISON ST.

Books marked *net* are such where ten per cent. must be added for postage. Thus a book advertised at *net* $1 00 will be sent postpaid on receipt of $1.10. Books not marked *net* will be sent postpaid on receipt of advertised price.

DOCTRINE, INSTRUCTION, DEVOTION.

ABANDONMENT. Caussade, S.J.	*net,*	0 50
ADORATION OF BLESSED SACRAMENT. Tesniere.	*net,*	1 25
ALPHONSUS LIGUORI, WORKS OF, ST. 22 vols. Each,	*net,*	1 50
ANECDOTES ILLUSTRATING THE CATECHISM. Spirago.	*net,*	1 50
ANGLICAN ORDINATIONS. Semple.	*net,*	0 35
ART OF PROFITING BY OUR FAULTS. Tissot.	*net,*	0 50
BIBLE HISTORY.		0 50
BIBLE HISTORY, EXPLANATION. Nash.	*net,*	1 60
BIBLE STORIES. Paper, 0.10; cloth,		0 20
BIBLE, THE HOLY.		1 00
BOOK OF THE PROFESSED. Vol. I, II & III. Each,	*net,*	0 75
BOYS' AND GIRLS' MISSION BOOK. By the Redemptorist Fathers		0 35
BREAD OF LIFE, THE. Complete Communion Book.	*net,*	0 75
CATECHISM EXPLAINED, THE. Spirago-Clarke.	*net,*	2 50
CATHOLIC BELIEF. Faa di Bruno. Paper, *net,* 0.15; cloth,	*net,*	0 35
CATHOLIC CEREMONIES. Durand. Paper, *net,* 0.15; cloth,	*net,*	0 35
CATHOLIC GIRLS' GUIDE. Lasance.	*net,*	1 00
CATHOLIC PRACTICE AT CHURCH AND AT HOME. Klauder.		
Paper, *net,* 0.20; cloth,	*net,*	0 40
CATHOLIC TEACHING FOR CHILDREN. Wray.		0 40
CATHOLIC WORSHIP. Brennan, LL.D. Paper, 0.20; cloth,		0 30
CEREMONIAL FOR ALTAR BOYS. Britt, O.S.B.	*net,*	0 35
CHARACTERISTICS OF TRUE DEVOTION. Grou, S.J.	*net,*	0 75
CHILD OF MARY. Prayer-Book for Children.		0 60
CHRISTIAN APOLOGETICS. Devivier.	*net,*	2 00
CHRISTIAN DOCTRINE, SPIRAGO'S METHOD OF.	*net,*	1 50
CHRISTIAN EDUCATION. O'Connell.	*net,*	0 60
CHRISTIAN FATHER. Cramer. Paper, *net,* 0.13; cloth,	*net,*	0 25
CHRISTIAN MOTHER. Cramer. Paper, *net,* 0.13; cloth,	*net.*	0 25
CHRISTIAN SCHOOL. McFaul. Paper,		0 10
CONFESSION. Paper,		0 05
CONFESSION AND ITS BENEFITS. Girardey.		0 25
CONFIRMATION. Paper,		0 05
COUNSELS OF ST. ANGELA.	*net,*	0 25
DEFENCE OF THE SEVEN SACRAMENTS, HENRY VIII.		
O'Donovan.	*net,*	2 00
DEVOTION TO SACRED HEART OF JESUS. Noldin, S.J.	*net,*	1 25
DEVOTIONS AND PRAYERS FOR THE SICK-ROOM. Krebs,		
C.S.S.R. Cloth,	*net,*	1 25
DEVOTIONS AND PRAYERS OF ST. ALPHONSUS.	*net,*	1 25
DEVOTIONS FOR FIRST FRIDAY. Huguet.	*net,*	0 40
DIGNITY AND DUTIES OF THE PRIEST. Liguori.	*net,*	1 50
DIVINE GRACE. Wirth.	*net,*	1 60
DIVINE OFFICE. Liguori.	*net,*	1 50
EDUCATION OF OUR GIRLS. Shields.	*net,*	1 00
EPISTLES AND GOSPELS. Large print.	*net,*	0 25

EUCHARISTIC CHRIST. Tesniere. net, 1 25
EUCHARISTIC SOUL ELEVATIONS. Stadelman. net, 0 50
EXPLANATION OF THE BALTIMORE CATECHISM. Kinkead. net, 1 00
EXPLANATION OF THE GOSPELS. Lambert. Paper, net, 0.15;
    cloth, net, 0 35
EXPLANATION OF THE HOLY SACRAMENTS. ILLUSTR. net, 1 00
EXPLANATION OF THE MASS. Cochem. net, 1 25
EXPLANATION OF THE OUR FATHER AND THE HAIL
    MARY. Brennan, LL.D. net, 0 75
EXPLANATION OF THE PRAYERS AND CEREMONIES OF
    THE MASS, ILLUSTRATED. Lanslots, O.S.B. net, 1 25
EXPLANATION OF THE SALVE REGINA. Liguori. net, 0 75
EXTREME UNCTION. Paper, 0 10
FIRST COMMUNICANT'S MANUAL. 0 50
FLOWERS OF THE PASSION. Th. de Jesus-Agonisant. 0 50
FOLLOWING OF CHRIST. Kempis.
    With Reflections, 0 50
    Without Reflections, 0 45
    Edition de Luxe, 1 25
FOUR LAST THINGS, THE. Meditations. Cochem. net, 0 75
GARLAND OF PRAYER. With Nuptial Mass. Leather. 0 90
GENERAL CONFESSION MADE EASY. Konings, C.SS.R. Flexible. 0 15
GENERAL PRINCIPLES OF RELIGIOUS LIFE. Verheyen, O.S.B. net, 0 30
GIFT OF THE KING. 0 60
GLORIES OF DIVINE GRACE. Scheeben. net, 1 60
GLORIES OF MARY. Liguori. 2 vols. net, 3 00
    Popular ed. 1 vol. net, 1 25
GLORIES OF THE SACRED HEART. Hausherr, S.J. net, 1 25
GOFFINE'S DEVOUT INSTRUCTIONS. 140 Illustrations. Cloth, 1 00
GOLDEN SANDS. Little Counsels for the Sanctification and Hap-
    piness of Daily Life. Third, Fourth and Fifth Series. Each, net, 0 50
GREAT ENCYCLICAL LETTERS OF POPE LEO XIII. net, 2 25
GREAT MEANS OF SALVATION. Liguori. net, 1 50
GREAT SUPPER OF GOD. THE. Coube, S.J. net, 1 25
GREETINGS OF THE CHRIST-CHILD — Poems. 0 60
GUIDE FOR SACRISTANS. net, 0 85
GUIDE TO CONFESSION AND COMMUNION. net, 0 50
HANDBOOK OF THE CHRISTIAN RELIGION. Wilmers, S.J. net, 1 50
HARMONY OF THE RELIGIOUS LIFE. Heuser. net, 1 25
HELP FOR THE POOR SOULS IN PURGATORY. net, 0 50
HELPS TO A SPIRITUAL LIFE. Schneider, S.J. net, 1 25
HIDDEN TREASURE. St. Leonard of Port Maurice. net, 0 50
HISTORY OF ECONOMICS. Dewe. net, 1 50
HISTORY OF CATHOLIC EDUCATION IN THE U. S. Burns. net, 1 25
HISTORY OF THE MASS. O'Brien. net, 1 25
HOLY EUCHARIST. Liguori. net, 1 50
HOLY HOUR OF ADORATION. Stang. net, 0 50
HOLY MASS. Liguori. net, 1 50
HOW TO COMFORT THE SICK. Krebs, C.SS.R. net, 1 25
HOW TO MAKE THE MISSION. By a Dominican Father, Paper, 0 10
ILLUSTRATED PRAYER-BOOK FOR CHILDREN. 0 35
IMITATION OF THE BLESSED VIRGIN MARY. Bennett-Gladstone.
    Plain Edition. net, 0 50
    Edition de luxe, net, 1 50
IMITATION OF THE SACRED HEART. Arnoudt, S.J. net, 1 25
IMMACULATE CONCEPTION, THE. Lambing, LL.D. 0 35
INCARNATION, BIRTH, AND INFANCY OF CHRIST. Liguori. net, 1 50
INDULGENCES. A PRACTICAL GUIDE TO. Bernad, O.M.I. net, 0 75
IN HEAVEN WE KNOW OUR OWN. Blot, S.J. net, 0 60
INSTRUCTIONS FOR THE CATHOLIC FATHER. Egger. net, 0 50
INSTRUCTIONS FOR THE CATHOLIC MOTHER. Egger. net, 0 50
INSTRUCTIONS FOR CATHOLIC YOUTH. net, 0 50
INSTRUCTIONS FOR FIRST COMMUNICANTS. Schmitt. net, 0 60
INSTRUCTIONS ON COMMANDMENTS AND SACRAMENTS.
    Liguori. Paper, net, 0.13; cloth, net, 0 25
INTERIOR OF JESUS AND MARY. Grou. 2 vols. net, 2 00
INTRODUCTION TO A DEVOUT LIFE. St. Francis de Sales. net, 0 50
LESSONS OF THE KING. 0 60
LETTERS OF ST. ALPHONSUS DE LIGUORI. 4 vols., each vol., net, 1 50

LIGHT FOR NEW TIMES. FLETCHER.	net, 0	60
LITTLE ALTAR BOYS' MANUAL.	0	25
LITTLE BOOK OF SUPERIORS.	net, 0	75
LITTLE CHILD OF MARY. A Small Prayer-Book.	0	35
LITTLE MANUAL OF ST. ANTHONY. LASANCE. Illustrated.	0	25
LITTLE MANUAL OF ST. JOSEPH. LINGS.	0	25
LITTLE MONTH OF MAY. McMAHON. Flexible.	net, 0	25
LITTLE MONTH OF THE SOULS IN PURGATORY.	net, 0	25
LITTLE OFFICE OF THE IMMACULATE CONCEPTION.	0	05
LITLE PICTORIAL LIVES OF THE SAINTS. New cheap edition.	1	25
LOVER OF SOULS, THE. BRINKMEYER.	net, 1	00
MANUAL OF THE HOLY EUCHARIST. LASANCE.	net, 0	75
MANUAL OF THE HOLY FAMILY.	net, 0	60
MANUAL OF THE HOLY NAME.	0	50
MANUAL OF THE SACRED HEART, NEW.	0	50
MANUAL OF ST. ANTHONY, NEW.	net, 0	50
MANUAL OF THEOLOGY FOR THE LAITY. GEIERMANN.		
Paper, net, 0.20; cloth,	net, 0	40
MARIAE COROLLA. Poems. HILL.	net, 1	25
MARY THE QUEEN.	0	60
MASS DEVOTIONS AND READINGS ON THE MASS. LASANCE.	net, 0	75
MEDITATIONS FOR ALL DAYS OF YEAR. HAMON, S.S. 5 vols.	net, 5	00
MEDITATIONS FOR EVERY DAY. BAXTER.	net, 1	50
MEDITATIONS FOR EVERY DAY. VERCRUYSSE, S.J. 2 vols.	net, 3	50
MEDITATIONS FOR MONTHLY RETREATS.	net, 1	25
MEDITATIONS FOR USE OF SECULAR CLERGY. CHAIGNON.	net, 4	50
MEDITATIONS FOR THE USE OF SEMINARIANS AND		
PRIESTS. Vol. I. BRANCHEREAU.	net, 1	00
MEDITATIONS FOR RETREATS. St. FRANCIS DE SALES.	net, 0	75
MEDITATIONS ON THE LIFE, THE TEACHINGS, AND THE		
PASSION OF JESUS CHRIST. ILG-CLARKE. 2 vols.	net, 3	50
MEDITATIONS ON THE MONTH OF OUR LADY.	net, 0	75
MEDITATIONS ON THE PASSION OF OUR LORD.	0	50
METHOD OF CHRISTIAN DOCTRINE, SPIRAGO'S. MESSMER.	net, 1	50
MIRACLES OF OUR LORD.	0	60
MISCELLANY. LIGUORI.	net, 1	50
MISSION BOOK FOR THE MARRIED. GIRARDEY, C.SS.R.	0	50
MISSION BOOK FOR THE SINGLE. GIRARDEY, C.SS.R.	0	50
MISSION BOOK OF REDEMPTORIST FATHERS. LIGUORI.	0	50
MOMENTS BEFORE THE TABERNACLE. RUSSELL, S.J.	net, 0	50
MONTH, NEW, OF THE HOLY ANGELS. St. FRANCIS DE SALES.	net, 0	25
MONTH OF MAY. DEBUSSI, S.J.	net, 0	50
MONTH OF THE SOULS IN PURGATORY, The Little "Golden		
Sands."	net, 0	25
MORAL BRIEFS. STAPLETON.	net, 1	25
MORES CATHOLICI; or, Ages of Faith. DIGBY. 4 vols.	25	00
(Easy payment plan, $1.00 down; $2.00 a month.)		
MOST HOLY ROSARY. CRAMER, D.D.	net, 0	50
MY FIRST COMMUNION, the Happiest Day of My Life. BRENNAN.	net, 0	75
MY LITTLE PRAYER-BOOK. Illustrated.	0	12
NEW MONTH OF THE HOLY ANGELS.	net, 0	25
NEW SUNDAY-SCHOOL COMPANION.	0	25
NEW TESTAMENT. Cheap Edition.		
32mo, flexible cloth,	net, 0	15
NEW TESTAMENT. Illustrated Edition.		
16mo, printed in two colors, with 100 full-page illustrations,	net, 0	60
NEW TESTAMENT. India Paper Edition.		
American Seal, limp, round corners, gilt edges,	net, 0	90
NEW TESTAMENT. Large Print Edition.		
12mo, large,	net, 0	75
NEW TESTAMENT STUDIES. CONATY, D.D.	0	60
OFF TO JERUSALEM. BENZIGER.	net, 1	00
OFFICE, COMPLETE, OF HOLY WEEK.	0	45
Cheap Edition, cloth, cut flush,	0	20
OUR FAVORITE DEVOTIONS. LINGS.	net, 0	75
OUR FAVORITE NOVENAS. LINGS.	net, 0	75
OUR MONTHLY DEVOTIONS. LINGS.	net, 1	25
OUR OWN WILL. ALLEN, D.D.	net, 0	75
PARADISE ON EARTH OPENED TO ALL. NATALE, S.J.	net, 0	50

PARISH PRIEST ON DUTY, THE. Heuser. net, 0 60
PASSION, A FEW SIMPLE AND BUSINESS-LIKE WAYS OF
    DEVOTION TO THE. Hill, C.P. 0 25
PASSION AND DEATH OF JESUS CHRIST. Liguori. net, 1 50
PASSION FLOWERS. Poems. Hill. net, 1 25
PASSION, THOUGHTS AND AFFECTIONS ON, FOR EVERY
    DAY OF THE YEAR. Bergamo. net, 2 00
PEARLS FROM FABER. Brunowe. net, 0 50
PEARLS OF PRAYER. 0 35
PERFECT RELIGIOUS, THE. De la Motte. net, 1 00
PIOUS PREPARATION FOR FIRST HOLY COMMUNION.
    Lasance. Cloth, net, 0 75
POCKET MANUAL. A Vest-Pocket Prayer-Book in very large type. 0 25
POPULAR INSTRUCTIONS ON MARRIAGE. Girardey, C.SS.R.
    Paper, net, 0.13; cloth, net, 0 25
POPULAR INSTRUCTIONS ON PRAYER. Girardey, C.SS.R.
    Paper, net, 0.13; cloth, net, 0 25
POPULAR INSTRUCTIONS TO PARENTS. Girardey, C.SS.R.
    Paper, net, 0.13; cloth, net, 0 25
PRAYER-BOOK FOR RELIGIOUS. Lasance. net, 1 50
PREACHING. Vol. XV. Liguori. net, 1 50
PREPARATION FOR DEATH. Liguori. net, 1 50
QUEEN'S FESTIVALS. 0 60
RELIGION OF SOCIALISM, THE CHARACTERISTICS AND.
    Ming, S.J. net, 1 50
RELIGIOUS STATE, THE. Liguori. net, 0 50
ROSARY, THE CROWN OF MARY. By a Dominican Father. 0 10
ROSARY, THE. Scenes and Thoughts. Garesche, S.J. net, 0 50
ROSARY, THE MOST HOLY. Meditations. Cramer. net, 0 50
SACRAMENTALS. Lambing, D.D. Paper, net, 0.15; cloth, net, 0 35
SACRAMENTALS — Prayer, etc. Müller, C.SS.R. net, 1 00
SACRED HEART BOOK, THE. Lasance. net, 0 75
SACRED HEART, DEVOTION TO, FOR FIRST FRIDAY OF
    EVERY MONTH. By Pere Huguet. net, 0 40
SACRED HEART, NEW MANUAL OF. 0 50
SACRIFICE OF MASS WORTHILY CELEBRATED. Chaignon, S.J.
     net, 1 50
ST. ANTHONY. Keller. net, 0 75
ST. FRANCIS OF ASSISI. Social Reformer. Dubois, S.M. net, 1 00
SECRET OF SANCTITY. St. Francis de Sales. net, 1 00
SERAPHIC GUIDE, THE. A Manual for the Members of the
    Third Order of St. Francis. By a Franciscan Father. 0 60
SHORT CONFERENCES ON THE LITTLE OFFICE OF THE IM-
    MACULATE CONCEPTION. Rainer. net, 0 50
SHORT STORIES ON CHRISTIAN DOCTRINE. From the French by
    McMahon. net, 1 00
SHORT VISITS TO THE BLESSED SACRAMENT. Lasance. 0 25
SICK CALLS. Mulligan. net, 1 00
SOCIALISM AND CHRISTIANITY. Stang, D.D. net, 1 00
SOCIALISM. Cathrein, S.J. net, 1 50
SODALIST'S VADE MECUM. 0 50
SPIRIT OF SACRIFICE, THE. Giraud. net, 2 00
SPIRITUAL DESPONDENCY AND TEMPTATIONS. Michel, S.J.
     net, 1 25
SPIRITUAL EXERCISES FOR TEN DAYS' RETREAT. Smetana. net, 1 00
SPIRITUAL PEPPER AND SALT. Stang. Paper, net, 0.20; cloth, net, 0.40
ST. ANTHONY. Keller. net, 0 75
ST. FRANCIS OF ASSISI, Social Reformer. Dubois, S.M. net, 1 50
STORY OF THE FRIENDS OF JESUS. 0 60
STORIES FOR FIRST COMMUNICANTS. Keller, D.D. 0 50
STRIVING AFTER PERFECTION. Bayma, S.J. net, 1 00
SUNDAY SCHOOL TEACHER'S GUIDE TO SUCCESS. net, 0 75
SURE WAY TO A HAPPY MARRIAGE. Taylor. Paper, net,
    0.13; cloth, net, 0 25
TALKS WITH LITTLE ONES ABOUT APOSTLES' CREED. 0 60
THOUGHTS ON THE RELIGIOUS LIFE. Lasance. net, 1 50
TRUE POLITENESS. Demore. net, 0 75
TRUE SPOUSE OF JESUS CHRIST. Liguori. 2 vols. net, 3 00
    The same, one-volume edition, net, 1 25

4

VENERATION OF THE BLESSED VIRGIN. Rohner, O.S.B.   *net*, 1 25
VEST-POCKET GEMS OF DEVOTION.   0 20
VICTORIES OF THE MARTYRS. Liguori.   *net*, 1 50
VISITS, SHORT, TO BLESSED SACRAMENT. Lasance.   0 25
VISITS TO JESUS IN THE BLESSED SACRAMENT. Lasance.   *net*, 0 50
VISITS TO JESUS IN THE TABERNACLE. Lasance.   *net*, 1 25
VISITS TO THE MOST HOLY SACRAMENT and to the Blessed Virgin
     Mary. Liguori.   *net*, 0 50
VOCATIONS EXPLAINED.   0 10
WAY OF INTERIOR PEACE. De Lehen, S.J.   *net*, 1 50
WAY OF SALVATION AND PERFECTION. Liguori.   *net*, 1 50
WAY OF THE CROSS. Paper,   0 05
WAY OF THE CROSS. By a Jesuit Father.   *net*, 0 15
WAY OF THE CROSS. According to Method of St. Francis
     Assisi.   *net*, 0 15
WAY OF THE CROSS. According to Eucharistic Method.   *net*, 0 15
WAY OF THE CROSS. According to Method of St. Alphonsus
     Liguori.   *net*, 0 15
WHAT THE CHURCH TEACHES. Drury. Paper, *net*, 0.20;
     cloth,   *net*, 0 40

JUVENILES.

ADVENTURE WITH THE APACHES. Ferry.   0 45
ARMORER OF SOLINGEN. Herchenbach.   0 45
AS TRUE AS GOLD. Mannix.   0 45
BELL FOUNDRY, THE. Von Schaching.   0 45
BERKELEYS, THE. Wight.   0 45
BEARNE, Rev. DAVID, S.J.
     SHEER PLUCK.   0 85
     MELOR OF THE SILVER HAND.   0 85
     THE GUILD BOYS' PLAY AT RIDINGDALE.   0 85
     NEW BOYS AT RIDINGDALE.   0 85
     THE WITCH OF RIDINGDALE.   0 85
     RIDINGDALE FLOWER SHOW.   0 85
     CHARLIE CHITTYWICK.   0 85
BISTOURI. By A. Melandri.   0 45
BLACK LADY AND ROBIN RED BREAST. By Canon Schmid.   0 25
BLISSYLVANIA POST-OFFICE. By Marion Ames Taggart.   0 45
BOB O'LINK. Waggaman.   0 45
BOYS IN THE BLOCK. By Maurice F. Egan.   0 25
BUNT AND BILL. Clara Mulholland.   0 45
BUZZER'S CHRISTMAS. By Mary T. Waggaman.   0 25
BY BRANSCOMBE RIVER. By Marion Ames Taggart.   0 45
CAKE AND THE EASTER EGGS. By Canon Schmid.   0 25
CANARY BIRD. By Canon Schmid.   0 45
CARROLL DARE. By Mary T. Waggaman.   1 25
THE CHILDREN OF CUPA. Mannix.   0 45
COLLEGE BOY, A. By Anthony Yorke.   0 85
COPUS, Rev. J. E., S.J.:
     HARRY RUSSELL.   0 85
     SHADOWS LIFTED.   0 85
     ST. CUTHBERT'S.   0 85
     TOM LOSELY: Boy.   0 85
DADDY DAN. Waggaman.   0 45
DAUGHTER OF KINGS, A. Hinkson.   1 25
DIMPLING'S SUCCESS. By Clara Mulholland.   0 45
DOLLAR HUNT, THE. Martin.   0 45
DOUBLE KNOT AND OTHER STORIES, A. Waggaman and Others.   1 25
EVERY-DAY GIRL, AN. By Mary C. Crowley.   0 45
FATAL DIAMONDS. By E. C. Donnelly.   0 25
FINN, Rev. F. J., S.J.
     HIS FIRST AND LAST APPEARANCE. Illustrated.   1 00
     THE BEST FOOT FORWARD.   0 85
     THAT FOOTBALL GAME.   0 85
     ETHELRED PRESTON.   0 85
     CLAUDE LIGHTFOOT.   0 85
     HARRY DEE.   0 85
     TOM PLAYFAIR.   0 85

FINN, REV. F. J., S.J. (Cont'd.)
PERCY WYNN.	0 85
MOSTLY BOYS.	0 85
"BUT THY LOVE AND THY GRACE."	1 00
MY STRANGE FRIEND.	0 25
FIVE O'CLOCK STORIES; or, The Old Tales Told Again.	0 75
FLOWER OF THE FLOCK, THE, and the Badgers of Belmont. EGAN.	0 85
FOR THE WHITE ROSE. HINKSON.	0 45
FRED'S LITTLE DAUGHTER. SMITH.	0 45
GODFREY THE HERMIT. SCHMID.	0 25
GOLDEN LILY, THE. HINKSON.	0 45
GREAT CAPTAIN, THE. HINKSON.	0 45
HALDEMAN CHILDREN, THE. MANNIX.	0 45
HARMONY FLATS. WHITMIRE.	0 85
HEIR OF DREAMS, AN. O'MALLEY.	0 45
HOP BLOSSOMS. SCHMID.	0 25
HOSTAGE OF WAR, A. BONESTEEL.	0 45
HOW THEY WORKED THEIR WAY. EGAN.	0 75
INUNDATION, THE. SCHMID.	0 45
"JACK." By a Religious of The Society of The Holy Child Jesus.	0 45
JACK HILDRETH AMONG THE INDIANS. 2 vols., each,	0 85
JACK HILDRETH ON THE NILE. TAGGART. Cloth,	0 85
JACK O'LANTERN. WAGGAMAN.	0 45
JUVENILE ROUND TABLE. First, Second, Third Series. Each,	1 00
KLONDIKE PICNIC. DONNELLY.	0 85
LAMP OF THE SANCTUARY. WISEMAN.	0 25
LEGENDS OF THE HOLY CHILD JESUS from Many Lands. LUTZ.	0 75
LITTLE MISSY. WAGGAMAN.	0 45
LOYAL BLUE AND ROYAL SCARLET. TAGGART.	0 85
MADCAP SET AT ST. ANNE'S. BRUNOWE.	0 45
MARY TRACY'S FORTUNE. SADLIER.	0 45
MASTER FRIDOLIN. GIEHRL.	0 25
MILLY AVELING. SMITH. Cloth,	0 85
MORE FIVE O'CLOCK STORIES. In Prose and Verse. By a Religious of The Society of The Holy Child Jesus.	0 75
MYSTERIOUS DOORWAY. SADLIER.	0 45
MYSTERY OF CLEVERLY. BARTON.	0 85
MYSTERY OF HORNBY HALL. SADLIER.	0 85
MY STRANGE FRIEND. FINN.	0 25
NAN NOBODY. WAGGAMAN.	0 45
OLD CHARLMONT'S SEED-BED. SMITH.	0 45
OLD ROBBER'S CASTLE. SCHMID.	0 25
ONE AFTERNOON AND OTHER STORIES. TAGGART.	1 25
OUR BOYS' AND GIRLS' LIBRARY. 14 vols., each,	0 25
OVERSEER OF MAHLBOURG. SCHMID.	0 45
PANCHO AND PANCHITA. MANNIX.	0 45
PAULINE ARCHER. SADLIER.	0 45
PETRONILLA. DONNELLY.	0 85
PICKLE AND PEPPER. DORSEY.	0 85
PILGRIM FROM IRELAND. CARNOT.	0 45
PLAYWATER PLOT, THE. WAGGAMAN.	0 60
QUEEN'S PAGE. HINKSON.	0 45
RECRUIT TOMMY COLLINS. BONESTEEL.	0 45
ROSE BUSH. SCHMID.	0 25
ROUND THE WORLD. Vols. I, II, III, IV. Each,	0 85
SEA-GULL'S ROCK. SANDEAU.	0 45
SHADOWS LIFTED. COPUS, S.J.	0 85
SPALDING, REV. H., S.J.:	
THE MARKS OF THE BEAR CLAWS.	0 85
CAVE BY THE BEECH FORK.	0 85
THE SHERIFF OF THE BEECH FORK.	0 85
THE RACE FOR COPPER ISLAND.	0 85
STRONG-ARM OF AVALON. WAGGAMAN.	0 85
SUMMER AT WOODVILLE. SADLIER.	0 45
TALES AND LEGENDS OF THE MIDDLE AGES. DE CAPELLA.	0 75
TALISMAN, THE. SADLIER.	0 60
TAMING OF POLLY. DORSEY.	0 85
THREE GIRLS AND ESPECIALLY ONE. TAGGART.	0 45
THREE LITTLE KINGS. GIEHRL.	0 25

6

TOM'S LUCKPOT. Waggaman. 0 45
TOORALLADY. Walsh. 0 45
TRANSPLANTING OF TESSIE. Waggaman. 0 60
TREASURE OF NUGGET MOUNTAIN. Taggart. 0 85
TWO LITTLE GIRLS. Mack. 0 45
VIOLIN MAKER, THE. Smith. 0 45
WAGER OF GERALD O'ROURKE, THE. Finn-Thiele. net, 0 35
WAYWARD WINIFRED. Sadlier. 0 85
WHERE THE ROAD LED AND OTHER STORIES. Sadlier and
  others. 1 25
WINNETOU, THE APACHE KNIGHT. Taggart. 0 85
WRONGFULLY ACCUSED. Herchenbach. 0 45
YOUNG COLOR GUARD, THE. Bonesteel. 0 45

NOVELS AND STORIES.

"BUT THY LOVE AND THY GRACE." Finn, S.J. 1 00
CARROLL DARE. Waggaman. 1 25
CIRCUS RIDER'S DAUGHTER, THE. Brackel. 1 25
CONNOR D'ARCY'S STRUGGLES. Bertholds. 1 25
CORINNE'S VOW. Waggaman. 1 25
DION AND THE SIBYLS. Keon. 1 25
FABIOLA. Wiseman. Illustrated. 0 90
FABIOLA'S SISTER. Clarke. 1 25
FATAL BEACON, THE. Brackel. 1 25
HEARTS OF GOLD. Edhor. 1 25
HEIRESS OF CRONENSTEIN, THE. Countess Hahn-Hahn. 1 25
HER BLIND FOLLY. Holt. 1 25
HER FATHER'S DAUGHTER. Hinkson. net, 1 25
IDOLS; or, The Secrets of the Rue Chaussee d'Antin. De Navery. 1 25
IN THE DAYS OF KING HAL. Taggart. net, 1 25
IN GOD'S GOOD TIME. Ross. 1 25
"KIND HEARTS AND CORONETS." Harrison. 1 25
LET NO MAN PUT ASUNDER. Marié. 1 00
LINKED LIVES. Douglas. 1 50
MARCELLA GRACE. Mulholland. Illustrated Edition. 1 25
MIRROR OF SHALOTT. Benson. net, 1 25
MISS ERIN. Francis. 1 25
MONK'S PARDON, THE. De Navery. 1 25
MR. BILLY BUTTONS. Lecky. 1 25
"NOT A JUDGMENT." Keon. 1 25
OTHER MISS LISLE, THE. Martin. 1 25
OUT OF BONDAGE. Holt. 1 25
OUTLAW OF CAMARGUE, THE. Lamothe. 1 25
PASSING SHADOWS. Yorke. 1 25
PERE MONNIER'S WARD. Lecky. 1 25
PILKINGTON HEIR, THE. Sadlier. 1 25
PRODIGAL'S DAUGHTER, THE. By Lelia Hardin Bugg. 1 00
RED INN OF ST. LYPHAR, THE. A Romance of La Vendée. Sadlier. 1 25
ROMANCE OF A PLAYWRIGHT. By Vte. Henri de Bornier. 1 00
ROSE OF THE WORLD. Martin. 1 25
ROUND TABLE OF AMERICAN CATHOLIC NOVELISTS.
  Complete Stories, with Biographies, Portraits, etc. 1 50
ROUND TABLE OF FRENCH CATHOLIC NOVELISTS.
  Complete Stories, with Biographies, Portraits, etc. 1 50
ROUND TABLE OF GERMAN CATHOLIC NOVELISTS. Illustrated. 1 50
ROUND TABLE OF IRISH AND ENGLISH CATHOLIC NOVELISTS.
  Complete Stories, Biographies, Portraits, etc. Cloth, 1 50
RULER OF THE KINGDOM, THE, and other Phases of Life
  and Character. Keon. 1 25
SECRET OF THE GREEN VASE. Cooke. 1 25
SENIOR LIEUTENANT'S WAGER. 1 25
SOGGARTH AROON. Guinan, C.C. 1 25
THAT MAN'S DAUGHTER. Ross. 1 25
TRAIL OF THE DRAGON. 1 25
TRAINING OF SILAS, THE. Devine, S.J. 1 25
TRUE STORY OF MASTER GERARD, THE. Sadlier. 1 25
UNRAVELING OF A TANGLE, THE. Taggart. 1 25
VOCATION OF EDWARD CONWAY. Egan. 1 25

WAY THAT LED BEYOND. By J. HARRISON.   **1** 25
WHEN LOVE IS STRONG. KEON.   **1** 25
WOMAN OF FORTUNE, A. By CHRISTIAN REID.   **1** 25
WORLD WELL LOST. By ESTHER ROBERTSON.   **0** 75

LIVES AND HISTORIES.

AUTOBIOGRAPHY OF ST. IGNATIUS LOYOLA.   Edited by
  O'CONOR, S.J.   *net,* 1 25
ANGLICAN ORDINATIONS. SEMPLE, S.J.   *net,* 0 35
BEGINNINGS OF CHRISTIANITY. SHAHAN.   *net,* 2 00
CHURCH HISTORY. BUSINGER.   0 75
GOLDEN BELLS IN CONVENT TOWERS.   *net,* 1 00
HISTORY OF THE CATHOLIC CHURCH. BRUECK.   2 vols.,   *net,* 3 00
HISTORY OF THE CATHOLIC CHURCH. SHEA.   *net,* 1 50
HISTORY OF THE PROTESTANT REFORMATION. COBBETT.   *net,* 0 75
LIFE OF BLESSED VIRGIN. Illustrated. ROHNER.   *net,* 1 25
LIFE OF CHRIST. Illustrated. COCHEM.   *net,* 1 25
LIFE OF POPE PIUS X.   2 00
LIFE OF MOST REV. JOHN HUGHES. BRANN.   *net,* 0 75
LIFE OF OUR LORD AND SAVIOUR JESUS CHRIST AND
  OF HIS VIRGIN MOTHER MARY. BRENNAN. 4to.   *net,* 10 00
     (Easy payment plan, $1.00 down, $1.00 a month.)
LIFE OF SISTER ANNE KATHERINE EMMERICH. WEGENER, O.S.A.
                                                        net, 1 75
LIFE OF VEN. MARY CRESCENTIA HOESS. DEGMAN, O.S.F.   *net,* 1 25
LITTLE LIVES OF SAINTS FOR CHILDREN. BERTHOLD. Ill.
  Cloth,   0 60
LITTLE PICTORIAL LIVES OF SAINTS. New, cheap edition.   1 25
LOURDES. CLARKE, S.J.   1 00
MIDDLE AGES, THE. SHAHAN.   *net,* 2 00
PATRON SAINTS FOR CATHOLIC YOUTH. 3 vols. Each,   0 60
PICTORIAL LIVES OF THE SAINTS.   *net,* 2 00
ST. ANTHONY, THE SAINT OF THE WHOLE WORLD.
  WARD. Cloth.   *net,* 0 75
STORY OF JESUS. Illustrated.   *net,* 0 60
STORY OF THE DIVINE CHILD. LINGS.   0 60
VICTORIES OF THE MARTYRS. LIGUORI.   *net,* 1 50

THEOLOGY, LITURGY, SERMONS, SCIENCE, AND PHILOSOPHY.

ANGLICAN ORDINATIONS. SEMPLE, S.J.   0 35
BENEDICENDA. SCHULTE.   *net,* 1 50
BREVE COMPENDIUM THEOLOGIAE. BERTHIER.   *net,* 2 50
BUSINESS GUIDE FOR PRIESTS. STANG.   *net,* 1 00
CANONICAL PROCEDURE. DOSTE.   *net,* 1 50
CHRISTIAN APOLOGETICS. DEVIVIER.   *net,* 2 00
CHRISTIAN PHILOSOPHY: God. DRISCOLL.   *net,* 1 50
CHRIST IN TYPE AND PROPHECY. MAAS, S.J. 2 vols.,   *net,* 4 00
CHURCH TREASURER'S PEW COLLECTION AND RECEIPT
  BOOK.   *net,* 1 00
COMPENDIUM JURIS CANONICI. SMITH.   *net,* 2 00
COMPENDIUM JURIS REGULARIUM. BACHOFEN.   *net,* 2 50
COMPENDIUM SACRAE LITURGIAE. WAPELHORST.   *net,* 2 50
CONSECRANDA. SCHULTE.   *net,* 1 50
DATA OF MODERN ETHICS EXAMINED. MING, S.J.   2 00
DIARY, ORDO AND NOTE-BOOK. Cloth, *net,* 1.00; flexible
  leather,   *net,* 1 50
ELEMENTS OF ECCLESIASTICAL LAW. SMITH, D.D. 3 vols.,
  each,   *net,* 2 50
GENERAL INTRODUCTION TO THE STUDY OF HOLY
  SCRIPTURES. GIGOT, S.S.   *net,* 2 50
GENERAL INTRODUCTION TO THE STUDY OF HOLY
  SCRIPTURES. Abridged Edition. GIGOT, S.S.   *net,* 1 50
GOD KNOWABLE AND KNOWN. RONAYNE, S.J.   *net,* 1 50
GOOD CHRISTIAN, THE. ALLEN, D.D. 2 vols.   *net,* 5 00

8